Because

Y♡U

Matter

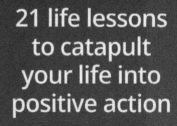

21 life lessons
to catapult
your life into
positive action

CHELLE VERITE
Empowerment Coach

Because You Matter

Chelle Verite

COPYRIGHT

Because You Matter
Chelle Verite

of liability that applied to all damages of any kind including (without limitation) compensatory, direct, indirect or consequential damages, loss of data, income or profit, loss or damage to any property and claims of third parties.

What the above says is I'm simply showing you what might be achieved not telling you what to do!

Cover Design by: Danje Designs

Illustrations by: Martin Richardson

Because Y♡u Matter

Chelle Verite

ACKNOWLEDGEMENTS

Yes get in! This book simply wouldn't have been in existence if it wasn't for the following people...

- ♥ My husband, best friend, and bestest supporter James. Thank you for being you. You are my rock even on the darkest hardest most challenging days, and on the days filled with sparkling colourful light.

- ♥ My children Oliver and Belle whom without them my stories and experience as a mother wouldn't have been half as much fun or filled with joy.

- ♥ My parents Mike and Jacquie, and my birthmum Margaret, for giving it their all, loving me, and the recognition that we are all human.

- ♥ Taryn for getting *'Because YOU Matter'* published (it only took three years to get to this point, patience, patience, patience), and Jos for getting her to call me in the first place!

- ♥ Claire for getting my words straight!

- ♥ Martin for your fabulous illustrations throughout, for making the stories told so bright by your brilliant art, and to your late brother Barry for introducing me to you.

- ♥ Dan for making the cover so amazing and for being so easy to work with (purple, white and green should definitely be seen!)

- ♥ Mike and Kenneth for your help creating all the exciting BYM social media. Bring on No1. Best Seller!

- ♥ Farhan for the awesome typesetting of *Because YOU Matter*. We've definitely been positively disrupted by your flair and styling!

- ♥ All the *'Lets Get BOMBCHELLED!'* lockdown attendees. You are simply amazing, and I want you to know it was all of you that inspired me to get this far and keep going. (If I can do 'It' you can too!!)

❤ My coaching superstars, previous teachers, family and managers that I've written about in the book; including Joanne, Rachelle, Max, Paul, Warren, Neal, Mr Findlay, Ben Williams, Aunty M, Evo and all the people named Matt, Chris, Mary, and Dave! Not to mention my dogs Yogi and Boo who kept me company along the way too.

❤ I also wanted in true Chelle "say it like it is, no bullsh*t" Scottish Tourettes fashion to say a big f*ck you to all the people who thought I would fail, who despite themselves have likely had to read this book. Karma always catches up. Shame on you!

❤ Thank you again to all of my loved ones. To everyone (and everything) all the trials, tribulations, challenges, hurts, pains and gains that have crossed my path to make me, me. Here's to the good, the bad, and the ugly. To my real friends (and real foes) for giving me the guts, the strength, the courage, focus and perseverance to keep going.

Book number 1 down.

Until next time and book number 2...

BE REAL... SHOW UP... BE SEEN and BE YOU!

Why do it?

Yup you know the answer.

Because Y♡u Matter

Chelle ☺ X

LiveLifeBE

DEDICATION

I dedicate this book to all of us who have doubted ourselves, who have felt at times utterly disillusioned, bruised or battered from a constant battle of trying to fit in, meet expectations, been simply overwhelmed at the pressure of creating a life of success, or felt completely ill equipped to be real, show up, or even if we want to be seen. I dedicate this book to all of us who got up this morning, despite how we are feeling, to be exactly who we were meant to be even when we didn't have a clue how. Sometimes we just need a nice cup of tea / glass of wine / some chocolate cake and a huge dollop of 'You're f*cking wonderful' so we can Live Life and BE. After all life was meant to be enjoyed not endured!

Why do it? Simple...

Because You Matter

Happy reading.

Chelle ☺ X

CATAPULT INTO POSITIVE ACTION

AND LIVELIFEBE

By Chelle Verite

A journey of a thousand miles begins with a single step.

Welcome to your first single step and the beginning of your empowerment journey that will positively disrupt your world, so you can **BE REAL... SHOW UP... BE SEEN...** and most importantly **BE** the truest, most valued and successful version of **YOU**.

You'll laugh, you'll cry, but most of all you'll re-evaluate your life.

Because Y♡u Matter

Chelle X

LiveLifeBE

Because Y♡u Matter

Chelle Verite

CONTENTS

Who is Chelle? Wake up, shake up, positively disrupt..........................11

LESSON 01. I am NOT normal. Absof*ckinglootly!..............................15

LESSON 02. Because YOU matter. Hello new world..........................27

LESSON 03. What's your MindF*ck? Non / Wrong / Their-DOing..33

LESSON 04. Human BEing. NOT Human DOing 49

LESSON 05. Self-awareness. The Crown of Acceptance................57

LESSON 06. Dissolving worries. Henry who?!....................................75

LESSON 07. Choice is limitless. God 'ERR☺ME'................................101

LESSON 08. Just BREATHE. Breathe and relax 125

LESSON 09. Choose life. Meet Matt, Chris, Mary and Dave............143

LESSON 10. Choice, power, change. What's in a name?.................181

LESSON 11. BE your own Superhero. The day reality shattered....201

Because Y♥u Matter
Chelle Verite

LESSON 12. Take the leap. Decide, bake and eat 223

LESSON 13. Valuing LOVE and HATE. Mirror, mirror..........................247

LESSON 14. Kick your Critical Mind. SDM versus PAM.......................267

LESSON 15. Feeding back to self. The 'BUNCHES' way 293

LESSON 16. Ridding UP and IF. Identifying emotional impact.......321

LESSON 17. Introducing HALT. Stop your emotional rollercoaster..345

LESSON 18. Who's for tea? Givers, takers, creating glow................409

LESSON 19. Making 'It' happen. The meaning of life 441

LESSON 20. Say 'Goodbye Hello'. Let in the new you.......................483

LESSON 21. Go BE. Absof*ckinglootly...499

APPENDIX Take the leap cakes. Chocolate muffin recipe.............517

Who is Chelle?

WAKE UP, SHAKE UP, POSITIVELY DISRUPT

Because You Matter

Chelle Verite

Hi, I'm Chelle Verite, Empowerment Coach, TEDx Speaker and Positive Disruptor. I'm an adoptee of Scottish / Caribbean descent, sufferer of Borderline Personality Disorder, and I grew up as the only non-white face in the beautiful, yet rather chilly, northern Shetland Isles. I'm a divorcee and now based, for the most part, in the UK with my family (and France in the summer).

This book will enable you to experience a truly transformational and life enhancing journey. *Because YOU Matter*, will empower you to grow, wake up, shake up and catapult you into positive action, so you can live the life you love AND love the life you live. To achieve transformational results, I live by the following premises.

1. **You are not broken.**
2. **You do not need fixing.**
3. **If you can create it, you can f*cking make it.**

Utilising my own life lessons based on overcoming hardships and adversity, and my values of integrity, passion and making a difference to create positive disruption, my motivational life toolkits will immerse you in a world of Scottish Tourette's like straight-talking and Positive Psychology.

Because YOU Matter is all about empowering you to **BE REAL... SHOW UP... BE SEEN...** and most importantly **BE YOU** by;

- ♥ Truly focusing on desiring, and deserving, success.
- ♥ Facing your darkest reflections and deepest fears head on.
- ♥ Finding and expressing your own truth.
- ♥ Equipping you with transformational confidence, clarity, and choices.
- ♥ Empowering you to be authentically present and **BE YOU**.

Because Y♥u Matter

Chelle Verite

You'll also be introduced to plenty of wine, prosecco, tea, chocolate, and cake along the way!

The only question left to ask is. why do I do what I do?

Simple.

Because Y♥u Matter

You really, really do.

Chelle X

> Nothing can dim
> The light that
> shines from
> within.

MAYA ANGELOU

LIFE LESSON

01

I am NOT normal

ABSOF*CKINGLOOTLY!

Because Y♡u Matter

Chelle Verite

Normal (adjective). *ordinary or usual; as would be expected.*

I am not normal. Thank God! Imagine aspiring to that? The expectation to fit in, to have to do stuff 'just because', or to be a specific shape as per the human expectation mould. As my Yorkshire born husband James would lovingly say:

'No, Chelle, you're definitely not normal. You're that crazy brown Scottish lady that grew up in the Shetland Isles, who's travelled and seen the world and who's *'BOMBCHELLED!'* thousands of people into positive action.'

Yes, get in! I am very proud of me, and you should be proud, too. Of you, that is. Not me. Although, it would be great if you were proud of me. There you go, your first introduction to my God complex, and it's within the first few pages of the book. Just you wait until you meet the gorgeous kilt-wearing, awe-inspiring **GOD ERR☺ME**. I am indeed a square peg in a round hole. A storm. Unique, challenging, and different.

Because Y♡u Matter
Chelle Verite

I am not normal. Thank f*ck!

Yes, that's right. Thank f*ck for that.

'Really, is swearing absolutely necessary?' Erm, well, yes. It's called expression and passion and it's me. So, if you're offended at the very start of this book, then you had better come to my LiveLifeBE *'Lets Get BOMBCHELLED!'* masterclasses instead. They're professional and non-sweary sessions that will help empower you with positive action. We still have a lot of fun and get a lot done. However, it's in no way the in-your-face-Scottish-Tourette's-say-it-like-it-is style of interaction that this book will offer you.

If you're still really offended and want to take this golden nugget of a book back for a refund, then be my guest. Although, secretly, I know you wouldn't dare, because…

Because Y♥u Matter

Chelle Verite

a) You bought it on Amazon, and it costs £4 to return.

b) You got a first print run edition that was likely personally signed by me, so that's a keeper.

c) I know you're only having a mini pretend strop to see if I'm listening and paying attention. I am.

d) You're already hooked on reading the book. I've been harping on about it for long enough.

e) It's a nice wee break from all of those 'must-read-because-I'm-a-grown-up' books. (My head is hurting for you already if you go for those options!).

f) This is your opportunity to catapult yourself into someone else's world for a bit. For you to relax and clear your day of your 'life pressures' and any gut-wrenching, debilitating anxieties and worries. Especially those 'Shit, I didn't do that!' or 'Crap, I've still got that to do!' moments.

Right, now we are sorted with the excuses, are you sitting comfortably?

Fabulous.

I do hope you have a nice glass of wine in your hand. Even if it's in the morning when you are reading this, it's afternoon somewhere else, so wine is totally acceptable. If it's not quite wine o'clock yet, substitute it for a nice cup of tea. If you do opt for wine, remember to drink responsibly. I cannot take all of you to AA or to A&E. Well, we could go to Alcoholics Anonymous seeing as that's now online (thanks, COVID). As for A&E, well, that's just way too busy dealing with all the noise and traffic from our new pandemic world (NHS, we salute you). Drinking sensibly means taking it easy. It also means no Buckfast (or *Bucky*, as us Scots call it).

If you do opt for the wine and are saving the tea until later, you can tell whomever it is that scorns you when you reach for that big bottle

Because You Matter

Chelle Verite

and glass that 'Chelle says I've to have this as part of my LiveLifeBE empowerment journey.' Better still, get them a copy of the book (you'll be writing in this one) and they will soon understand the need for wine! Working with me does that, you know.

Also, in case you were worrying (which we will soon put a stop to with our **Worry Dissolver** in Life Lesson 6), you'll be relieved to hear that if you don't have any wine in stock, I've got a five-litre white wine box that I've just opened. That ought to do us, and a huge drawer full of chocolate (70% dark chocolate, as I needed plenty to create my **Take the Leap** chocolate muffin cakes, the recipe for which is in the appendix).

However, as you are yet to get to the part of the book with the recipe in, you won't have done the obligatory Amazon pink spatula shop yet for the making of your muffins. The chocolate in the Take the Leap muffins tastes delicious. I can also recommend inhaling chocolate straight into your mouth. That does the trick, too. Just be sure to take the foil off when you eat it. (If you don't, it will give you quite a shock when the metal hits your fillings.)

Wine, prosecco, tea, chocolate and sofa sorted?

And reeeelaaaaaxxxx. Let's get back to our little chat.

If, however, you're not connected to Scotland (which everyone is really), you can be like my husband, James, and settle in the lolloping, rolling hills of the Yorkshire countryside. Just don't do Barnsley. I still to this day cannot understand a word they say. They are very friendly though, and to be fair, after living in the white rose country rather than the thistle, haggis and tartan country, I do sometimes catch myself saying the Yorkshire "love" after words rather than the more direct Scottish Tourette's "f*ck".

Because Y♡u Matter

Chelle Verite

James continually asks me, "Chelle, how on earth do you manage to say whole sentences that contain the F word five times out of six words, and it still makes sense?!" To which I merely smile and reply time and time again, "Why, that's the joy of having Scottish Tourette's, darling."

There I go again. Defiance. Go on socially acceptable police, I dare you. Make me stop. As if you will be able to catch me. Yes, to carving my own way in the world and making up my own rules, like pen-knifed 'I love you' messages on a tree or knocking on doors and running away (love that game). That's the best part of being who I am, and you being who you are, no, not the door knocking, but the fact that we are not meant to be 'normal'. If I had been 'normal', this book (and my *'Lets Get BOMBCHELLED!'* motivational life toolkit sessions) would never have been born. I wouldn't have succeeded in doing all the wild and wacky things I have, either (including jumping 12,000 feet out of an aeroplane and standing on the TEDx red carpet, both of which were equally terrifying and exhilarating).

Instead, life would have just broken me.

Life hasn't exactly been an easy ride, due to my often misunderstood whirlwind of a personality, recently diagnosed Borderline Personality Disorder and just about every other 'label' life seems to have gifted me. Life has pushed me, like it has for many of us, to the limit. Life has a habit of doing that, doesn't it? We regularly feel pushed, prodded and squished into the categories of acceptability. Playing the 'being accepted as normal' game in the adventures of the everyday, whether we're a working parent, or inhabiting the business world. Who the f*ck wants that? And what on earth is 'normal', anyway? It's certainly not a domain I aspire to.

You're meant to create your own world. You're meant to design your own life rules. You are there to honour and listen to your own voice,

Because Y♡u Matter
Chelle Verite

to live the life you love AND love the life you live. You are free to adore yourself and be adored by everyone around you. You are able to adore what you achieve, or cleverly choose not to achieve. You can, and you will, revel in the pride element of life. Your life should be easy, simple and understandable, a kind, contented experience, just like love should be. Your life should also be a welcoming, safe and empowering place that puts you firmly in the driving seat of your journey. YES! Here's to you getting a handle on your critical mind and catapulting yourself into positive action so you can feel empowered and be you.

As civil rights activist Maya Angelou said.

'Nothing can dim the light that shines from within.'

It's exactly true. This is what it's all about.

It's also one of the many reasons I wrote this book.

Because Y♡u Matter

Now, I fully realise that this book may not be beautifully written (it is, after all, my first attempt... and won't be my last!) However, what I can promise is that this book, written in its real, raw, unfiltered-story glory will transform, empower and re-energise your life. It will equip you with a new mindset full of possibilities and wants, and the means to achieve them. It'll make you laugh. It'll make you cry. At times, it'll even make you scratch your brain out with pain. Then, in the same breath, it'll make you spit your tea out with laughter and joy because you've found new ways of being you.

This book is all about you taking charge of your inner world. Kicking into touch your often debilitating and highly critical **Sabotaging Devil Mindset**. Dissolving the crippling, all-consuming, self-confidence-zapping **Woe-is-me Worries** that get in your way. It's about not handing power to others who have previously ruined your life. It's about getting a handle on those **Catastrophising Chris, Meltdown Mary** and **Devastating Dave** moments when life overwhelms you and paralyses you from creating and making what you need and want to make you smile. It's about equipping you with motivational life toolkits, to help you get your backside off the sofa and throw out all the debilitating and damaging internal thoughts, beliefs and negative ways of interacting with the world. Instead, you can create the life you actually want and need, so you can live the life you love AND love the life you live.

Because YOU Matter will help you, and others in your lives, recognise that you are enough. It will help you recognise that you are wonderful and exactly how you are meant to be. It will gift you time to stop and time to breathe. Regardless of how good or bad you feel, how lost or found, how confused or focused, how overwhelmed or calm you are about life or love. This book will empower you to realise that you always, always matter.

Because YOU Matter has been written so that, despite the emotional, physical or mental stresses, strains, upsets, challenges or joys that come your way, you can find your inner truth, your inner soul and your inner you. By doing this, you can consciously choose to positively respond rather than automatically react, enabling you to find ways to take responsibility for what you want and who you are. You will be able to stand up and truly look at your reflection and recognise, acknowledge, engage and act in ways to unlock love, compassion and gratitude, and generate trust in asking for and ultimately receiving what you truly want.

The stories and life lessons in this book will show ways to seek the truth, to stop pain and celebrate feeling good (or at least better) about yourself, and provide accessible ways to transform the world you live in. *Because YOU Matter* is about refocusing your personal beliefs. Beliefs that you are loved, wanted, accepted and respected, providing ways of empowering your BEing to enable you to take positive actions and make positive differences to your life. Despite all the pressures and anxieties we place on ourselves, we can have all that we wish for.

Because Y♡u Matter
Chelle Verite

If we want it, we can dream it. If we can dream it, we can create it. If we can create it, we will f*cking make it!

Life Lesson 01

WE ARE NOT NORMAL

You are not broken. You do not need fixing. In fact, it's only now I've hit the ripe old age of forty six that I am ready to unpeel and share my search for truth. I am ready to unravel the layers of my life. Years of loss, misunderstanding, identity struggles as a mixed-race child being adopted into a white Jewish agnostic family, growing up in a land of cultural strangers in a strange land, later finding myself plunged into the depths of divorce, a single struggling career mother, fighting low self-worth, a stigmatised personality disorder, and drowning in diminished self-confidence. Years of loss to help you catapult into a world of transformation and positive action instead. With all the complexities of society's expectations and lack of acceptance, I fought a constant battle between valuing and honouring myself. I felt a constant need to reprogramme me away from a life of sabotaging reactions, devaluing myself, lack of boundaries, and a severe inability to drop control, let people in or let go. All of which, up until now, had a devastating and debilitating effect on my life, my heart and my inner soul. Me. The Empowerment Coach, Positive Disruptor, TEDx Speaker, mother and now wife. However, I was brave. I took the leap and now I can say, with the most definite pride...

'I am NOT normal!'

Because Yöu Matter

Chelle Verite

I am a **Human BEing**. Just like you. We are all special and unique. Only it took me a lifetime of sadness, loss and fight to truly know how to express how I wanted to **BE REAL... SHOW UP... BE SEEN...** So here I am. Welcoming you into your new world. For you to laugh with, laugh at, and learn from. For you to scorn, to understand, to challenge, to ignore, to put down and to cherish.

Here's to the next few hours, days, weeks and months we spend together as you read this book. Bend it. Write in it. Laugh with it. Cry with it. Above all, know that even at times when it doesn't make sense, the fact you're reading it means that I did it. And if I can do this and can stop fighting debilitating internal battles and catapult myself into positive action, then you, my friends, can do it, too.

Whatever the Marmite rollercoaster experience this book, and your journey, provides you, I can assure you that you'll unleash way more self-awareness about what you want and how to get it. You'll create and have more freedom to choose ways to positively disrupt and enhance your world. You'll have more freedom to choose love, happiness, abundance, ease and contentment for your world. You'll reduce your anxiety, stress, worry, angst and anger, and you'll boost your low self-worth and self-confidence, empowering yourself to create your world exactly the way you want it to be. This journey will give you truthful context about your world. The things that most people don't talk about. The things that most of us find difficult to face and to function with.

Be sure to listen to the audio book version, too (when I get around to recording it). You'll get my voice in full Scottish-walking-down-Sauchiehall-Street Glaswegian slang.

'Aye, man. That's braw. Ya f*cking dancer, I cannae wait.'

And, also, my Edinburgh-Morningside-ladies-who-lunch-prime-of-Miss-Jean-Brodie-akin-to-Mrs-Doubtfire accent.

Because Yöu Matter
Chelle Verite

'Ooooh yes, m'dear. I'm awfley thrilled to start our wee journey.'

Translated from both Glaswegian and Edinburgh accents as.

'Brilliant, I'm most excited to get started!'

Yes, time in Scotland is required; it's such an expressive world. In the absence of Scotland being available, let this book and my voice transport you there. To be clear, there is no skirting round the edges. No naming of pink elephants in this book (well, actually, there are, but you'll learn all about that later). There's no bullshit. No fluff. None, nada, not a sausage. You'll get the truth, the whole truth and nothing but the truth. I've stripped myself bare so you don't have to. Whatever you've gone through, whatever hardship or struggles you have faced, you will be recognised and relieved to know that you are not alone.

Here's to you being you. Here's to your name being up in lights. Here's to you being utterly honest, open and available. Here's to you being *'BOMBCHELLED!'* into positive action and living AND loving the life you live. If I can be brave and face this world, you can, too.

Yes! We are not normal.

Thank f*ck.

Yes! We are not normal.

Thank God.

Yes! We are **NOT** normal.

Absof*ckinglootly!

Bring it on.

Why do it?

Why take your **first step** on your **new empowerment journey?**

Simple.

Because Yöu Matter

Who looks outside
dreams. Who looks
inside, awakes.

CARL JUNG

LIFE LESSON

02

Because YOU matter

HELLO NEW WORLD

Because You Matter

Chelle Verite

Is it morning already?! F*ck. Can I not just hide under the covers for that little bit longer? In fact, if I breathe really slowly and pretend I'm not here surely no one will see me...?

I'm sure we all recognise this feeling.

Or perhaps you bounce out of bed in the mornings, full of enthusiasm for the day that will unfold? Whichever aspect of waking up you recognise we all know it can be tough to get our backsides out of bed in the mornings. After all, it's not all fluffy marshmallows and pink unicorns, is it? Putting one foot in front of the other to get all the stuff done we need to get done in the day can be hard. Let alone figuring out how we are meant to make sense of all the life stuff, pressures and lessons that unravel in ways we are all supposed to magically know how to deal with.

I mean, what is with growing up? Being an 'adult' and getting 'it' right? Yup, I feel your pain. I really do. I should have paid attention when my parents told me that school years are the best years of your life. Being an adult, a grown up, often means putting up with shit that we shouldn't have to deal with. It means the pain of not being where we thought we would be by now, the pain of not knowing, the pain of not going, the pain, the pain... and that's just peeling your eyes open in the morning.

So, here's the thing. What if you didn't have to go through that pain anymore?

What if I could offer you ways to positively disrupt your world so instead of feeling pain, you create a life that not only makes you smile, it also makes you high five it, saying a huge, earth shattering, exhilarating, 'Yes, get in!' as you go? What if you could create a world where you consistently *wanted* to get out of bed, rather than sinking into the mattress with that full on body weight and 'I don't want to'

Because Y♡u Matter
Chelle Verite

strop, 'Do not come near me, I'd rather die than put one foot out of the covers and have to get up to face what I have to do.' Or as I would say in Scottish, 'Aww, dinnae man. Get te f*ck.' Instead, how about you create a world that surrounds you with an abundance of refreshingly genuine availability, and you become an awesome new you?

How would that be for you? It would likely change things a little, wouldn't it? It did for me.

In a way that simplifies the hard stuff.

With none of the *what ifs*, the *should haves*, the *ought tos* or the *oh, f*ck, I shouldn't haves* **Unchangeable Past** regrets.

And none of the devastating debilitating worry anxieties either. *What if this catastrophising crap of the imagined future happens?* or *I won't be able to cope* or *I won't be able to do it.*

And definitely none of the *'I'm not worthy, I don't deserve a life that's wonderfully kind, awesome and fulfilling'* or being stuck in an irrelevant, fruitless and insignificant distraction bullshit.

HELLO!!! This is about putting you at the heart of your world. Kicking that critical **Sabotaging Devil Mindset** to touch this instant!

I truly cannot wait to hear you say, 'Chelle, I f*cking did it!' That however, does mean that you need to pledge allegiance to you.

Life Lesson 02

BYM FIGHT CLUB

Welcome to **BYM Fight Club**

Welcome to your new way of being, an authentically present aspiring human.

Authentically:
an emotionally appropriate significant purpose and responsible mode of human life

---

Present:
finding acceptance for who you are

Aspiring:
directing hopes and ambitions

Human:
being unique and special

Your transformational and empowering journey begins.

Because Y♡u Matter

Chelle Verite

Fill in the following.

Hello new world. Hello new equipped, responsive, compassionate, and contented me.

I, _____ , *(write your name here, afterall, it's your book, your journey and your pledge to you)* agree that this is my pledge to **BE REAL… SHOW UP… BE SEEN…** and truly BE me.

I matter because**	
** *detail your reasons why you want to fight to stop internal struggles and instead empower and equip yourself with a life that you live and love*	

Reason 1	
Reason 2	
Reason 3	
Reason 4	
Reason 5	
Reason More!	

I pledge and promise that as a result of reading, listening, engaging with and learning from this book, I will stand up for me and take positive action for my life, because I matter. (Also a perfect excuse to get on Amazon and purchase some nice stationery, some pens, a journal… the list is endless)

Because Y♡u Matter

Chelle Verite

I also promise to...

- ♥ Read this book, all of it.
- ♥ Complete the life lessons in it. Properly.
- ♥ Drink tea / eat cake / devour chocolate / consume wine, prosecco or favourite equivalent (diet and health permitting) while processing content from this book.
- ♥ Share this book with the people I love.
- ♥ Keep this book away from enemies, fren-emies, or rivals otherwise I understand that Chelle will have to 'dekneecapitate' them (chop their legs off at the knees!).
- ♥ Give the **'Take the Leap chocolate muffin cake'** recipe a go (it's in the appendix ready to be made).
- ♥ Use all of the **God ERR☺ME** breathing, life responses and life lesson approaches so I can **Go BE ME**.

Bring on my new world.

And why will I do it?

The answer is simple.

Because I matter.

Signed _____

Dated _____

Yes, get in!

Here's to your transformational journey.

Because Y♡u Matter

> "
>
> ---
>
> The trick in life is... learning how to deal with it.
>
> **HELEN MIRREN**

What's your MindF*ck?

NON / WRONG / THEIR-DOING

Because You Matter
Chelle Verite

Why choose to empower you? Why actually bother? Other than the fact you've just pledged allegiance already. I know, I know, there are so many boxsets and TV programmes that will gift you entertainment instead of personal growth. (I've heart Game of Thrones is a *'I can't switch it off'*, and Jane the Virgin keeps a lot of us amused). Needless to say TV can be a great distraction from the drudgery of life and from reading the 'normal' self-help or personal development books, which can be full of drivel or nonsense that proclaims to *help you achieve your dreams, revolutionise your life* or *change your world*. Blah, blah, blah. Oh, you utter cynic you.

Cynicism (or as I've named it that Mindfield of a **MindF*ck**. **MFs** aka **MindF*ck** for short) is your habitual internal belief systems and thoughts, that zap you of your confidence, diminish your ideas, your plans and your creativity. That internal voice that says you're not up to scratch or you can't handle the pace, or constantly tells you that you just don't matter. Well, that's simply not true. How about instead of beating yourself up and limiting yourself with internal noise, you could identify and obliterate your debilitating **MFs** states and float in a bubble of absolute ability, empowerment and contentment? Not to mention you'd have a load more time to do what you loved, and what feels good too, right? Ermm, that's quite a few things to contend with now, isn't it?! Hand on heart, you recognise one, two or three guises of the negative impact your **MFs** state of mind has had on your life, don't you? Think back. For some of you it'll only be a few minutes ago!

I mean, come on, even the most successful personalities you know all suffer from one or several of those things I have mentioned so far. Besides, I know you've woken up and are at least thinking about getting your backside out of bed.

Positive disruption. Positive action. Positive you.

Because You Matter
Chelle Verite

Right, let's do this. Go on get out of bed. Put your big girl pants on (or your Yorkie-man-eating-chocolate-bar boxers) and imagine your life as less stressful and easier. Where you're way more in control and focused on you being you. A world where you get picked up, shaken down and lovingly given back that feeling of being alive, rather than being terrified about doing right or wrong. Or worse still, completely apathetic.

I'll keep myself busy with life admin stuff. That's simple and avoids the fact that I don't know what else to do, or how to be me.

Urgh to that. Computer says no. Well, actually it says, 'Oi you, slimy wee self-important nasty wee bastard of a **MindF*ck** mind. Think you can take me? Dinnea think so, you can get tae f*ck man.' (West coast, really broad Glaswegian Scottish accent required here, think Begbie from the film Trainspotting). And to top it all off, he does the Begbie glass toss over the shoulder, smash of the glass in the face violent action too. Regardless of whether it's Begbie, or a wee bit of polite yet direct Miss Jean Brodie, the result is the same, your debilitating and limiting **MF** state of mind will be glass smashed and rugby ball kicked into touch. Instead, this is about you empowering yourself into positive action so you can **BE REAL... SHOW UP... BE SEEN...** Create a world where you are wildly celebrated for being your whole human 'BEingness' (yes, that is a word. Well, it's a Chelle-ism now so it totally counts) and where you can calmly and contentedly be you. Where you can feel confident and motivated and zap the **MF** state of mind (try saying that after a few glasses of wine). I'll even make it easy with just the right amount of challenge and support so you can **Go BE**.

Right, enough of me ranting. Where exactly is your state of mind then? Let's take a moment to start noticing what's going on. Start picking up on and positively disrupting your **MF** status quo ways of doing things and shaking yourself out of the pressures of being 'normal'.

Because Y♡u Matter

Chelle Verite

Which ones, up until now that is, have played a part in your world? And if you fib, avoid the truth or blatantly lie, I will know. Come on… tell all. What type of **MF** have you got?

Which do you recognise most?

A) Non-DOing. The *I'm so overwhelmed*, the *I'm lost, haven't a clue*, or the *I'm just not confident of what I want and how I'll get what I want, in fact I'm totally unsure, so I'll just procrastinate, wait and worry* aka **Non-DOing?**

☐ **Yes**   ☐ **No**

B) Wrong-DOing. The *I'll put myself under immense pressure of getting it right*, the *I'll beat myself up*, the *I'll convince myself that I will make stupid mistakes*, or the *Nope, that's a risk that I won't be taking as it's not worth the chance that I won't be successful* aka **Wrong-DOing?**

☐ **Yes**   ☐ **No**

C) Their-DOing. The *I'll give myself freely to other people as they keep taking*, the *I keep saying yes, I'll do it*, the *Where does my time, my life, or my wishes go? I'm so busy all the time*, or the *I'd rather do it for you than for me because I'm not worthy, but you are* diversion tactics and immersion focus aka **Their-DOing.**

☐ **Yes**   ☐ **No**

Well? Where exactly is your MF state of mind?

Ok, for all you wonderfully, logically inclined people, I've made it easy for you and compiled it all into a little questionnaire. Firstly, because it's easier to digest. Secondly, we all secretly love books where we can tick boxes and do some *Yes, I'm intelligent, let me use my basic GCSE/Standard Grade maths at least once this week.*

Thirdly, it's a great excuse to get up, head to the kitchen and go and get a pen (I mean fill up that wine glass).

Remember that this just the beginning. We will be going into way more detail about kicking your **Critical Mind** in Life Lesson 14. For now, this is us getting to grips with you. Opening up your eyes, ears and mind so you can begin to notice the impact your internal state of mind has on yourself and your world. It'll also help you see how your logical and your emotional selves are entwined in your approach to things. Or indeed if they are at all.

Life Lesson 03

SO WHAT MF ARE YOU?

♥ **How often do you find yourself in the following situations?**

Score yourself on the following questions by circling the answer that best represents you.

Ⓐ Always | Ⓞ Often | Ⓢ Sometimes | Ⓡ Rarely | Ⓝ Never

Because You Matter
Chelle Verite

Non-DOing

Q1. I feel overwhelmed when faced with lots of things to do.
Ⓐ Ⓞ Ⓢ Ⓡ Ⓝ

Q2. I can at times feel lost and often unable to decide what or how to do things.
Ⓐ Ⓞ Ⓢ Ⓡ Ⓝ

Q3. I don't feel very confident or able to do things.
Ⓐ Ⓞ Ⓢ Ⓡ Ⓝ

Q4. I worry so much I procrastinate and put things off for another day.
Ⓐ Ⓞ Ⓢ Ⓡ Ⓝ

Wrong-DOing

Q5. I put myself under immense pressure to get things right.
Ⓐ Ⓞ Ⓢ Ⓡ Ⓝ

Q6. I beat myself up if I get things wrong.
Ⓐ Ⓞ Ⓢ Ⓡ Ⓝ

Q7. I convince myself I'll make stupid mistakes.
Ⓐ Ⓞ Ⓢ Ⓡ Ⓝ

Q8. I'd rather not do something if there is a risk that I won't be great at it.
Ⓐ Ⓞ Ⓢ Ⓡ Ⓝ

Their-DOing

Q9. I say yes even to things I don't want to do to get recognition from others.
Ⓐ Ⓞ Ⓢ Ⓡ Ⓝ

Q10. I'd rather do things for others, or life admin tasks, instead of things for me.
Ⓐ Ⓞ Ⓢ Ⓡ Ⓝ

Q11. I feel that I am not worthy of attention.
Ⓐ Ⓞ Ⓢ Ⓡ Ⓝ

Q12. I worry I come across as needy.
Ⓐ Ⓞ Ⓢ Ⓡ Ⓝ

Total up your scores and see what you get.

Always	Often	Sometimes	Rarely	Never
4 points	3 points	2 points	1 point	0 points

YOUR MF SCORES			
Non-DOing		TOTAL:	/ 12
Q1. ① ② ③ ④	Q2. ① ② ③ ④	Q3. ① ② ③ ④	Q4. ① ② ③ ④
Wrong-DOing		TOTAL:	/ 12
Q5. ① ② ③ ④	Q6. ① ② ③ ④	Q7. ① ② ③ ④	Q8. ① ② ③ ④
Their-DOing		TOTAL:	/ 12
Q9. ① ② ③ ④	Q10. ① ② ③ ④	Q11. ① ② ③ ④	Q12. ① ② ③ ④
		OVERALL **MF** SCORE:	/ 36

And your overall **MF** score out of 36 was… wait for it… [   ] Ta da!

(By the way anything over 8 overall MF score we need to have a chat.)

EXPLANATIONS OF THE MFS

Let's see what the **Non-DOing, Wrong-DOing**, and **Their-DOing** states of mind look like.

Non-DOing Your state of mind is constantly processing information. You are your own worst enemy as you constantly gather more and more data until you overwhelm your system and break down into emotional '**Meltdown Mary'** moments. This provides you with a world awash with emotion, tears, procrastination and a to do list longer than your arm, and then some. You are often crippled with self-doubt, limiting beliefs and a feeling of inadequacy, which up until now has often prevented you from taking the leap.

Wrong-DOing Your mind is task and logic focused. You are highly critical of your achievements (or lack of them) and can be very fixed into patterns of being simply downright nasty to yourself. You will happily spend time quietly (or even loudly) chastising yourself about how stupid, rubbish and totally pants you are... even when the reality and facts say you aren't bad at all. You can come across as a dismissive, strict, unforgiving, arrogant twat (or '*wa*' as we say in our family, dropping the 't's in public makes it way more acceptable to say than the four-letter word equivalent). Up until now you haven't given yourself an inch, let alone a f*cking mile.

Their-DOing Your mind is focused on the importance of other people. You spend the majority of your time doing what others want you to do, sacrificing what you want and feeling bad in the process. You are highly affected by how people treat you and give value to other people's demands. In short, you can come across as a bit of a push over, a wet blanket, or even a martyr, depending on how much your state of mind has to say on the matter. Rescuing others has up until now become a default state of mind. *I don't deserve goodness in my world so you can have it instead.* Blah blah blah. You get the picture.

LET'S LOOK AND PROCESS

♥ **Have a look at your scores. What do you notice?**

♥ **Which MF state is most prominent / least prominent for you?**

Because You Matter

Chelle Verite

❤ **What impact is your MF state having on situations in your life?**

❤ **What impact is your MF state having on your relationships?**

❤ **What impact is your MF state having on you?**

Because Y♥u Matter

Chelle Verite

Right. Stop. STOP! Stop and actually think about those questions.

This is important. It's the rules of *Because YOU Matter*. Remember, we are fighting for you to empower you. This is my God complex talking here. Stop whizzing over the deep and meaningful, touchy feely, *I'm not sure I really want to investigate myself* questions that you just answered. Stop being impatient. Stop the mindset that you don't want to or you're scared to find out. Keep calm, you've got this.

Pop the kettle back on, make a nice cup of tea, get a bit of cake out (or your favourite snack), or pour a nice wee glass of vino or prosecco. Now you're sorted, go back and re-read through the definitions, locate your scores and go through the questions and explanations again. This time actually take a minute to stop, think and truly consider yourself.

Cake, tea, prosecco and your Life Lesson processing all finished? Well done. Now read on. Remember your **BYM Fight Club** pledge promise? Full commitment required.

WHAT YOU REALLY NOTICED

♥ **Well, what did you really notice?**

(About the MF states and scores that, up until now, featured most in your world?)

Were you...

Non-DOing?	
Wrong-DOing?	
Their-DOing?	

The higher the scores, the more you are opting for the Critical **MF** Human '**DOing**' option, and if you scored more than 8 in the total score section, keep reading. If you scored less than 8, get your little black book out and contact all the people you love to go and teach your methods.

For those of you who are new to identifying and recognising your **Non-DOing, Wrong-DOing,** and **Their-DOing** states, have a real think about the following.

Because You Matter
Chelle Verite

♥ **What exactly do you want more of, or less of, in your life so you can positively disrupt your world and focus on the things that make you feel good and grow?**

♥ **What actions will you now take?**

♥ **How will you respond to life events rather than automatically reacting to events that happen?**

Because Y♥u Matter

Chelle Verite

One thing… regarding the first Life Lesson recap question. *What did you really notice?*

Did you spot that I said 'Did notice' (past tense) and not 'Do you notice' (future tense)? Ah, you probably didn't. However, I wanted you to know that I did that on purpose. The reason being is that I am going do exactly what I do on the side-line of a rugby pitch when my son, Oliver, is playing a game. I'm going to shout to your **Non-DOing**, **Wrong-DOing**, **Their-DOing** mind when it dares get in the way of your progress.

'FLATTEN THEM, OLI!' Meaning rugby tackle anyone or anything that gets in the way!

I know that's not exactly politically correct as he's eleven years old and has only just started playing touch rugby, but hey, f*ck it, I'm only showing my support. I am going to show you my support by detonating your **MF** the same way.

So, here I am, cheering you on to kick your **MF** state into touch, and by the way, I must really want to help you because it's *f*cking baltic* (Scottish term for very, very, cold) out on the rugby pitch side-lines. I also have Reynard's disease in my hands, which means they are currently turning blue, and my ears have practically fallen off because I forgot my earmuffs. In short, I am totally dedicated to you getting a handle on your mental well-being.

Here we go.

'Watch out _____ '*(your name)*

'Flatten them _____ '*(your name)*

'F*cking flatten them!'

'Yes, get in!'

Because Y♥u Matter

Chelle Verite

I will scream, whistle, rant, shout and run like a loonball with my coat over my head stating, 'You did it, you did it!' as your **Non-DOing, Wrong-DOing, Their-DOing** state of mind gets a severe kicking and trampled on. You will then continue to flatten the living hell out of your **MF** mind, picking it up and kicking it like a rugby ball into touch. Best kick ever and the game is won! Cheeeeerrrs all around the pitch, high fives, smiles all round, and a lost voice to Chelle.

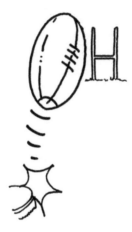

And why do it?

Why notice your **MindF*ck** critical mind states and kick them to touch?

Why notice all that **Non-DOing, Wrong-DOing, Their-DOing?**

Why choose to positively **Respond** rather than automatically **React?**

Simple.

Because Y♥u Matter

"

We do not become
humans just by
thinking, reasoning,
feeling, choosing or
even by just doing
something. We
become humans
by being.

VICTORINO Q ABURUGAR

LIFE LESSON

04

Human BEing

NOT HUMAN DOING

Because Y🙂u Matter
Chelle Verite

Remember, as much as we give it a huge shot, run ourselves ragged and habitually gift ourselves negatively with being so busy doing things, not doing things, and beating ourselves up about things, we have learned to be defined by what we do (or don't do). Helloooooo new world. We are not a **Human DOing.** We are a **Human BEing.**

Human BEing = Unique and Special.

Clue is in the name, people. We aren't supposed to be constantly on the go and defined by what we do. Yet there we have it. It's the first question we all ask when we meet someone new, whilst doing the obligatory handshake (well, now it's the nod hello and facemask check).

'Hello, what's your name, and what do you do?'

As if by magic it will mean something. The assumptions we all make about what we do. We measure our worth by what we do. Although, to be fair, thanks to Coronavirus-induced lockdowns hitting the world, people often now answer, 'Well, I haven't got the foggiest about what I actually do. Except work from home, attempt to juggle home schooling of the kids, pretend that Zoom comes naturally, and hold down the day job without being made redundant or having my house, or sanity, repossessed.' Oh, the irony that life used to be so different. When we were allowed to go out without sticking a face mask on our heads and having to social distance by about three hundred metres. I miss that world!

The journey of life... it's an interesting one, isn't it? Self-awareness. The more you know the more you can see, and once you've seen it and become aware of something, you can't just unsee the f*cker. It's like the bear hidden in the Toblerone logo, or the arrow hiding in the FedEx logo. (Sorry if you hadn't noticed these amazing little details. Quick, log into your phone (or laptop) that's by your side pretending not to zap your attention and access that interweb thingy. Give it some love and affection by Googling the Toblerone and FedEx logos and see if you can spot what I'm talking about. Ta-da! See, now you can never un-see it.)

Self-awareness, as it says in the name, is looking for the meaning in who we are and what we do, to somehow define our success in all the things we actually do. However, you are not a **Human DOing**. You are a **Human BEing**. Yet where is the instruction manual on how to be the latter? To just **Go BE** you and accept, acknowledge and love yourself just as you are? Yup, hello people, this is the start.

Life Lesson 04

HUMAN DOING VS HUMAN BEING

Have a think about what you have just read.

- ♥ **What have you unearthed so far about enjoying BEing human? What's surfaced from your unconscious mind into your new self-awareness?**

Hmmmm, that may be a bit of a deep, sit on the couch, tell me all about it question. So, here's the easier version and (yay!) another activity. Brilliant, an excuse to get those pens out again.

Because You Matter

Chelle Verite

This is what I'm like and how I experience the world when I am a **Human DOing**	This is what I'm like and how I experience the world when I am a **Human BEing**
(e.g. Busying myself with trivial tasks like loading the dishwasher, running around after the family, work tasks, to do lists, not enough time, or feeling pressured.)	*(e.g. Recognising what I need. Acknowledging what's important. Listening to what is in my heart and mind. Recharging my energy.)*

Referring back to the table you've just completed answer the following:

Because Y♥u Matter

Chelle Verite

💜 **What are the key differences in you when you focus on being a Human BEing rather than a Human DOing?**

💜 **What do you notice?**

💜 **What are the key differences for you and your internal processing of emotions and thoughts when you are a Human DOing and a Human BEing?**

Because You Matter

Chelle Verite

❤ **What actions will you take so you can grow to BE a Human BEing more in your life and positively impact your internal thoughts and emotions and Live the Life you Love AND Love the Life you Live?**

I will (Action 1)...

I will (Action 2)...

I will (Action 3)...

Have you answered all these questions properly? No skipping just because you can. Remember, this is your world that you are creating. You made a promise to fight for you, to create positive action and instil a calm, contented and confident life.

Why do it?

Why concentrate on becoming a **Human BEing** not a **Human DOing?**

Simple.

Because Y♡u Matter

"

> Inner peace begins the moment you choose NOT to allow another person or an event to control your emotions.

PEMA CHODRON

LIFE LESSON

05

Self-awareness

THE CROWN OF ACCEPTANCE

Because You Matter
Chelle Verite

Thinking about our self-awareness. Being aware of self… it's a good thing, right? Yes, it definitely is. It has to be, doesn't it? I mean, it's one of the many reasons you are on this empowerment journey and why you are engaging in this in the first place. Except with self-awareness, that in itself means you have to make conscious decisions. Decisions to support and help your life, rather than decisions that hinder you and who you are. Decisions of acceptance so you can be fully content and the fulfilled version of yourself, and where you can focus on **BEing Human** and complete yourself mentally and emotionally. And you know how important it is to be a **Human BEing** and NOT a **Human DOing** now, don't you?

Or as I like to call it, creating and celebrating the **Crown of Acceptance.**

The **Crown of Acceptance.** Unconditional acceptance for all that you offer your life and for the beautiful **Human BEing** that you are. Since I was a very young child, I've searched for just that. acceptance of self. Self-worth, self-honour, self-respect. Yet somehow, I've always felt there was something missing (you'll get more of my story in Life Lesson 11).

Because Y♡u Matter

Chelle Verite

Something missing in that I had to rely on other people to fill the void of uncertainty, that chasm of who I am or was supposed to be. Who could I model myself on? Who would accept this frizzy brown haired, brown skinned, spontaneous whirlwind of a personality with no siblings of my own and no cultural input about my heritage? I've pondered the question often. *How, if I don't understand my identity in the world, can I actually be accepted and seen for who I am?*

For some of you reading this story afresh (or if you haven't seen my TEDx talk), it's likely that, other than the brief mention at the beginning, you won't have known I was adopted.

Also, for the majority of you, unless you have experience of adoption in some way, the majority of you will have no idea of the depths of loss it can cause. You will already have those parental reference points. Those childhood experiences that you can look at and rely on to give you a bearing and a handle on how things should be done, to help you build a jigsaw of who you are, how you show up, and how you can be seen in the world that you create. You'll also have added to this picture the choices you've made about what you love to do, your passions, and your world of work. (If you made conscious decisions, that is, and didn't just go with the crowd or fall into something).

So, if you're 'lucky' (and I use this word in a positive sense, you'll understand why I point this out as you read later Life Lessons), all of this understanding sits like a golden crown of confident acceptance on your head that you can wear with pride and assurance that you are indeed a wonderful human being, unique and special, defined only by you.

However, for some of you reading this book (me included), the journey is a little less clear and certainly a f*ck load wobblier. Sadly, the **Crown of Acceptance** is not on our heads. Instead, what should have been a glowing, diamond, twinkling halo has slipped past our foreheads

Because You Matter
Chelle Verite

and face and is now sitting around our neck, quietly choking and suffocating us, as we scrabble around for people to free us and replace the crown because our hands are tied. We are fixed into the mentality that it is only other people who can place the crown on our heads and define whether or not we are able to be seen, are good enough to be seen, or somehow worthy enough to be seen. That's just crazy, isn't it? You'd like to think so. Except my husband says I'm a smart, beautiful, professional, capable, fiercely independent woman who up until fairly recently looked to other people for acceptance, for guidance, for recognition. To feel okay about me. To fill my *Chelle* (oh the irony of my new name), fill my void, so I could somehow be comfortable with being me. Being Real, Showing Up and Being Seen.

My crown had slipped. It was choking me. Choking me in my work life. Choking me in my home life. Choking me in my life full stop. The sad thing was I truly believed my hands were tied, and because of that I couldn't breathe. I *was* choking but the only person that had tied my hands was... ME.

And they were really tied. At least, I believed they were.

For those of you whose hands were also tied, or that you thought were tied because you were waiting for someone else to give you permission to release them, or you were simply obeying orders and giving your power away, we need to have some time together. A lot of time. I'd say all of this book time. You see, the impact of looking to others to define you, the impact of having other people's words, wants, or wishes to gift you a feeling of acceptance, the impact that their words somehow release you isn't helping you, it's suffocating you. Waiting for their opinion or rating of your worth, their God-like nod giving you permission to be you, that *kind* word. Waiting for them to have an epiphany moment and truly *see you* for all that you are, for all that you offer. For you to matter and for you to be accepted.

Because You Matter

Chelle Verite

In many situations, this is simply a catastrophic waiting game. It's like chasing your tail. You never quite reach it, and with that energy you end up spiralling out of control. Expecting acceptance from other people, instead of placing that **Crown of Acceptance** on your own head and being proud of who you are, is a killer. Putting God-like powers in someone else's hands, even when you don't know if they will care for your well-being and waiting for them to decide if you can or can't join in or if you are enough. We've all been there. Some of us occasionally, but for some of us who suffer from low self-esteem and lack of self-worth, we've been there a lot. That game of waiting for acceptance will mean you feel like you never quite make the grade, or even know what the f*ck the rules of the game are at times as they seem to change so much.

'We'll accept you if you do this... and this... and this... and this...and this...' or 'We won't accept you for that... and that... and that... and that.' You get the picture.

No matter what they do, and no matter what you do, they simply won't put that god damn crown on your head. I mean, put yourself in my shoes. Imagine being told, 'We don't want to get to know you further' and 'We don't want to have you in our life' and 'We don't want to accept you because...' (wait for it) 'we feel threatened by you because you are too fat, too thin, too nice, too pretty and look too alike.'

Too nice?! Too pretty?! And I look too alike?!!

On that basis, being told to talk to the hand. Not being accepted or allowed to interact with a newly found family, or being rejected because of those very reasons? Ermm, ok, changing goal posts. I mean, what should I do? Make myself uglier, nastier and get plastic surgery?! What on earth are the rules of admission? What are the rules of the acceptance game exactly?!

Self-awareness

Because You Matter

Chelle Verite

To put things into context, I'm referring to my newly found brother. I'd found out after doing some research in 2013 that I was one of seven siblings (one father, six different women!). The next few years riding that emotional life rollercoaster marked one of the most wonderful and emotionally treacherous experiences of my life. Imagine the emotions. I grew up as an only child, then after almost twenty years of searching, I found and met my siblings, my ten nieces and nephews, and extended family that went into the tens and hundreds. Family. My family. I was utterly ecstatic.

Growing up there had been three of us. My mum, my dad and me, and a few cats and dogs, but it had really just been the three of us. Instead, there I was, finally getting my life's wish to be included, explaining why I wanted to be a part of a huge family, a real family, instead of ticking the family history box *unknown*. I had found my full blown, full-on, real blood heritage family. Something that I had dreamt of, like Father Christmas was out there on the table and I was as vulnerable as a baby lamb. After a lifetime of waiting to be accepted and recognised for myself. A sister to a brother. An aunty to nephew and nieces. I had landed. Being invited into a place in the world where I was finally the same and I had a basis of comparison. I was so excited to be seen. To be accepted.

Then to be told, after a few months into developing an immensely positive relationship, that nope, you're not welcome because. 'We think you're too nice, and too pretty.' And despite being a struggling single mother. 'You're too successful.' And. 'It's uncomfortable being around you because you make your brother too happy.' It was like seeing a party that I wanted to join in but there was an impenetrable glass wall stopping me, and only me, from entering.

I bet we've all been in that place, looking in from afar and wishing we were inside.

Because You Matter

Chelle Verite

- ✕ Like not being invited to a party at school.
- ✕ Like not having your ideas taken up by the people at work for new initiatives.
- ✕ Like someone taking the last cake at the delicatessen or when you go out for dinner, and them knowing you wanted it but not being gifted it.

(Do not take my cake. This is **BYM Fight Club** remember.)

So, what did I do? What was my fight? My fight for me to be accepted?

I wrote a letter.

I wrote a letter to my brother (bear in mind this is a man who had told me he loved me and couldn't believe how fortunate he was to have me in his life). All my wishes, my justifications, my heart, and for the biggest part, pretty much all of my love and my soul. I wrote and finally finished a hand-written letter. Five pages of blood, sweat, tears, dreams, disappointments and all of my wishes for my heart, his heart, my family and his family. Everything. I posted it. Then I hoped and hoped and hoped. Then I waited and waited and waited.

And I waited.

Days went by.

Weeks went by.

Months went by.

In fact, twenty one months went by. I waited for a response, wishing that I was a good enough reason to write back to. Wishing that my heart-breaking honesty and vulnerability was enough, and that I was enough, to be accepted and wanted. It was like I was holding all of my breath for someone to make a decision on whether I was allowed to be in an exclusive club, except it was a gateway to my heritage,

Because You Matter
Chelle Verite

connection, everything that I had wished for. Would I be deemed valuable enough? Would I be seen to meet the criteria? Would I be important enough, worthy enough, or credible enough to be seen and accepted?

As every day passed of those twenty one months (and six days, three hours and thirty seven minutes to be exact), I lost a little bit more of my soul. A little bit more of myself disappeared. A little bit more of the carefree bubbly 'too nice' personality disappeared. To be replaced with something that felt deeply, deeply rejected; a sad, empty, worthless and less connected version of myself. Every day I looked at what I did to brighten other people's lives when I coached, trained, got out of bed. I stood up and I inspired and motivated others. Every day that passed I felt like I had been in a fatal car crash, that I'd lost my mind, my dignity, my understanding and my zest for life.

I'd lost my fight.

I'd lost me.

All because I'd put my fate and my power for acceptance in the hands of someone else. My hands were tied. All along, my **Crown of Acceptance**. My Crown. The Crown that I should have placed on my own head, was slipping. Slipping to strangle me. Slipping and preventing me from breathing in all aspects of my life. Every aspect of my life suffered. My health. My relationships. My sanity. My work.

All of it.

Twenty one months, six days, three hours and thirty seven minutes after promises of breaking that silence (we hadn't spoken for all that time) and for me to brave and ask the question.

'Did you actually get the letter?!'

Because You Matter

Chelle Verite

To receive the replies.

'Yes, we got the letter.'

'Yes, I'll write.'

'Yes, I've been meaning to reply.'

'Yes, I started but didn't quite get there.'

'Yes, I will.'

'Yes.'

Blah, blah, blah. False hope after false hope. After blatant pretences, I realised. I don't just mean a small, dawning realisation. I mean it was a huge smack-me-in-the-mouth-knock-me-sideways-and-into-smithereens dawning *Chelle, WTF are you doing?!* realisation.

I was waiting for another person to define me.

I was waiting for someone else to gift me my **Crown of Acceptance**.

It was never going to come.

That was when it broke.

No, not my spirit. Although that wasn't far off. There were days when I just didn't want to be in the world. There were days when I just didn't want to get out of bed. Yet instead of my spirit breaking, what broke was my hands from being tied. They simply released. My self-awareness hit me like one last truck. I flexed my previously immobile hands. I picked up that crown from around my neck and for the first time I placed it on my head. My crown. My **Crown of Acceptance**. For me, to love honour and respect me as I am, and for all that I am. To be a **Human BEing**, unique and special.

To be me.

Because You Matter
Chelle Verite

What I realised that day, as the sheer exhaustion of running a life on pure hope, anger and devastating disappointment crushed me, is that we cannot rely on anyone else to define how we are allowed to be seen in this world. We cannot wait for other people to tell us we are enough. We cannot wait for other people to tell us that we are worthy. We cannot wait for others to accept us. We must accept ourselves for who and what we are.

How on earth do we do that so it feels good and so we don't keep creating the same patterns over and over again?

And that got me thinking. F*CK! I'd done it all my life. It's like changing the way you dress. Changing your accent. Changing your likes or dislikes so you fit in, even when you don't.

It's like waiting for the person who's been bullying you, just because they can (or because they're running scared from themselves or they want you to feel uncomfortable) and you do what you can to show up and be recognised for what you offer, expecting them to stop bullying you. Yet you're still putting yourself in that punchbag position.

It's like waiting for someone to be nice to you. In my case, when I worked at a huge online retailer, no matter what I did or how I did it, my mentor would move the goal posts. Little did I know that she begrudged me because she had wanted my job and not got it. Every Wednesday for six months, she'd set me tasks that I would fail and would continually berate and belittle me to the point where I was beyond crushed, barely able to function and became very ill. Still I waited for her to grant the magic words. 'You are accepted' and 'You are good enough.' It's like being in a toddler group with your baby and never quite fitting in because all the other mums seem to know the rules and you're not part of the 'Mummy knows best' club.

Because Y♡u Matter
Chelle Verite

Sadly, it's like me waiting for my brother to write that letter of recognition, understanding or kindness. To acknowledge that I am a good person, a worthy person, allowing me access to him and his family, while I put all other elements of my life on hold until he decided that I wasn't getting it wrong, whatever *it* and *wrong is.* In doing so, during that period, I put my life on hold. I stopped living and started sabotaging all that I had instead.

We put so much power into people's hands. Except here's the thing. my brother didn't ask for it. He didn't demand that he had that power over me. Neither will anyone you've gifted your **Crown of Acceptance** to. The power to decide whether or not we should be accepted and accepted enough to be seen in life. I did that. I gifted that power away. I can also guarantee you've done it too. Sometimes without even consciously thinking you're doing it. Sometimes as a trade for that ever-elusive affection, love or connection. Sometimes it's *just because.* That's the biggest, saddest, most crushing thing of all, we weren't forced. We weren't held at gun point. The saddest thing is, we gave the power away of our own free will. Every time.

So, I say NO!

I say.

- × Stop giving people the power of your **Crown of Acceptance**.
- × Stop relying on others to make the decision that you are good enough or acceptable enough to **BE REAL... SHOW UP...** and **BE SEEN...**
- × Stop waiting for your value to be defined by someone else.
- × Stop giving you away for others to decide your fate.
- × **STOP. STOP. STOP!**

And instead.

- ♥ Fight. Fight. Fight.
- ♥ Decide. Decide. Decide.
- ♥ **Be. Be. BE!**

Fight and decide that YOU, and you alone, are going to release your tied hands, for they are not tied. YOU are going to place that **Crown of Acceptance** proudly back on top of your head, exactly where it belongs. It may or may not be twenty one months since you've done that or you may never have done it (up until now). Whatever the situation is, YOU are the one that defines your own acceptance. This is your head. This is your crown. You decide when and how to wear your **Crown of Acceptance**. This is your life to live and love. This is your life to decide.

I did it. Yes, it took me a while. In fact, it took me a lifetime. Yes, there are days I wished I hadn't gone through the pain, that waiting and wishing game, that *I want to feel accepted* game. I wish to God that someone had explained to me as soon as I could walk, talk and laugh that the biggest belief in life is self-belief and self-acceptance. It wouldn't have been My Little Ponies, or cars in the dirt, or roller-skates that I would have been concentrating on. It would have been taking on the world like I was completely invincible, rather than imagining I was invisible.

Instead, I had to wait forty six years to see it for myself. See me and accept me, for me.

I had to want to fight. **Fight. Accept. Decide.** Well, I did fight, I did accept and I did decide. I haven't looked back. I can guarantee, when you do it too, neither will you.

Life Lesson 05

YOUR CROWN OF ACCEPTANCE

♥ **Who, what and when have you given/are you giving your Crown of Acceptance away to?** And when I say 'crown' I mean the power over you to decide if you are to be seen or not. Let's dig deeper and find out.

STEP 1. YOUR PEN AND TIMER

Pick up a pen and grab a timer (egg timer or phone, whatever is to hand) and set it for 3 minutes (just long enough to boil an egg). When you've read the instructions below, I want you to write non-stop in the Step 3 box on page 69. Your pen cannot leave the page, just keep writing all your thoughts. You are going to figure out why you've given your power away.

STEP 2. GETTING READY

When you write, I want you to think of all the people, all the situations, all the times you've given someone else the power to judge whether you are to be accepted, or not.

Because Y♥u Matter

Chelle Verite

Write down all the times (or as many as you can remember) when you have given the power of your Crown of Acceptance away to someone or something else.

Before you start... pay attention, this is important! This is **your** list. No-one will be reading this except you. Remember, if anyone wants to borrow this book, you'll either buy them a copy or you'll be giving them a link to buy one of their own. What's written in this book is yours and yours alone.

This is not a pretend *I'll write it to please other people* list. This is your **BE Real** list. This is the list of when you have previously given away your **Crown of Acceptance** power. This is the list of when you were waiting for someone else to decide your worthiness. (It's important to note here, that when you write this list will bring emotions up from within you. It's a list of things you may not have thought about for quite some time. A list that will have potentially caused you pain, struggle and loss of hope. So, if when you write it, it doesn't bring up hurt, it's not your **BE Real** list).

Use the following life areas as a prompt for how you focus your thoughts.

This is about the good, the bad and the ugly.

- ♥ Dreams
- ♥ Disappointments
- ♥ Friends
- ♥ Finances
- ♥ Family
- ♥ Hurts
- ♥ Health
- ♥ Relationships
- ♥ Work

Here's some of the power items from my list.

- ✕ My brother, the letter I wrote and me waiting for recognition.
- ✕ Not being told that I was loved by my parents, or that I was doing something that they were proud of.
- ✕ Putting myself down and giving power to my **Sabotaging Devil Mindset.**

(See? I told you...We are all human and this is about **BE**ing **Real**.)

STEP 3. YOUR 3 MINUTE THINK TIME

Timer, pen, paper and prompt list at the ready?

> ♥ **Who, what and when have you given away your Crown of Acceptance power to?**
> (Your 3 minutes think time starts now. GO!)

Because You Matter

Chelle Verite

Beep! 3 minutes is up! Stop writing, pens down please. You did it. You made your **BE Real** list. Take a moment to look at your list. This is now your time. Your time to stop giving away your power. This is the time to untie your hands. This is the time to take the crown away from around your neck. This is the time to finally put that **Crown of Acceptance** firmly back on your head.

Yes, get in!

So, let's make all the 'up until now' pain, hurts and disappointments worth it by figuring out how you can stop them and start **BEing** the real you.

> ♥ **What is the first step you need to take to stop that person, or that situation, having the power of playing God and dictating your Crown of Acceptance?**
> (First steps are great. Remember every journey of a thousand steps start with a single step.)

Because Y♡u Matter
Chelle Verite

> ♥ **What specifically do you need to stop (or prevent) people from taking your 'Crown'?**

> ♥ **What do you need to start so you can put your 'Crown' firmly on your head?**

> ♥ **What will you do more of / less of to ensure your Crown of Acceptance stays there for good?**

Because You Matter

Chelle Verite

This is about your life. Your fight. Your choices. This is about **BEing Human**. This is about **BEing YOU** so you can Live the Life you Love AND Love the Life you Live.

Make sure that you have really answered the questions and not just given them lip service.

Make you proud of you.

I'm watching you!

Why do it?

Why keep the power of putting your own **Crown of Acceptance** on your head and stop gifting your power away?

Simple.

Because You Matter

Instead of worrying
about what you
can control,
shift your energy
to what you
can create.

ROY T BENNETT

LIFE LESSON

06

Dissolving worries

HENRY WHO?!

Because Y♡u Matter

Chelle Verite

'Because YOU matter. Simple.'

'To be, be me, and realise that I do actually matter.'

'Wow, that sounds f*cking awesome, Chelle!'

Except, what I realised while I was doing what I do just to get out of bed and do life and positively delivering training masterclasses on Zoom 'TV', is that deep down in the unconscious part of our self-critical brain, we spend most of our time worrying. Regardless of how good we are, how much experience we have, or what we know about the subject in hand.

We worry if we fit in. We worry if we don't fit in. We worry if we get it right. We worry if we get it wrong. We just plain worry about it! Am I enough? What will they think? Who are they? This is reality, people. Hands up if you have been in this situation? It's like some imaginary friend who expects us all to have achieved even though we don't quite know what the rules of the game are. I mean, it's like turning up on sports day to play rugby with a football in your hand. No-one tells you the rules, then we spend the majority of our waking and sleeping hours beating ourselves up. And worrying about *it* all. What is *it* anyway?

For some of us, we know that *it* is a tiny, insignificant ball of anxiety and worry that bears no relation to our lives. For others, the aspiration of getting *it* is just f*cking huge. I call it the **'Worry-woe-is-me Dance'**. It's like doing the hokey kokey, in out, in out and shake it all about. The pretence that we all actually know what we're doing, yet none of us actually have a clue. It's about feeling okay about yourself, and with yourself, rather than getting eaten up in a pile of catastrophising worry rubble. **'Worry-woe-is-me Dance'** is like a huge earthquake of stones avalanching on our heads, burying us alive. Richter Scale 9.

Because Y♥u Matter
Chelle Verite

For some of us though, the curse of **'Worry-woe-is-me Dance'** is that it's more than rubble. It's just plain paralysis with complete and utter fear. Like riding that terrifying *Smiler* in Alton Towers. Who was the nasty person who named that rollercoaster? It's grimacing and nasty, not a smiler. It's white knuckling fear. For me, fear was Count Dracula in my bedroom cupboard. That cupboard door just looked at me, looming with the evilness that was going to pounce out of it in only the way a fanged, blood dripping, black clothed Count Dracula could. I knew it wasn't real and only a clothes cupboard, but try telling that to my mind and its subsequent adrenaline-filled rush of fear. Honestly, I've never been so afraid, other than riding Smiler. Oh, and maybe when I grew up and found that I needed to pay bills and step out into the world as an adult and go and be amazing. That, my friends, is just f*cking terrifying.

Fear. Fear. Fear.

Or the **Fear Monster**, as I call it. That social dance of acceptability. Fear of understanding how we actually do life. Fear of failure aka **Atychiphobia**. Sounds like a nasty sneeze *(Aty-chi-phobia)* or a chip butty *(Aty-chiphobia)*. We also worry ourselves stupid about the opposite. The fear of success, or as Google likes to call it **Achievemephobia**. *Yes*, that's really the name. **Achieve-me-phobia**. Before we get all label happy here, we are talking about fear and the worry and anxiety that goes with both fear of success and fear of failure. Fear, fear and more fear. Yes indeed, there is so much pressure for us to fit in. We worry about the fear of being accepted. Fear of being successful. We worry about whether or not we should be the same as everyone else, or is it better not to be the same as everyone else? Do I stand out? Do I not stand out? It's ironic, isn't it? It's not that easy, you can't just say, 'F*ck it, I am normal' or 'F*ck it, I am NOT normal.'

Because You Matter
Chelle Verite

There's always a dilemma (except if you are using the *I am not normal* statement to start a book that is. And just wait until you meet Henry. Oh, how the irony will all make sense).

The thing is, we tell our kids, 'Do the best you can.' We tell our friends, our loved ones. In fact, we tell everyone around us, 'Be proud of who you are and what you achieve.' Yet as our adult self we often crumble under the pressure of being different. That dilemma of being within the parameters of *normal* acceptability, and we constantly worry ourselves stupid.

For example, writing this book. Will it work? Will I be brave enough to finish it? To actually write it? To have people read it? To have me out there? What if it isn't good enough? What if it fails and doesn't work? Have I got the guts to be me? Urghhhhh! Really. **Aty-chiphobia** seriously! You can, 'Get ef e.' (Welcome back Begbie, and my Scottish Tourettes). Worse still, what happens if it's a success? What happens if people actually like it? **Achievemephobia** will rear its head and that'll mean even more people analysing and scrutinising whether or not I'm good enough. Whether I fit in. Did I do *it* right? Did I do *it* wrong? Worry. Worry. Worry!

And I'm the Empowerment Coach, the Positive Disruptor, the TEDx Speaker, mother, and not to mention loving wife. Equipped for the last twenty two years, (and despite crippling Borderline Personality Disorder), I've helped thousands of people empower themselves. The irony is that **Fear Monster** doesn't discriminate. It can, and does, rear its head. The **Fear Monster** and '**Worry-woe-is-me Dance'** happens to us all, regardless of who we are, what age we are, what sex we are, where we live or what we do. My **Fear Monster** chases my arse so much it literally sets itself on fire most days.

However, if you're fortunate to have an anxiety that is so small it doesn't exist, and you glide effortlessly through life being continually proud of who and what you are, then I congratulate you. I ask you what did you do to make that work? I also have to ask you why the f*ck are you reading this book? And where the f*ck were you when I (and the rest of the 99% of the population) needed you? You would have saved us all the angst of this *Because YOU matter* learning and self-awareness journey. However, to be fair, it would also have put me out of a job as this book would have gone unwritten. Every cloud, Chelle. Do not chastise these lovely people.

Or perhaps you are the type of person who doesn't worry because your self-awareness has yet to be awakened, like a slumbering bear in the midst of a complete life hibernation. WOW, you will be in for a bit of a rollercoaster ride. Oh, and by the way, lack of self-awareness and not having a clue, or being unaware that you have a **Worry-woe-is-me Dance** does not count towards gaining life brownie points!

Alternatively, maybe, just maybe, you are the type of person that continually just wallows and spends all of your waking hours being consumed by worry, because...

A.	it's a habit	☐
B.	it makes you feel good	☐
C.	it's all you have ever known	☐

(Tick which option applies to you)

Being the introverted extrovert that I am, I have ticked all three of those boxes many, many times when consumed by the **Fear Monster**, and that's just getting out of bed. In fact, so much so that if worrying was an Olympic sport I would be sure to have won gold medals many, many times over.

Because Y♡u Matter

Chelle Verite

Here's the thing. I could leave you to worry yourself stupid over things but you'd end up throwing up all over yourself, or worse still, projectile vomiting over me. But what would be the use in that? I mean, I'd get to go shopping for some new clothes. Also, if you spent all your time worrying and throwing up, I'd lose my cake eating, prosecco / wine drinking and tea making buddy and that would simply be a downright shame. We are having such a lovely time together.

I thought instead of losing you to a heap and puddle of catastrophising worry rubble and tears, I'd gift you with a **Worry Dissolver**, so you can say a big FU to that back-and-forth **Worry-woe-is-me Dance**. (I'll let you fill in the gaps for FU, however I think you've got the picture.) No, that doesn't mean you need to give back your gold medals, you can keep them with my blessing. However, what it does mean is that we will be expending our energy on way, way, way more fun and productive things, like living and loving your life. Of course, doing something new will mean replacing habitual ways of doing things and

Because Y♡u Matter

Chelle Verite

concentrate on **BE**ing the new you. You've already made your **BYM Fight Club** pledge promise and I know you want a new way of **BE**ing you. That, and you really don't fancy the wrath of me; I'm amazingly encouraging, however, I'm also a devil when it comes to decapitating knees. Trust me, the former is way nicer than the latter, which makes it very difficult to walk.

Talking of things to concentrate on. 'Worrying is like a rocking chair. It gives you something to do, but never gets you anywhere.' Or so says Erma Bombeck, and I have to agree.

So, what exactly is it? That worrying thing? Worrying for a lot of us is a self-destructive habit. It's something we do automatically without thinking, and often not because it offers anything positive. Usually we do it because it feels like a worthwhile distraction. Except it's not worthwhile at all. The back and forth, back and forth, sadly, has huge negative opportunity costs in our world. Opportunity costs as in losses due to the amount of energy we expend, and the amount of lost time doing the worrying itself. We can waste hours and hours worrying about the smallest (and biggest) of things. Things in our life

Because Y♥u Matter

Chelle Verite

that we either aren't going to fix, aren't real or aren't going to change, so we are merely left with energy being spent back and forth, back and forth.

Worrying = no time for much else and very little energy.

(Sad faces at the ready).

In short, worrying is a big fat waste of time, a habitual distraction, and often has hugely detrimental physical and mental wellbeing costs. To top it all off, while worrying keeps us busy, it stops us from doing other things which means that to do list gets bigger and bigger and that **Non-DOing MindF*CK** state of mind is back with a vengeance. That and the fact that worrying only serves to heighten anxiety, not reduce it. The act of worrying, therefore, rarely makes us feel good.

Ermm, remind me again, why the f*ck do we do it?

Worrying is all about pink elephants.

Pink Elephants called Henry. Ah, there you go. You're probably thinking *What the f*ck is Chelle going on about?* A few minutes ago, she was talking about rocking chairs and now it's pink elephants. Has she lost her marbles? No, I can assure you I haven't.

However, shall we take a few minutes to worry about if that was a *normal* thing to say or not? Pink elephants. 'Pink elephants called Henry,' I hear you say. 'Pink elephants. What about pink elephants? Oh God, I don't know anything about pink elephants! And what about the name Henry, shouldn't it be something different? Why is it Henry? Where is Henry? Should I know Henry? Why don't I know that it's Henry?'

See? Exactly. That was just a brain dump of nothingness but worry about Henry the elephant of all things. It gave you something to do but in doing so meant absolutely f*ck all. Okay, okay, before you disappear into your catastrophising worry rubble, let me explain. Worrying is all to do with something called the Ironic Process. Love that name. Cool, isn't it? Let me show you what I mean.

Do not think of a pink elephant.

Do not think of a pink elephant called Henry who's just come through the door of the room you are sitting in.

Do not think of a pink elephant called Henry who's wearing a pink tutu and roller-skates and eating a chocolate bar.

Do not think about Henry.

Et voila. What are you thinking about?

A pink elephant called Henry of course.

Because You Matter

Chelle Verite

Ironic, right? You see, this is Daniel Wegner's 1987 Ironic Process Theory at play. A psychological concept that says that the more we concentrate on what we don't want, the more it becomes lodged in our brains and the more we think about it. It's the same as when you're on a diet and have stopped eating chocolate. Firstly, what the f*ck is wrong with you?! Chocolate is awesome and should be eaten 24-7. Secondly, if you had really stopped eating chocolate and all you said to yourself was *Don't think about eating chocolate. Don't think about eating chocolate. Don't think about eating chocolate.* Then, low and behold, all (and I mean *all*) you would think about is eating chocolate.

Now, where are those bars?

Because You Matter
Chelle Verite

Right, I'm back in the room. Chocolate eaten. Thanks Henry.

As for worrying, some of you will believe it's there to prevent you from getting upset about the situations you are in. If you think about it and worry about it, the mere act of focusing your energy on it will mean it will disappear. Duh, will it f*ck. We've just spent the last ten minutes talking about 'not' thinking about Henry! When you start to worry, it will appear as a huge amount of emotional, gut-churning, lurching stress and anxiety in your stomach, like a washing machine. For others, worrying is like getting hit by a truck. For some, worry shows itself as lack of sleep, palpitations, sweaty hands, lack of concentration, snippiness and lack of patience around people, and general nastiness. Gosh, it sounds so delightful! Where do I sign up?! Nope, it isn't delightful. In fact, it's anything but. So just how do you get a handle on this worrywart rollercoaster and those distortions of reality in your world?

It's all to do with filters. The way you see things; your reality. Those cognitive distortions that can be displayed as expecting the worst, black and white extreme thinking. Those catastrophising thoughts and emotions which get your knickers in a twist and then some. Or often, your cognitive distortions appear as taking responsibility and blame for everything. Even the things that had nothing to do with you, you'll take responsibility for.

Urrrrrgghh, that's so exhausting.

The list is long about how the world is shaped and because of the distortions, and your habits and patterns, it's not that easy to stop worrying, is it?! How can you take away the anxiety that worrying creates? Getting rid of worrying means reprogramming yourself differently. It means instead of automatically doing '**Worry-woe-is-me Dance'** and focusing on what the problem is, you will focus on creating a different response that will positively impact your outcome instead. Now, that sounds like a great plan. Thankfully, yes, I have a plan for you. Say hello to the magic **Worry Dissolver**. Yay! It's another Life Lesson. Remember, watching you, watching you. **BYM Fight Club** promise alert. Get those lovely thanks-for-the-delivery-Amazon pens at the ready. Ooooh, and a nice cup of tea or glass of wine.

Life Lesson 06
WORRY DISSOLVER

STEP 1. ACKNOWLEDGE WORRIES EXIST

Say after me...

"Hi. My name is (say your name) _____ **and I'm an alcoholic"**

Nope that's the wrong one Chelle!

Repeat after me...

"Hi. My name is (say your name) _____ **and up until now I was a worrier"**

Yup, bingo.

The first thing you need to do with your worries is to stop giving them airtime. You need to recognise and acknowledge that they are there, however, fixating on *I should have done this* or *What if this happens*?

or *Oh no, that won't work* or *What if I can't cope?* and on, and on, and on every five seconds seriously doesn't leave time for much else now, does it? I for one know that you have way more interesting things to do, rather than losing half of your life to the world of catastrophising! Even if you have done up until now, from now on you are choosing a different option.

STEP 2. ALLOCATE FU WORRY TIME

Still, you do need to recognise and acknowledge that your worries exist. Except, instead of being a **Woe-is-me Worrier** and eating yourself up with fear about things at every opportunity, you are going to focus your attention on **BE**ing a **Worry Dissolver** instead. To do that you need to have dedicated **FU Worry Time**. For twenty minutes. Instead of being filled with dread, anxiety and stress, you are going to take the bull by the horns and go for twenty minutes full on **Worry Time**. A maximum of twenty minutes per day, every day (only once per day though), and at a specifically planned time of the day. This is your time, time when you get to focus on and full-on rant and moan about absolutely everything you are worried about. And I mean all of your worries. All of them. Every single one.

Journals are great. In them, you can rant to your heart's content if you like to write. It's also another excuse to get onto Amazon. However, if you don't want to write, get yourself to a place where talking out loud to yourself won't call out the men in white coats, and have a good old rant with yourself.

Timewise, I'd recommend a time such as 4pm/5pm or mid-afternoon. Avoid first thing in the morning and last thing at night as this might not help your mental health. Remember, it's for no more than twenty minutes and once it's done it's done. If you forget stuff when ranting, you'll have to save it for the next day.

Right let's get ranting… for the purpose of learning.

Give it a go now for ooooh, let's say three minutes.

Get a timer and get into position to rant.

Go! Your FU Worry Time rant starts now!

Go on, really rant. You know you want to. What are you worried about? What's getting in your way? What do you want to say that's consuming you with worry?

Excellent! See, that didn't need much persuasion now, did it?

STEP 3. DISSOLVE WORRIES IN 7 STEPS

Right, once your daily **FU Worry Time** rant is over (which usually takes about ten minutes of your allocated twenty minute timeslot, and this practice run only took three minutes), I want you to actually do something constructive with your head and your heart and figure out what to do with your worries. After all, we are all about catapulting you into positive action and I can hardly leave you hanging on by a thread going, 'Chelle, Chelle, what do I do with my **Worry-woe-is-me Dance** rant stuff now?!' Because that, my friends, would be like a film cutting out just as it gets to the big finale. Aka shit.

So here we go… (this is where the magic happens)

Drum roll please…

Introducing the…

Worry Dissolver Matrix

DISSOLVE your worries in 7 steps. Yes, get in!

1. **Recognise & Write**
2. **Identify**
3. **Notice & Acknowledge**
4. **Challenge**
5. **Analyse Power**
6. **Accept & Choose**
7. **Engage, Breathe & BE**

1. Recognise & Write

From your list of today's FU worries, that you have just ranted about, write your worries below

2. Identify

Now identify your worries by initialling them into

(P) = **People**

(F) = **Finances**

(S) = **Safety**

(For S = Safety worries, split them further into SE Emotional, SP Physical and SI Intellectual or whatever short-hand symbols you prefer.)

(SE) = Emotional | (SP) = Physical | (SI) = Intellectual

3. Notice & Acknowledge

Look at your worries in the (P)(F)(S) categorised list and ask yourself

♥   What do I notice?

Because You Matter

Chelle Verite

♥ What themes are there?

♥ What exactly is it I'm worried about?

Dig deep here. It is not at the first surface level, or first question, that your worry lives. It's usually at the third or fourth time you question yourself and truthfully acknowledge it. This is at the 'Pandoras Box vulnerable level'. Stay at that point until you get an answer (it will be from your unconscious mind, not your logical mind, so it may take a minute or so to appear).

Once you've had time to let your answers appear, and digest the above questions, ask yourself this one regarding your worry rubble.

Because Y♥u Matter
Chelle Verite

> ♥ **Considering what's come up as my worry rubble,**
> **What's really going on for me?**
> Write what your real worry is here.
> (This is just for you remember so be truthful!)

---

4. Challenge

Now you know what your worries are really about, you need to test how robust they are and challenge whether the worries you are focusing on are emotion or facts.

> ♥ **Looking at your worries, how factually true are they?**
> Without fantasising that your answer was real, ask yourself that question again. Really listen to the answer and write your thoughts.

Because You Matter
Chelle Verite

Now you've got your thoughts written down, next ask yourself the following question

> ♥ **How is what I am saying to myself helpful?**
> What lesson is in there? Or are you simply wasting time and energy? Be honest!

Your results will then become clear. Please note this challenge process will ping out a lot of objections, reasons or justifications that simply aren't real. When this happens (which it will), you need to write that problem down on another piece of paper, tear or scrunch it up and chuck it as far away as possible. It's now ditched, gone, dissolved and cannot re-enter your head or your heart; it is well and truly banished from **BYM Fight Club**. If you don't write and scrunch it, I guarantee it will stay a worry.

So be sure to recognise it, acknowledge it, and well and truly challenge it.

Because Yｏu Matter
Chelle Verite

5. Analyse Power

For those worries that are left, this is when fun re-programming begins. For the worries that haven't been banished, we need to analyse their power. Do this by asking yourself the following questions.

Worry 'X...'

> ♥   **Can I control you? Yes / No**

> ♥   **Is it important that I do something about you? Yes / No**

> ♥   **If I do take action, will you add value to my life? Yes / No**

> ♥   **Are you solvable? Yes / No**

---

6. Accept & Choose

If the answer is NO to any of the **Analyse Power** questions, then you ditch it. The worry gets written, crumpled, and chucked. In other words, you fully recognise and acknowledge it by writing the problem down on another piece of paper, scribble it out, crumple it up and chuck it far, far away. It is not welcome in your world. It adds no value and is now banned, gone, insignificant. When, or if it comes back into your world, go back to Step 2 and start the process again. (You'll be able to kick it into touch completely when we get to Life Lesson 14 **Kick your critical mind**).

However, if the answer is YES to all the **Analyse Power** questions, then complete the following. Accept that you need to choose to take action and focus on the present, which gives you three options.

💛 **Option 1. Choose to take action now.**

Get off your arse and choose the best, most positive, present focused, and results driven response.

💛 **Option 2. Choose to defer action to a later planned date.**

No this is not procrastination, it's planned commitment.

💛 **Option 3. Delegate the action.**

Choose to give the action to someone else for them to do it.

(It has to be agreed, otherwise you need to choose Option 1 or Option 2 instead).

7. Engage, Breathe & BE

Now you have accepted that you need to choose to focus on the present and take action or to ditch, you now have a way forward. Relax. You are now **BE**ing you. Plans are in place, actions are **BE**ing completed, and you are breathing more easily. Focus on the present, focus on the now. Let the magic happen.

Like I said before, if your catastrophising worry rubble dares to come back, we will do the same thing again. Or head to Life Lesson 14 and we will rip it to bits along with any '**Sabotaging Devil Mindset**' situations that occur. Yes, there is always a way. You've got this... and breathe.

So now you have a plan. Now you know how to go from **Worry-woe-is-me** to **Worry Dissolver** in 7 steps. We've realised that this is real. Roll on thinking about other things. Do not think about pink elephants called Henry... got you! (You'll spot that Ironic Process everywhere now.) We are agreed. Here's to you focusing on what you want rather than what you don't want.

Just for the record, there is very little real understanding of what being *normal* or getting *it* right constitutes. I, for one, have no idea what it is like to have inner calm, no pressure and a feeling of being normal. Remember, you are YOU. You are your own ideas. You are your own ways of working, thinking, feeling and being. Some of which works brilliantly, other ways not so much, which is why I'm here to show you some different ways of being (the **Worry Dissolver** was one of them). One thing is for sure. we now know you have a way to minimise that worry rubble and are well on your way to being worry free. It's all about focusing your mind on what you desire (not what is going wrong) and ditching our beloved Henry.

Because Y♡u Matter
Chelle Verite

Habits form in 22 times to 66 times of repetition, depending on how stubborn you are. The more stubborn a personality you are (to be fair, it's likely you are stubborn if you've picked up this book to read it!), the more you have to do something new for it to stick and the higher the habit number is to 66. We have done the **Worry Dissolver** only once. So now you can cut you and your learning curve some slack, only another 65 more times to go and you'll have cracked it. Stop with the **Worry-woe-is-me** useless-energy-stealer-rocking-chair habit. Remember, until you stop something, there's no room for anything new.

Choose to dissolve your worries. I use it all the time. And I promise I won't ask you to do anything I can't, or won't, do myself. I may not have *the* answer, however, I do have *an* answer. As you can see, it'll be a nice wee chatty *'Because YOU Matter'* journey as it unfolds. Start living the life you love and loving the life you live. You never know, you might even enjoy it. I mean who could say no to that?

Other than your critical mind of course! Hahahahahaha.

Did you see what I did there? **Worry Dissolver**, here we come. And if your **Worry Dissolver** is kicking up a huge stink at the challenge part, then that's because you haven't yet got your critical mind in check. Head back to Life Lesson 3 and do the **MindF*ck** questionnaire again. Have **'Flatten Them Oli!'** in your mind, that will help. Also know that as well as the FU **Worry-woe-is-me** rant, we also have more in-depth discussions about your **Sabotaging Devil Mindset** and your **Pioneering Angel Mindset** to come. So, if your critical mind is a bad ass and still lingering around just to piss you off, then you can say a big FU to it, once and for all, very, very soon. To make it even more accessible, here is the **Worry Dissolver** in picture format too.

Because Y♡u Matter

Chelle Verite

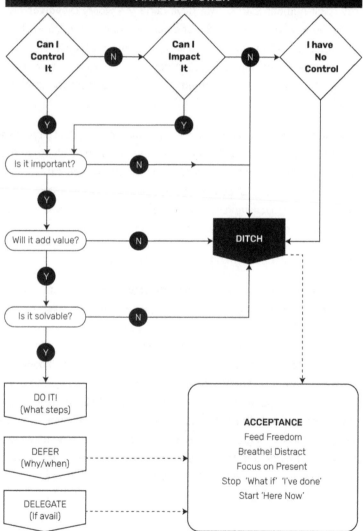

SEE WHAT	SEE SPECIFICS	CHALLENGE
Finances/People/Safety	What exactly am I worried about?	True? Helpful? More (+ve) way?

ANALYSE POWER

Can I Control It — N → Can I Impact It — N → I have No Control

Y ↓   Y ↓

Is it important? — N →

Y ↓

Will it add value? — N → **DITCH**

Y ↓

Is it solvable? — N →

Y ↓

DO IT! (What steps)

DEFER (Why/when)

DELEGATE (If avail)

ACCEPTANCE
Feed Freedom
Breathe! Distract
Focus on Present
Stop 'What if' 'I've done'
Start 'Here Now'

Because You Matter
Chelle Verite

Why do it?

Why take the time to truly process your stuff, ditch your **Worry-woe-is-me** approach and use the **Worry Dissolver** to catapult your life into positive action instead?

Simple.

Because You Matter

Read on my friends, read on.

Everything in life is a reflection of a choice you have made. If you want a different result, make a different choice.

KAMAL RAVIKANT

LIFE LESSON

07

Choice is limitless

GOD 'ERR☺ME'

Because You Matter

Chelle Verite

Choices, choices, choices. This is your Life. That big red book where all of the stories about you are conveyed. Do you remember that TV programme? I do. I recall, when I was younger, it being Michael Aspel who did that show, and then there was even that one off special with Trevor McDonald in January 1990. Love a bit of Trevor. He always made me smile. The concept of the programme was surprising a guest with that big red book of their life. Priceless. The surprise element was always so important. Not to mention the bit I didn't know is that the shows were broadcast live. Brave people, brave! However, here's the thing. What are your life stories actually like? Or as they say in the trade, what's your backstory, your why and your what?

I mean, what if someone nominated you, and your world, for *This is Your Life* (I can even hear the theme tune music. *T H I S   IS YOOOOOUUUURRRR   LIIIIIIIIIIFFFE.*   SURPRISE!!!) Would you say, 'Oh my God, it's me. I am so chuffed and tremendously proud. What a fabulous experience, just look at how my life stories have panned out.'

---

or

Would it be more like a monumental, cringeworthy, experience instead? 'Oh shit, I've f*cked up royally and now everyone gets to see and hear all about it.'

Maybe it's only me that woefully wakes up in the morning with a horrendous hangover and then has the dawning realisation that all that dancing on tables at 2am in the morning, smashing plates, pretending I was Greek wasn't quite the memorable life story that I wanted to create? Well, we've all got some stories we'd rather keep quiet about now, haven't we?

So, to help you create the right type of *This is Your Life* stories that will positively disrupt and cocoon you in exhilarating pride, rather than make you throw your guts up with shame, frustration, disappointment or disillusionment. Let me introduce you to an invaluable Life Equation and some great Life Characters.

Life Lesson 07

EQUATIONS, GOD

AND LIFE CHARACTERS

Life Equation = **God ERR☺ME.**

Firstly '**God ERR☺ME**', he's simply awesome. In a few moments you will be able to carry that magnificent diet coke specimen around with you and heaven sent you will be.

Because Y♡u Matter
Chelle Verite

Also, once you've got your head around **God ERR☺ME** then you'll meet the fabulous **Motivating Matt**, who does exactly what it says on the tin and keeps you inspired, motivated and engaged in creating a world that positively enhances your experiences.

Now, of course, this won't be a proper LiveLifeBE *Because YOU Matter* guide with real stuff in it, if I didn't introduce you to the flip side of the coin of life. Welcome to the dark side of your life.

The Dark Side

I wish I could say that human nature is such that we are always fully satisfied with the good stuff that goes on in our world, however, I'd have to *eckkhem* clear my throat and say, 'C'mon, let's get real here.' There is a f*ckload more negative responses in human nature than positive. Fortunately, this is where I come in and we figure them out together so we can rugby tackle what I call those utter balls of shitness moments to the floor. We get our rugby balls out and. **'Flatten them, Oli. Flatten them!'**

Breathe, Chelle, breathe! Calm down so you can talk to these lovely people.

That got me thinking. What if we put a label on the utter balls of shitness moments? Where we could get to the point of being able to recognise them, and do something proactive with them? 'Now that,' I hear you say, 'sounds like a plan, Chelle.' It's either that, or we get them in a boxing ring, we are after all in **BYM Fight Club**, aren't we?

Let me introduce you… *ding ding*… in the blue corner we have the **Dark Side**.

Catastrophising Chris, **Meltdown Mary**, and **Devastating Dave**. Three in one go? That's a bit much, but we can handle anything that this life throws at us, especially with **God ERR☺ME** and **Motivating Matt** on our side. So, bring it on!

Choice is limitless

Because Y♡u Matter

Chelle Verite

Creating your stories and having a fabulous *This is Your Life* moment is all about recognising and choosing your responses, and understanding the concept that choice is indeed available. In fact, one of the most important limitless (rather than limiting) things that has ever happened to me, was when I discovered that I actually had control over my world. I mean, yes, I was an utter control freak (we'll come to that later), but I don't mean it that way. I mean control over how it played out for me, and my success. It's all down to self-awareness, conscious choices, where you put your energy, focus and your will, and it's all about consciously choosing your responses. Except to be able to choose you need to increase your understanding and see things as they truly are (rather than a dodgy Snapchat filter).

Once you truly recognise, acknowledge and see, you cannot unsee. Just like the Toblerone Bear. (Love a bit of Toblerone, especially the massive bars you get when it's near Christmas time. Don't get me started. Do not think about chocolate. Do not think about chocolate. Chelle! Do not think about chocolate... Oh, hello Henry. Damn that Ironic Process.)

Welcome back to the curse of the normality **Worry-woe-is-me Dance**, meaning many of you have, up until now, been frantically rocking back and forth consumed by false views of your reality, often filled with an infinite amount of anxiety, worry and feeling overwhelmed by the sheer fullness and heaviness of life.

Well, you were, until you got your hands-on the **Worry Dissolver**, that is.

You are worthy. You are worthy. You are worthy.

Because You Matter
Chelle Verite

As you now know, a world full of worry rubble and fear means you will be living in a world consumed with adrenaline. Adrenaline is brilliant if you are an Olympic athlete. It's not so great when you are a gold medallist in the worry arena and that ball of anxiety and all the utter balls of shitness hit you like a truck or build up that much over time that you literally can't breathe. However, you are now armed with your **Worry Dissolver** so you can save that for your twenty minutes of **FU Worry Time** rant later on today. Love it when a plan comes together.

Right back to the here and now. When faced with emotional, mental or physical challenges, you are either a fighter, flighter or a freezer. Not literally a freezer. Although when I was growing up my mum did have a big white chest freezer that seemed to have an endless supply of frozen Shetland lamb meat joints. (Remember I grew up on on the Shetland Isles, which you'll hear more about soon or alternatively, you may have seen my TEDx talk "Impossible to I'm possible").

When I was a little girl, or a 'wee bairn' as us Scottish folks say, I once checked in my mum's chest freezer in case there was a dead body stored away in there. I also believed that my dad was a spy. I did seriously believe that he was a spy. I was convinced. I soon realised that was indeed my overactive imagination, which may have had something to do with the fact that I grew up on an island 263 miles from the UK mainland, with no TV.

So whatever fight, flight or freeze adrenaline responses you have in your body, whether it's the fight (to stay in the moment and react), the flight (you want to run away) or the freeze (like a rabbit in the headlights, or in my case a frozen meat joint not a dead body), I want you to know that you have a choice.

A life choice.

Because You Matter
Chelle Verite

A choice that you can control your world and implement choices that are limitless. The choice for you to positively impact on the outcome of your world. The choice to respond and not run with what you just automatically react to. As my very first boss Ben Williams, Corporate Psychologist, in my post-graduate job in Edinburgh, said to me with his infinite wisdom.

'It's all about $E + R = O$.'

'$E + R = O$?' I said

'Yes,' he replied. '**Event** + **Reaction** = **Outcome**, of course.'

Ah, of course. Simple when you know the f*cking answer. Like a crossword puzzle. Great when you know, not so great when you don't have a clue. (*Boo-Boom-ching*. I'm here all week!)

However, it seems even after twenty two years of me being in the Corporate Psychology and self-development field, this little equation has been around for many a year. Even your man Paul McGee from the *Shut Up and Move On* (SUMO) book spends quite some time discussing it. (Great book by the way, I'd recommend it, along with *F*CK IT*. No, not another bout of Chelle's Tourette's moments, however it is a good read, written by John C Parkin, about being able to let go and getting on with your life.) Now me being me, I changed the $E + R = O$ equation. Yes $E + R = O$ was fitting for some of the processing of life events, but it didn't quite give me what I needed for LiveLifeBE / *Because YOU Matter* / being BOMBCHELLED! into positive action, which was limitless choice.

So, of course, I changed the equation, I did. Pinched it, used it with pride and developed it so you can actually use it.

Because You Matter
Chelle Verite

This is Chelle, name changer extraordinaire (a reference you'll get very soon in the **'What's in a name'** Life Lesson 10). I changed the Equation from 'E + R = O' and instead it became

Life Choice Equation

$$E + R + R = \text{☺}ME$$

Ta-da! Welcome to **ERR☺ME**. I thought it sounded rather like a Greek God. **ERR☺ME**. It may even catch on. Zeus, Athena, Errome. Yes, it has a certain regal ring to it, don't you think? I can see it now, tattooed across many a forearm, muscles rippling, torso sparkling, Diet Coke in hand, tartan kilt…

Chelle… Chelle… Chelle! *Oi FFS! Get yersel back in the land of the living.*

Sorry for that slight interlude. It was all that God talk, ripped torsos and kilts. Well, I am Scottish and *ye cannae beat a good looking man in a kilt now, can ye?* So, other than the thought of a Greek / Scottish God appearing with rippling muscles, where was I? Oh yes, that's right.

$$E + R + R = \text{☺}ME$$

It stands for. **Event + Reaction + Response = Outcome**
and a happy **ME** ☺.

E for Event

Something happens in your world, you see something, something is said, or done, and an activity and **Event** occurs. Remember, even the best of your control freak tendencies cannot control what events happen in your world. They happen, people, they happen!

R for Reaction

The **Event** happens in your world and you **React** to it. Immediately. This is your adrenaline fuelled fight-flight-freeze response. It's an automatic **Reaction**, without any real logical or emotional thought. It just happens. **Reaction** is like the way we talk in our mother tongue (in my case English / Scottish-Tourette's / a bit of Yorkshire-ism thrown in for good measure), we don't really think about the impact, we just do it. If the event is unchallenging and not one that has a real, possible impact on your world, there is a fifty-fifty chance that you will actually get the outcome that you want. However, the fact that it's done out of habit without conscious choice, and often for self-preservation, or protection, would indicate that when it's a challenging **Event** that really matters, a **Reaction** like that won't give you what you actually need.

Now here's the thing. Most of you do yourselves an injustice. This is the *This is your Life* creation of story moment. Up until now you have only utilised the **Reaction** element of the story to generate the **Outcome**. Sometimes the **Reaction** leads to a positive **Outcome**, although more often than not it ends up as a regretful, or getting it totally wrong, experience. It's like we just react to the gut kick or fatal blow to our solar plexus, we just react automatically without thinking. And there you have it, it's an *ooops* or an *oh bollocks* as a result.

Instead of relying solely on your automatic **Reactions** to provide your **Outcomes**, I suggest that you do the following positive actions instead.

From now on …

- ❤ You accept that **Events** will happen, and that most of the time you don't have much control over them.

- ❤ You accept that you will immediately and automatically go to either a fight, flight or freeze adrenaline fuelled **Reaction**. This happens to all of us within three seconds. (For example 'Whoo hooo you've won the lottery' or 'We've just gone back into totally lockdown again'…) **Events** happen we all automatically **React**.

- ❤ However, instead of acting on those automatic and immediate **Reactions** (aka what your body and mind is screaming out to do, or even in some cases may already be halfway through acting out), you consciously choose a different and more positive **Response**.

R for Response

This is the newest bit in our **God ERR☺ME** Life Equation. It's also the most important.

Take a moment to apply the brakes and consciously **Stop -> Breathe -> Think-> Focus.**

Because You Matter

Chelle Verite

♥ **Stop** = Stop acting on your **Reaction**. Instead, stop, recognise and acknowledge that it's there. You can do this by breathing.

Stop -> Breathe

♥ **Breathe** = Once you've stopped in your tracks, take a moment to breathe, and I mean really breathe. Breath in, sharp breath out, breath in, sharp breath out. This stops your adrenaline from completely taking over and will allow your emotional **Response** to dissipate. So instead of doing an immediate *oops, f*ck, I regret that* **Reaction** that will lead to a potentially destructive or negative **Outcome**, your logical mind will engage and you will consciously ask it to spring into action.

Stop -> Breathe -> Think

♥ **Think =** This means thinking about what it is that you specifically want. This means you are at the beginning stages of exploration and choosing what may be a potentially different action. In other words, a different **Response**. To do this you must consciously choose to stop acting on your **Reaction**, start breathing to reduce your adrenaline, so your logical brain can become available. Bearing in mind that your impulsive way of being will be to react and act on impulse, which will then get a potentially undesired **Outcome** that you have to bail yourself out of. You will instead be teaching yourself by stopping, breathing and thinking in order to proactively choose a **Response** so you get what you actually want.

Easier said than done.

Because You Matter
Chelle Verite

You may get a little resistance from yourself as you choose a **Response** rather than automatically **React.** That sounds a bit grown up, doesn't it? The amount of resistance to changing your habitual patterns, to recognising and acknowledging **Reactions** and instead choosing **Responses**, will depend very much on how stroppy and stubborn you are, how ingrained that pattern of **Reaction** is within your psyche. And whether you actually want to do something about it in the first place and make a positive **Response**. (I refer back to previous Life Lesson when I mentioned the twenty to sixty six times something has to be done to make it a habit. But only if you want to change it in the first place. Let go of the old and let in the new go on! Go on!)

Which leads us on to...

Stop -> Breathe -> Think -> Focus

♥ **Focus** = This is key. This is the bit, my friends, that will work wonders in your world if you are able to truly do it. You can go through all that work. **Stop -> Breathe -> Think**. Only to fall flat on your face at the last hurdle, which is **Focus**. For you to get what you want you need to **Focus** on what that looks like and ensure that it will give you the desired and positive **Outcome** you need in the appearance of a particular event. **Focus** takes practice, an adult frame of mind and at times, when real challenging events appear, a f*ck load of guts.

Putting God ERR☺ME into play

Congratulations. You've stopped. You've breathed. You've thought. You've focused. The key to success is that you have to choose to implement your chosen **Response**, and whether you can reprogram your world for the better. This is when you get to be grown-up and properly assess the event situation you find yourself in, then choose a **Response** that will positively impact on the **Outcome** you actually want. If you are in tune with what you need and want, then you will be able to choose this option. If you are able to keep a lid on your emotions and allow your logical mind access to your choices, then you will be successful.

Trust me, there will be times (a whole load of times) when your brain goes *nope I do not want to get to an adult positive* **Response**. In fact, that would be a huge *FU no!* as the damaging **Reaction**, which, if you acted on it unfiltered, would simply not get you (or your world, for that matter) anywhere. Sometimes in those utter balls of shitness moments, consciously choosing a positive **Response** is not high on the agenda. Especially if you are having a stroppy day. However, I want you to know that you can, and will, have limitless choices in your life to **Respond** rather than to **React**, and with it you will get a more positive **Outcome**. I promise. You've already chosen to place the **Crown of Acceptance** on your own head. This time you can also choose to have limitless **Responses** and a bucket load of good *This Is Your Life* choices, so you catapult yourself into positive action rather than into a whole pile of self-destruction.

O for Outcome

A happy ME positive **Outcome** comes from being able to translate your mother tongue reactions and become fluent in a new response language. Oooooh yes, fluency, I'm up for that. (At least it would mean that I could order a decent bottle of wine when I'm in France.) You will firmly be able to stop habitually reacting like Pavlov's Dog to any nemeses in your life. Yes, yes, yes! I know that by consciously choosing how to **Respond** will gift you with more ease and clarity and is way better than being faced with the physical, mental and emotional stress of being beholden to habitual **Reaction**. I opt for limitless choices every day of the week and encourage you to do the same. It also means you can stop beating yourself up when automatic **Reactions** happen and know that yes, they will happen, and no, they don't define you, and yes, you can and will make a different choice for your **Response**. I can recommend it, after all it makes getting out of bed in the mornings way easier when you know you have a life choice strategy. Want to join me?

$$E + R + R = \text{☺}ME$$

Events + Reaction + Response = Outcome and a ☺ Me.

We are in the hands of God. **God ERR☺ME**, we love you.

As Dr Seuss would say...

You have brains in your head,

You have feet in your shoes,

You can steer yourself,

In any direction you choose.

Yet, here's the thing. When you are focused on achieving the **Outcome** you actually want, with no games and total focus on being an adult (not a stroppy child), all of these limitless choices come into your awareness. You will find ways to choose your **Responses** rather than **Reacting** automatically. Which means you will actually get what you want and, as a bonus, feel good in the process.

Yes, indeed. Thank you, Dr Suess, for being on this journey, and thank you too, **God ERR☺ME.**

E + R + R = ☺ME

Events + Reaction + Response = Outcome and a ☺ Me.

As you know now, **God ERR☺ME** is the start of getting used to making choices in your world. So, let's see if you are actually aware of what conscious choices, if any, you've made to positively impact the **Outcome** you have achieved. Once we do this, we can see how those Life Characters of **Motivating Matt**, **Catastrophising Chris**, **Meltdown Mary** and **Devastating Dave** feature in your world (they're coming up very soon too).

Life Lesson 07

CREATING GOD ERR☺ME

STEP 1. IDENTIFY EVENTS

> ♥ **What important and recent Events have gone on in your world in the last 24 / 48 hours / week / month?**
> List them below.

STEP 2. DIG DEEPER

Pick one **Event** from the list above that was important to you and answer the following questions (go through this process for as many as you wish).

Because You Matter

Chelle Verite

♥ **What was the Event?**

♥ **What made it important to you? Why did it matter?**

♥ **When this event presented itself what was your initial automatic / emotional / gut Reaction?**

Because You Matter

Chelle Verite

♥ **What was the Outcome to the Event?**

♥ **If you could have chosen a Response (different to your automatic Reaction) to achieve a more positive Outcome what would / could you have done differently?**

Choice is limitless

Because Y♡u Matter
Chelle Verite

♥ **Think this through for other important events on your list... what do you notice? What patterns emerge?**

♥ **What was the difference between your automatic Reactions and your chosen Responses?**

(Were they the same? Were they different, and if different, what made them so?)

STEP 3. MAKE A PLAN

Creating a positive action means...
Consciously making a plan and using it!"

> ♥ **What limitless choice Responses can you choose that will mean you will get a more positive Outcome and make you ☺ ME?** (Be specific on your answers here. What will you personally do? Hint refer back to **Stop -> Breathe -> Think -> Focus**).

> ♥ **What conscious Responses will you now definitely choose to positively enhance the Outcomes you get?**

Because You Matter

Chelle Verite

> ♥ **How will you ensure**
> **Stop -> Breathe -> Think -> Focus**
> **as a positive life strategy features more in your world?**

See, it's all down to choices; choosing to catapult yourself into positive action and choosing to **BE YOU**.

For many of us, being an aspiring human and life explorer while maintaining our truest essence without compromising ourselves can be a challenge. As an adoptee and divorcee living with BPD, it's been apparent that I for one have missed achieving this many, many, times over, if the number of mistakes I've racked up are anything to go by! Except, here's the thing, all of us are human. All of us have taken a wrong turn and made choices that haven't empowered our life journey. Yet, despite how many decisions we have made, we will find strength to focus on what and how we can add value to our world in ways that gift us rather than taking from us. As I always say. 'If you can create it, you can f*cking make it.' We may not know where our journey will take us, however, we are all heroes in our own story of empowerment and transformation. The transformation from being closed, to being open. From being open and vulnerable, to truly living life and **BEing**. It takes guts, and yet when we **Take the Leap**, we unearth ways that add value to our world in a golden and empowering way.

Because You Matter
Chelle Verite

This is about you choosing to be you. **BEing YOU** shouldn't come at a cost. You are wonderful, creative, resourceful, whole and beautiful just as you are. Relax into what that means.

Enjoy your new journey.

Remember to fight.

Here's to your chosen transformation unfolding.

Choices mean you create your own world, and from a chrysalis you will emerge a beautiful butterfly. Here's to your fight for your new dawn, new day and new you. Remember, regardless of how you feel, what anyone says, and what huge challenges are in front of you, you've got this!

Why do it?

Why let the all empowering **God ERR☺ME** into your world?

Why choose to **Respond** rather than **React**?

Why **Stop -> Breathe -> Think -> Focus** on conscious choices to create positive **Outcomes** in your world?

Simple.

Because You Matter

66

Feelings come and go like clouds in a windy sky. Conscious breathing is my anchor.

THICH NHAT HANH

LIFE LESSON

08

Just BREATHE

BREATHE AND RELAX

Because Y♡u Matter

Chelle Verite

Inhale the future. Exhale the past. Ta da. You are now a grown up. You now know how to **Respond**. You know how to get *it* right in this society, don't you? Ermm, except no, not really. That's what we are working on, isn't it? You being the truest representation of you. I mean, how did it happen? One day you were a child, with no real knowledge of the world, running around with your coat above your head in the wind, pretending you were invincible, and then, voila! You are now a grown up like Mr Ben, suddenly appearing in life but without the right costume.

However, all is not lost. What we do know is that our **Responses** don't always have the most positive **Outcomes** and you, lucky people, you're already equipped with your **God ERR☺ME** life response situation. You now know a way to help you process your world, but you also need to get a grip on your adrenaline **Responses** and calm those down too. Except you're not often told how to do that. A friend of mine who sparked this Life Lesson (thanks Warren, you are a gem) mentioned that when our paths originally crossed in our MoneySuperMarket days (a long time ago), I had introduced him to some breathing techniques during a training session. Well to be fair, being highly asthmatic, he had already figured some out otherwise he wouldn't be standing to tell the tale. If he wasn't around, I would miss him dearly. So that got me thinking, it would be a great idea to have some breathing techniques as part of this journey.

Now, I am no yoga teacher, and I don't profess to be a mindfulness guru or a black belt in getting yourself centred and focused forever (there are plenty of ten day silent retreats for that, or a whole lifestyle choice that involves mountains). This is about getting to grips with when you feel adrenaline taking hold of you and using oxygen and focus to help ground you, so you have choices. (*Disclaimer alert. if you have a health issue then I am definitely not suggesting you do*

Because You Matter
Chelle Verite

this instead of going to see a fully trained professional like your GP.) I am, however, saying take a moment out of your busy schedule to calm the f*ck down and recognise there are other options.

Empowerment, conscious choice and breathing have an awful lot to do with how successful that ever illusive self-awareness journey is. Most days you don't even notice you are doing it. Breathing is so automatic yet critical to your survival. Most days you carry the weight of the world on your shoulders, they are up by your ears as a standard stance, until someone like me comes and long and says, 'Oi, drop your shoulders. Drop them.' I can guarantee that little instruction alone has made you think about your shoulders and dropped them down a little. If you haven't done so yet, then drop them. Those shoulders. Get them down, and that's an order! See, there you go, even the most chilled personalities will hold tension somewhere.

Your body hold tensions in lots of places. Your shoulders. Your back. Your arms. Even your brain. Resulting in disturbed sleep and failure to recharge your batteries. Or you become so tired you are unable to process information when you need to. It's a big bad world out there. You need your wits about you to survive it, and that's just the children / dog / life jumping on your head in the mornings. In fact, our new Newfiedoodle puppy, Boo-Boo, keeps doing that (when I wrote this, she was a mere fifteen weeks old).

Breathing is a way of tapping into reserves. A way of getting oxygen into your system and helping calm everything down by creating a state of coherence. Olympic athletes do it. You'll see them, zoning themselves at the start of their event in anticipation of focusing all of their mental and physical energy into their performance. Getting centred and getting ready physically and, as a result, mentally and emotionally. Now, I'm not suggesting for one minute that you are an Olympic sprinter at the peak of your physical fitness about to run a hundred metres in under ten seconds, however, when I came across the coherence and HeartMath Institute and the wonderful ways of breathing, I realised that you didn't have to be an Olympic athlete to benefit from it.

For us lay people, just getting out of bed to face the world is stressful enough, but I'm up for anything that makes our lives easier, releases stress and stops draining emotions such as frustration, irritation, anxiety and anger. If breathing helps us to feel positive, focused, calm and energised instead, then it must be a good thing. I thought. *I know, I'll combine my own knowledge of breathing, the HeartMath Institutes approach, as well as a previous life mentor's offering to give you three options that will help you get a handle on your world so you can spend more time being a* **Human BEing** *rather than a* **Human DOing**. I'm also going to do it in such a way that you can actually access the f*cking information rather than attempting to do a Buddha pose and getting pins and needles for a fortnight.

BREATHE AND RELAX

So here you go. Let me introduce you to.

> Sigh Breath.
>
> Hello World Breath.
>
> Seven Wonder Breath.
>
> Just BREATHE.

All of which will ensure you have what you need to relax at your fingertips.

SIGH BREATH

Love this technique. It's so simple. You just sigh. Yup. **Sigh**. Exhale all of the air out at almost one hundred miles an hour. **Sigh**. Go on, sigh! Make that funny noise form your chest and mouth like all the stuffing has been punched out of you.

Sigh.

There you go.

Now you are going to hunch up your shoulders up to your ears and breathe in, then shove your shoulders down violently while making your huge, guttural **Sigh**.

Because You Matter

Chelle Verite

Shoulders up... breathe in... get ready... and **Sigh**.

Now, at the same time, add in your arms and your hands.

Breathe in until your chest is bursting, pick your shoulders up so they touch your ears, then shove your arms down violently while sighing, shaking your hands like you have something disgusting on them that you simply have to get rid of. You might even find that your body wants to shake too, like a dog shaking water off its body. (Just avoid plonking your butt down on anyone's head while you do it. You are considerably heavier than a fifteen-week-old puppy, with or without the I-need-to-lose-some-weight-from-drinking-too-much-wine-and-eating-too-much-chocolate detox.)

Breathe in... shoulders up... chest bursting... keep breathing in... big breath **Sigh**... huge, guttural war cry noise out of your mouth from your chest... push shoulders and arms down to the ground (like they are going to be wrenched out of their sockets)... shake your arms and hands.

Ya dancer. (Aka) you did it.

In your head, that is. To be fair, you probably did attempt a little **Sigh Breathing** but you didn't really engage fully, did you? You probably just looked a bit odd flexing your shoulders up, giving a tiny little **Sigh** and then waggling or flailing a hand or an arm about a bit.

So now it's your proper turn. (You signed your **BYM Fight Club** pledge, remember.) Let's have a proper go.

You need to do three of these in quick succession and, yes, make as much f*cking noise with your big ass **Sigh** as you can.

Because You Matter
Chelle Verite

Breathe in... shoulders up...**Sigh** and breathe out... downwards shake with your arms and hands. Come on. Breathing in deep... raise those shoulders... make some noise as you let your **Sigh Breath** out... violently shake your arms and hands. That's it.

And again...

Breathe in... shoulders up... **Sigh** and breathe out... downwards shake with your arms and hands. Come on. Breathing in deep... raise those shoulders... make some noise as you let your **Sigh Breath** out... violently shake your arms and hands.

Yes, well done.

And again...

Breathe in... shoulders up... **Sigh**... arms down... shake...

You get the picture.

Whoop, whoop, you did it! Do a little dance around the room. Oh, and I might add, whilst being present with this exercise there is the possibility you may be picked up by the men in white coats. My advice, pick the places you do the **Sigh Breath** wisely! Remember, should the men with the white coats come close, you do have a life caveat.

You are not normal! 'Of course, I'm not,' I hear you say!

Phew, thank f*ck for that lucky escape. The men in white coats have backed off and your lack of normality lives for another day. Yes, get in!

Which leads us to **Hello World Breath**. You'll like this bag of tricks.

Talking of bags of tricks, it's very important to ground your energy. Once you've sighed and shaken up and moved the energy around your body, it's really important that energy can find ways out. A very simple and easy addition to the **Sigh Breath** is a wiggle of the toes.

Do it now. Put your feet firmly on the ground and give your toes a wiggle or scrunching up as I like to call it. Wiggle your toes and move them in your socks, your shoes or your slippers. If you're bare footed then watch them as they wiggle about. Scrunching and wiggling your toes means that your energy will start to flow out of your body via your toes and into the solid floor. Do that for even just a minute or two and you will feel a whole lot more grounded. Lovely.

HELLO WORLD BREATH

A big hello to you from **Hello World Breath**. This one is so lovely. It's about appreciation (even in challenging times with challenging people), replenishing the good feelings in your world, getting to grips with reality and recognising that you have the choice to **Respond** differently. The more you breathe concentrating on your heart, the more you will be able to step away from what is overwhelming you.

And it will only take as long as it takes to boil an egg.

However, don't by any means feel restricted; if you're feeling very zen you can do it for way longer. Here's to you saying 'Hello world!'

STEP 1

Stand or sit, whichever you find yourself or where you are genuinely most comfortable.

It could be at your desk in your working from home office, your lovely sofa in the living room, on your bed (just don't fall asleep), in the conservatory in a relaxing tub chair, or in the garden. The latter is great so long as it isn't pissing it down with rain, or so baltic it'll freeze your nads off.

STEP 2

Take a moment to centre yourself and focus your attention in the area of your heart.

Take a deep inhale breath in, and deep exhale breath out.

STEP 3

Slow inhale breathe in take your time, slower than usual, be considered. Focus your attention on the area of your heart.

Exhale breathe in the same deliberate gentle manner. Imagine that your breath is flowing in and out of your heart and chest.

Feel that energy flow in your body.

Inhale breathe in. Concentrate on your heart.

Exhale breathe out. Concentrate on your heart.

Inhale breathe in. Concentrate on your heart.

Exhale breathe out. Concentrate on your heart.

Because Y♡u Matter

Chelle Verite

STEP 4

Now take a moment while breathing to pause.

Pause your emotional and physical **Reactions** to what's going on in your world or that situation that you find yourself in.

As you inhale in and exhale out, remove yourself from that situation in your head, as if you are in a helicopter.

Keep breathing in and breathing out, noticing the flow in and out of your heart and chest. Focus on your breathing from your heart and take a moment to appreciate that helicopter view, looking down on yourself.

Look down from that helicopter view and see you. You heart breathing, you caring and you looking after you. Take a moment to connect to a positive feeling such as appreciation, happiness, or care for the situation or person that this involves, for that person that you can see in your helicopter view. The helicopter view of you.

Notice that connection to positivity, to appreciation, to care for that person, and shower them in that energy.

STEP 5

Staying with that helicopter view, imagine if you were a different person. As you breathe and consider, ponder for a moment on the following questions.

Because You Matter
Chelle Verite

♥ **What do you think is going on for that person?**

♥ **What is their reality of the situation that person finds themselves in?**

♥ **What would you say to them to be kind, appreciative, positive, caring and loving towards them?**

> ♥ **What words would you offer them?**

> ♥ **What can you do to support them?**

Ask each question. Then say your answers to each question out loud.

STEP 6

Now gently come back from the helicopter view, back into yourself. You are now back in your body. Breathing in, focusing on your heart, and breathing out, focusing on your heart.

Recall those helicopter view words and feelings of positively, appreciation, happiness and care.

Repeat those words out loud and say the following mantra.

'I choose the following words to be part of me today... (say your words)'

'I choose that I want those words to replenish and re-energise me.'

'I choose that I want my world to be... (say your words and wants)'

*'I choose with pride how I want to **BE ME**.'*

STEP 7

Inhale breathe in and concentrate on your heart.

Exhale and breathe out concentrate on your heart.

Inhale breathe in, and exhale breathe out.

Stay in the moment with you for 3, 2, 1 seconds.

And you're back in the room. Replenished and re-energised and most importantly way more appreciative of you.

Ahhhhhhhh. Now we get to go, 'And reeeeellllllaaaaaaaaaaaxxxxx.'

That's so nice, isn't it? Spending time with you. **Hello World Breath** is all about choosing what you want to think and what you need. It's so rewarding to step away from the **Reactions** of life and choose to stop and breathe. It will help you think and focus, which means you will be able to consciously choose how best to **Respond** to get the positive **Outcome** you truly want.

Remember it's your choice, your world, and those choices are limitless.

And as I say, 'If you can create them, you can f*cking make them!'

SEVEN WONDER BREATH

This breath is about creating a meditative state of calm energy. For those of you with busy lives, it can be done on the go too (when you get the chance). In the car, for example, travelling and strategising. I have yet to try it sleeping as I do recognise it needs a bit of a conscious state to complete it. I named it the **Seven Wonder Breath** because I use up to the count of seven. (Although when I started, I could only get up to a count of three so go easy on yourself.)

Ready to meet your new wonder?

Let's get you comfy and then we will begin. Standing, sitting upright or lying down. (The latter option only works if you're sure you won't fall asleep.) Breathe and inhale in, then breathe and exhale out. Place your hands by your sides. Relax your body. Relax your shoulders and wiggle your toes gently for a few seconds. Then, when you are ready again, breathe and inhale in deeply through your nose. Breathe and exhale out through your mouth (sighing is good here).

Now you are going to start to breathe to a count of seven. Breathe and inhale in through your nose for a count of seven (or as big a count as you can, start off with a count of three, or four if it's easier).

Breathe in through your nose... 1, 2, 3, 4, 5, 6, 7.

Hold the air for a count of seven... 1, 2, 3, 4, 5, 6, 7.

Breathe out slowly through your month for a count of seven... 1, 2, 3, 4, 5, 6, 7.

Because You Matter
Chelle Verite

And repeat.

Now you understand what the breathing pattern is...
inhale for 7, hold for 7, exhale for 7.

Just so you know, this one will require practice. If it's easier, build up to 7 until you get used to it.

Ready? Let's do it again. This time as you breathe, I want you to imagine the air flow going around your body. Here we go.

Stand (or sit), relax, wiggle your toes and shake your hands gently. Get ready to breathe and ground yourself.

Breathe in for a count of 7. Imagine the air...

1. **Going up your nose into the front of your head**
2. **Going up to the top of your crown**
3. **Down the back of your neck**
4. **Travelling all the way down your back**
5. **Reaching the bottom of your spine**
6. **Flowing from the bottom of your spine**
7. **Through your waistline ending up in your belly button**

Hold the air in the place of your belly button for a count of... 1, 2, 3, 4, 5, 6, 7.

Breathe out slowly for a count of... 1, 2, 3, 4, 5, 6, 7.

(As you push the air on your breath out, imagine that the energy is travelling from your belly button up your chest. If it's easier, bring your hands up as a guide as you think this.)

And repeat.

And again, closing your eyes this time.

The whole point of this is to impact positively on your body, to reduce your levels of stress and anxiety, and to relax.

While we are still all gooey in our zen relaxation state, I'll offer you another great way to create positive energy quickly, which is to **Just BREATHE**. A nice wee reminder in case your lives get too busy to count. (Although to be fair, before the COVID-19 lockdowns I did do the **Seven Wonder Breath** a lot when I was driving to and from work. I just had to make sure that I didn't get too relaxed.)

JUST BREATHE

Keep this little life enhancer close by.

Use the **Just BREATHE** toolkit and I promise you the adrenaline will stop being such a crippler.

> Just BREATHE
>
> B = Breathe in the future, exhale out the past
>
> R = Roll your shoulders
>
> E = Extend your arms and legs and wiggle your toes
>
> A = Adjust your posture, consciously release tension
>
> T = Talk, connect and rant
>
> H = Hydrate (water, tea, or wine)
>
> E = Exhale and sigh!

And there you have it.

Sigh, Hello World, Seven Wonder and Just BREATHE.

Breathing.

So simple yet it's something that we rarely spend time focusing on. 23,040 is the number of breaths we experience every day. Yup, who would have thought? I'm very sure we can use a few of them to feel good.

Remember this is your world.

These are your choices.

Why do it?

Why consciously choose to **Just BREATHE**, feel good and relax?

You know why.

Because Y♡u Matter

"

Rise above the storm and you will find the sunshine.

MARIO FERNANDEZ

BE REAL... SHOW UP... BE SEEN...

LiveLifeBE

LIFE LESSON

09

Choose life

MEET MATT, CHRIS, MARY AND DAVE

Because Y♥u Matter

Chelle Verite

So, now you know that you are going to be choosing your **Responses**, and **God ERR☺ME** is in your midst. You know how to **Just BREATHE** so you don't keel over, you're fully energised and you have not been dragged away by men in white coats. There is a God.

Now, let's delve into what type of **Reactions** and **Responses** are available to you. And I mean really available. Ideally, of course, you want all your **Outcomes** from the chosen **Responses** to the events in your life and world to be the Yes, get In! variety, rather than the stressful type.

So, say hello to your *This is Your Life* characters. By the way, I made the characters fun rather than tediously boring like most serious Psychological development self-help books. (This is a personal transformation book remember.)

Because Y♡u Matter
Chelle Verite

Life Lesson 09
CHOOSE LIFE

Enter *This is your Life* character **Motivating Matt.**

Because Y♡U Matter

MOTIVATING MATT

I love **Motivating Matt** and what he brings to our worlds. He's the one who has boundless energy and keeps us smiling and motivated, and he's that feel good factor in life that we really want. Yes, I am fully aware he is a dog. Dog aside, let's focus on what he is all about. **Motivating Matt** is all about positive, logical, considered **Responses** that make you feel genuinely good.

When you are full of endless enthusiasm, positivity, curiosity, contentment and satisfaction, your angel mindset is in play with a positive, happy filter. In other words, you'd be one happy mother f*cker constantly. Like that immensely happy **Human BEing** and Buddhist Monk Mattiueu Ricard, or you'd live in a world where you would forever be encapsulated in the *everything is awesome* dance moments of that Lego Movie.

Here is the reality check. **Motivating Matt** moments, as much as they are wonderful, sadly don't naturally happen all the time in our worlds. However, we do want to encourage these moments to appear more than the **Dark Side** characters of **Meltdown Mary, Catastrophising Chris** and **Devastating Dave**. Unless we make a conscious decision to choose our *applaws*, or to get our fix of positive impact on our world, then as human beings we will sadly (and often) veer to the **Dark Side** and it will all go to shit. It's three times as likely that we will go to the **Dark Side**, rather than head to **Motivating Matt** Yes Get In feel good. Sad faces at the ready. So, I ask you to step away from the **Dark Side**. Step away! It's all down to the impact these **Responses** have on your life.

UNDERSTANDING CHOICE

REACTION IMPACT

Let me explain. Every **Reaction** to an event, regardless of whether it's a **Motivating Matt** feel good or on the **Dark Side** feel bad, depends on the intensity of pleasure or pain that it brings to your world. All are rated on a 1-10 scale or 0-100% scale depending on your preferred choice of measurement.

For example, good things that have happened in my world recently.

- ♥ I made Spaghetti Bolognese, people ate it, enjoyed it, and didn't die of food poisoning.
- ♥ Despite Covid we got to go to France as a family as soon as COVID-19 restrictions ended.
- ♥ I wrote this book and it got published!! Eeeek.

Now this is about taking all the good things and placing them in what I call the Room of Renewal, where we can truly acknowledge that they bring us pleasure in our world.

So, what scores on 'Yes Get In' impact would they get?

- ♥ Spaghetti = 3/10 (secret recipe made me smile at lot).
- ♥ Going to France = 8/10 (Ahh yes, relaxing, in the middle of nowhere to write, relax and drink wine).
- ♥ Writing this book and publishing it = 10/10 (pinch me, pinch me, off the scale moment, still running around the garden in disbelief).

Because You Matter
Chelle Verite

All of these things made me feel good. Well getting this book published so you can read it genuinely made me feel ecstatic. Definitely a big **Motivating Matt** moment. Well, actually, it would be more like me saying, 'Ya f*cking dancer, yes, get in!' However, perhaps you are a little more reserved and refined? Ah f*ck it I bet when you have 10/10 in your world you too, you'll be screaming from the roof tops. As for the 3/10 Spaghetti Bolognese making, yes, it's not as high as the 8/10 or the 10/10s, but it still registers as a feel good **Motivating Matt** moment none-the-less.

However, herein lies the difference. **Events** will happen in your world, and you will **React**. When it's good, however, sometimes you might forget to actually notice and focus so you can register that it is a feel-good experience. The thing is, I have to be pleased I actually cooked and no one died of food poisoning; it most definitely registers up there on the scale of positive feel good **Responses** regardless. The fact that people rated it as the 'best Bolognese they have ever eaten'… well, now that I think about it a little more, it may even shift from a 3/10 to a 5/10 feel good **Motivating Matt** so that it becomes a proper notice, focus, choose **Response** moment. Nice! Choosing **Responses** rather than being led by your **Reactions** is, as we know from **God ERR☺ME**, utterly key. It means you can start to have a positive impact on how you experience life and what the **Outcomes** are.

Your turn…

Because Y♡u Matter
Chelle Verite

STEP 1. IDENTIFYING GOOD THINGS
IN YOUR WORLD

Take a moment to stop and think. You've been busy doing stuff lately, like getting out of bed and reading this for a start! What other good things have happened to you in the last 24 / 48 hours / week / month / year / decade? Have a think and list them in the table below (leave the **Motivating Matt** impact score column blank for now, we'll get to the scoring in a moment). Be sure too to write down a minimum of three for this game please and be sure that you focus only on good things. 'Get te fe,' as our Begbie would say to your critical mind. We will kick it into touch if it even dares to attempt to surface.

	GOOD things / events in your world	What feelings did the GOOD things evoke?	Motivating Matt Impact Score
1.			/10
2.			/10
3.			/10

Because You Matter
Chelle Verite

STEP 2. WHAT'S YOUR SCORE?
―――――――

Good. You've got the events and the feelings written down. Now look over what you've written and decide what score they would get out of 10 for each (e.g. was it 3/10 Spag Bol or 10/10 getting a book published).

STEP 3. WHAT DO YOU NOTICE?
―――――――

♥ What do you notice about the good things in your world?

♥ How highly did you rate them out of 10?

Because You Matter

Chelle Verite

♥ **How positive are the Responses you recalled?**

♥ **How easy was it to find positive Motivating Matt moments in your world?**

♥ **How often do you Respond with a positive Motivating Matt Response?**

☐ Most of the time

☐ A lot of the time

☐ Sometimes

☐ Occasionally

☐ Rarely

Because You Matter
Chelle Verite

♥ **What impact would it have if you chose to have more Motivating Matt in your world?**

Remember, **Motivating Matt** moments are connected to your limitless choices. Perhaps you weren't up until now but you are in charge of how you frame your world. Brilliant news, thanks to you and our lovely **God ERR☺ME**. Except some of us, who haven't yet mastered the art of being that lovely *pawsome* **Motivating Matt**, you may indeed have a tendency to revert to the **Dark Side**. Now, I do not expect you to be super awesome all of the time and I do fully acknowledge there will be moments (and sometimes huge moments) that you will spend with our characters. After all, for us to appreciate light, we must experience the dark. Being on the **Dark Side** all the time is a very bleak energy-zapping and utterly shit place to reside.

However, all of the life characters have a place in your life.

These **Dark Side** characters. **Catastrophising Chris**, **Meltdown Mary** and **Devastating Dave** all have an impact. The impact, unfortunately, is just negativity and pain. So the sooner we can recognise when we have these in our lives, the faster we can deal with the **Dark Side** and what life lessons they need to teach us. The faster we can choose to reframe them and make the decision to deal with what helpful things (if any) they have to offer, the faster we can well and truly kick them into touch. And **Just BREATHE!**

Because Y♡u Matter

Chelle Verite

Getting back on track with our mate **Motivating Matt** is most important. He focuses on hope, solution and positivity. Got it? 'Almost, Chelle, almost', I hear you say. Okay, let me explain further.

Motivating Matt is above the line, in the happy, pleasurable and positive place. However, **Catastrophising Chris**, **Meltdown Mary** and the most negative, destructive, the darkest of the dark **Devastating Dave** are all below the line and provide only negativity, pain and pessimism. They focus on problems, fear and worry.

Here they are. See which ones you recognise.

CATASTROPHISING CHRIS

Catastrophising Chris is the *OMG NO! Everything is going to go wrong. The worst will happen. How did we get into this mess? I wish I could have, should have, ought to have done XYZ. The world is going to implode.* (It doesn't matter what it is that you should have done here, it's the fact that a particular event has happened and caused a problem for you).

The focus for **Catastrophising Chris** is a reaction that isn't focused on the present. The focus is on what's gone wrong, what will go wrong, and how you won't be able to cope with it when it does. Or worse still, you spend your whole time in **Worry-woe-is-me** mode catastrophising *what if this or that happens* when you haven't even

Because You Matter
Chelle Verite

gotten there. You're lost, confused, don't understand the landscape of your world, and often spend time in the cellar of despair in a Bitching, Moaning and Whining mentality (BMW but not the car). Or even worse still, you become a negative mood hoover. There is definitely nothing joyous here.

It reminds me of my Aunty M who lived in Glasgow. She was forever moaning about how difficult the world was. She'd moan about everything and anything; it was always doom and gloom, even down to the smallest of things. Well, to be fair, her washing was a big deal. She would spend most of her life talking about it!

'Washing's done, Aunty, shall I pop it out on the line to dry?'

She'd reply, 'Ochhh no, it's too dreech (aka wet and rainy). I cannae put my washing ooot, it'll never dry in this wet weather, and I cannae bring the washing inside, it takes up far too much room in ma wee hoose, and I cannae put it on the radiators, it looks a mess, and my hoose wilnea warm up if it's stuck on them, then my windows steam up, I cannae shut my blinds properly, and I cannae have my neighbours peeping in, to see all of my life...'

OMFG Aunty M, seriously? It's washing!!! Can you imagine a world where washing consumes the majority of your time? Thankfully, I know that you are talking about things that matter in your life, not just washing.

However, we get stuck.

- × **What if this happens?**
- × **What if that happens?**
- × **What if we can't cope?**

Yep, this is well and truly in the world of **Catastrophising Chris**. Lo and behold, you are exhausted too (and that's without irons, washing, pegs and weather!). Your adrenaline goes utterly crazy and your mind starts to race into the unknown, thinking up all sorts of awful things that might happen. It can stop you sleeping, eating and doing any action; in fact, it pretty much stops you functioning. And then you die! Goodness, it's exhausting. And no, you don't really die. It's just what you think will happen when you choose the world of **Catastrophising Chris**. Which, by the way, if you do find yourself in it, it's because you are focusing on the past or the future, rather than staying in the present.

STAYING IN THE PRESENT

For many of us, having a **Catastrophising Chris Reactions** occurs because we lose focus on what's important and what we can control and do something about, rather than what we can't. You now know it's based on fear, problems and worry, yet your brain will get hold of it and start to unravel it and go down pathways that make you think about knock on effects. Like a big batch of ten pin skittles. The ball of fear comes trundling down and knocks one skittle over, which then sends a whole whack of skittles flying in all sorts of directions. It's a huge explosion of negative energy, which throws us spiralling into *OMG, I can't cope and my whole world is going to implode* mode.

Except, it isn't real. It's a pattern of behaviour. It's an automatic **Reaction** to events that have happened. It's a habit. Here's the best thing. when you recognise that you have gone into **Catastrophising Chris Reaction** mode, you can choose to get your backside off the sofa and stop being a **Woe-is-me Walker**. You can choose to be brave, **Take the Leap** and consciously choose a different **Response**. Remember, if you want a different result, make a different choice.

Because Y♡u Matter
Chelle Verite

Some of you, however, need a bit of a helping hand to make the choice to bid **Catastrophising Chris** goodbye. Even those of you who are a dab hand at getting little old **Motivating Matt** back in the room may struggle from time to time because shit does really happen and yes, you are human. Like I said, all three of these **Dark Side** characters will appear in your life, it's just when you notice them, and how long you allow them to loiter, that will make the difference.

Let's have a look and see when **Catastrophising Chris** appears in your world.

Think back to a bad **Event** that happened recently in your world. It might be a decision you had to make about work, an illness, a divorce, a change in circumstances, or even the kettle breaking (yes that really was huge for a client of mine, **Catastrophising Chris** was at a number 10 level!). For me, one of the major factors has to have been COVID-19 and lockdown. 2020 was supposed to be my year. My year of being brave in business. Except in a flash, in less than 24 hours, all of my work running face to face training events and conferences, my whole livelihood and way of being, went up in smoke. *Poof. Just like that.* And I don't mean in a good way with Tommy Cooper humour, I mean all of it. My business model. My capability to pay the bills. All of it, gone, with a bang. To be fair, I was better off than Tommy. He died. I have not.

However, my ability to engage with **Motivating Matt** took a serious nosedive. It was not good. I definitely reacted. I'm sure for all of us having gone through 2020, you can all fully appreciate that it was a very different year. **God ERR☺ME**, where were you when I needed you? Taking a f*cking vacation by the looks of things. My thoughts were through the roof and I spiralled like crazy… for about three days. I was lost in my worry rubble and my adrenaline hit the roof. How was I going to pay the bills? What was I going to do? How was I going to reach my clients? How was I going to provide for my family and do my job? I mean, I couldn't live on baked beans forever.

Because Ÿou Matter

Chelle Verite

I went through what I call the House of Change. Room by f*cking room. I went through the Room of Contentment. *I'll just focus on the other stuff, la, head in the sand.* I went through the Room of Denial. *nope it's not there, COVID-19 I can't seeeee you, I'll just carry on as normal.* I went through the fear moments. *COVID-19 you can f*ck off *pointing finger* I'm so angry at you I just don't believe it.* Then it was the BMW Cellar of Despair situation. And then the Paralysis Pit of not being able to focus.

I said a big hello to **Catastrophsing Chris**.

Then I got a grip. I got a grip because instead of fear, I decided to choose where my focus was going to be. Except I wasn't quite there yet. **Motivating Matt** wanted to come out to play but **Catastrophising Chris'** automatic **Reaction** still had a hold. Which meant I was focusing on the problem, which was mostly how I was going to do what I loved whilst in lockdown and still pay the bills! I was continuously focusing my energies on the **Unchangeable Past** or wishing that things had stayed the same and COVID-19 was a figment of my imagination. The *what should haves* and the *if onlys* and the *what ifs* of the **Imagined Future,** which meant that I wasn't going to get anywhere except stay in the problem.

I had to figure out what were the little wins that I could put in the **Motivating Matt** category instead. That way, once I had broken down elements of my situation, I could decide what I wanted to do. So, you see, even I am consciously aware of the **Dark Side** and battle **Catastrophising Chris** (and **Meltdown Mary** and **Devastating Dave** which I'll explain next) moments that appear.

Remember. **Events** happen, we **React**. The **Outcome** of the situation, however, is not defined by our automatic **Reaction**, it's what we decide to choose to **Respond** to that matters. **God ERR☺ME**, there you are! I choose for us to find ways to stop **Catastrophising Chris** and invite **Motivating Matt** back.

Right, enough of my world. Let's find out how much negative impact **Catastrophising Chris** has had in yours.

STEP 1. CATASTROPHISING CHRIS APPEARS WHEN?

> ♥ **Take a moment to list events you considered to be bad or negative that have happened in the last 24 / 48 hours / week / month / year / 18 months.**
> List them below.

Next, have a look at your list and recognise which ones sent you spiralling into *what if* skittle catastrophising reaction. Mark these with a befitting icon, e.g. an **X** or a ☹ are good choices (an **!** works too, whatever the mood strikes.) Et voila, welcome to you being able to identify your **Catastrophising Chris** moments.

STEP 2. CATASTROPHING CHRIS HAS WHAT IMPACT?

Next, let's see how much negative impact those moments had on your world. **Go back up to your list and place a score out of 10 next to each of the Catastrophising Chris moments.** This is like the **Motivating Matt** scoring system except this time, sadly, it's not a positive impact. It's how much negativity it gave you. 10/10 = 100% negativity, 1/10 = 10% negativity.

Now let's see if there is a correlation between your score out of 10 and where you focused your mind when you processed these bad events.

Go back to your list. Pick a ⊗, X or ! marked event and answer the following.

❤ **When you processed this event and thought about it, how did you spend your energy and thoughts?**

A) Focusing on the past

- ☐ Most of the Time
- ☐ A lot
- ☐ A little
- ☐ Not At All

B) Focusing on the future

- ☐ Most of the Time
- ☐ A lot
- ☐ A little
- ☐ Not At All

C) **Focusing on being present**

- ☐ Most of the Time
- ☐ A lot
- ☐ A little
- ☐ Not At All

Repeat the exercise for at least two of the bad catastrophising events that you have identified.

♥ **What do you notice?**
(Where was your focus, mostly past, present, or future?)

♥ **How often do you choose to engage with Catastrophising Chris as opposed to Motivating Matt?**
(Be honest)

Because You Matter
Chelle Verite

Remember, this is about choices.

♥ **What Life Lesson can Catastrophising Chris give you?**
When is it good to catastrophise? When is it too long to be
stuck in that **Reaction?** How will you know when to stop and
choose to focus on a solution, hope and **Motivating Matt**
instead?

Remember, **God ERR☺ME**. This is about understanding and
recognising that **Events** will happen and you will **React**. Despite this,
it's about your conscious decision to choose a different **Response**
that will give you a different **Outcome**. **Catastrophising Chris** can be
ok for a few minutes, however, the driving of your BMW does get a little
tedious after a while longer.

Like that 1980s TV series *Why Don't You?* Why don't you just switch off
your television set and go do something less boring instead?

(I am such an 80s child.)

Choices, choices, choices. How will you recalibrate so that you stop
the negative impact of **Catastrophising Chris** in your world? That's
the aim of the game. To consciously choose to reframe the **Dark Side**
and walk toward the light, the light, the light...

Life Lesson 09

MELTDOWN MARY

Now, unlike **Catastrophising Chris** who focuses on the logical responses to life events,

Meltdown Mary is rather different. **Meltdown Mary** is the sobbing, heart breaking, hide under the covers, beyond duvet day character. She's tearful, she's emotional, she sobs, she feels like she can't face life and everything is *Woe is me, my life is so hard, I really can't cope.* She cries floods of tears and throws tantrums and toys throwing, even cake and wine won't sort this one.

For us girls, it gets harder with the time of the month, when we will break down in floods of tears at the drop of a hat. Men, it's when your other half has eaten all of your Yorkie chocolate bar, you have thrown out all your toys and had a bit of a metrosexual pink shirt strop and sob at the unfairness and unjustness of it all. You can't figure it out and your processing capabilities have disappeared and been replaced with a sobbing mess of, *I can't understand the world no matter what I can do. I'm useless. It's useless. My life is so unfair.* Yup.

Now remember, this is an automatic **Reaction** to **Events.** It can kick you in the solar plexus so hard it will wind you and **Meltdown Mary** will go, 'Surprise, I'm here! And guess what? There is f*ck all you can do about it.' We can attempt to get a grip. However, here's the thing, you are full, full, and even more full, of emotions. When you are in full emotional **Reaction** it means logic has been well and truly chucked out of the window.

Hello Meltdown Mary

Look back at your list of bad events that you created in the **Catastrophising Chris** Life Lesson. Which of them did you **Respond** to as a **Meltdown Mary**? In fact, add to your list, and let's see when **Meltdown Mary Moments** appear in your world.

♥ When was the last time you had a Meltdown Mary Moment (MMM) and what was it all about?

To put this into context, I've had **MMMs** to the biggest of life changing events. I've also had **MMM** with the smallest events like someone eating the last piece of chocolate, taking the last earbud, or the fact that there is no toilet roll (the latter is a big **MMM** event, being caught short is never a nice experience). Usually, my **MMMs** happen when it's been a big, busy day and I'm tired. Yup, an event happens and lo and behold, out pops Mary. I'll have a huge, snot filled breakdown moment over the last earbud?! Seriously, I am a grown woman. However, in saying that, **MMMs** can be soooo cathartic as a chosen **Response**. Instead of an automatic uncontrollable **Reaction**, they can be beneficial at times, if you get yourself in a place where you actually gift yourself a **MMM** (a 2-5 minute one, that is).

For example.

- ♥ Bawling your eyes out to one or two songs in the car.
- ♥ Taking a moment to have a tantrum to yourself.
- ♥ Wailing at the top of your lungs about how hard life is.

Recovering from a two to five minute **MMM** is easy. It's a self-hug or a hug from a friend, a nice cup of tea, a sit down in the sunshine in your favourite chair, a magazine buy, wine drinking or chocolate eating. Yup, totally doable. I would say though, the impact of an extended **Meltdown Mary Moment** may mean you'll be sporting a snot filled face, coupled with tears rolling down your cheeks for days. Not much of a good look. Needless to say, you wouldn't get much done and you would have to spend time recovering physically, emotionally and mentally by scraping yourself up off the floor, recovering from crying constantly, dusting yourself down, and giving yourself a good talking to. It would be pretty damaging to you and your world. All those tears and tantrums require a lot of sleeping off the stress of them. You cannot afford to lose days or the energy that goes with them. So, yes, have **Meltdown Marys**, but as a **Response** choice that last a matter of seconds to a couple of minutes at most. Having a **MMM** as an automatic, habitual **Reaction** is not going to serve you, or the life **Outcome** you need, well at all. You are in control of you, remember.

Just BREATHE. You've got this.

Because Y♡u Matter
Chelle Verite

YOUR MELTDOWN MARY MOMENTS

♥ **When was the last time you had a MMM?**

♥ **What was it about?**

Because You Matter

Chelle Verite

♥ **How long did it last?**

♥ **What impact did it have on your world?**

Up until now, how often have you had **Meltdown Mary Moments**? Have a look at your list of bad events that you created in the **Catastrophising Chris** Life Lesson. How many of these were **MMMs**?

Because You Matter

Chelle Verite

♥ How often have you actually chosen (rather than just Reacted) to put aside time to consciously engage in a Meltdown Mary Moment?

♥ What would it be like if you did choose to Respond rather than React?

♥ What steps can you take to move Meltdown Mary Moments to Motivational Matt Yes Get In! Moments instead?

Because You Matter
Chelle Verite

See. You're getting to grips with this. **Events** will happen and you will have an automatic **Reaction**. If that **Reaction** isn't serving you, make a different choice to engage in a chosen **Response** that will help get a positive **Outcome**. **Stop -> Breathe -> Think -> Focus**.

Except what about when the shit really hits the fan? When we don't just stick with **Catastrophising Chris** or **Meltdown Mary** as a reaction, and we're nowhere close to **Motivating Matt**? When we go to adrenaline fuelled Defcon 5. Well, more like Defcon 5000. For some of us there is no middleman. No positive Matt, no logical Chris and no emotional Mary. We go into full *NO WAY, my way or the highway, talk to the hand, I will destroy you, stay away from me or I will annihilate you and everything around me* mode. In short, FU mode.

Ahhh, yup, that will be Dave then.

DEVASTATING DAVE

Welcome to the nuclear explosion, self-sabotaging and destroyer of relationships **Reaction**. Meet **Devastating Dave**. This negative **Reaction** is usually triggered by people or situations that bring out the worst in us. When people engage with us and operate in a way as to undermine our thoughts, feelings or input. When our values are disregarded, we aren't being listened to or we're being controlled by other people's intentions. In **Reaction** to events like this we automatically default to *Screw you*, I'm going to focus on my agenda. This is the *I'm just plain angry with the world/you and explode like a grenade to destroy everything in my way*.

This automatic **Reaction** happens so fast it's like a dog biting someone's hand or leg and simply not letting go. Typical 'attack the postman' situation. As a result, people don't want to be around you. You aren't responsive or available to discuss anything at this stage. You are plain nasty *f*ck you, f*ck off, this is my world*, and you see things with *my eyes only* agenda. This is emotional and logical combined and utterly devastating. Hence the name **Devastating Dave**.

When this happens, your agenda, self-protection mode and general distrust or disgust of the other person, is so strong that bridges will be most definitely burnt. It also takes a really long time to recover relationships and your physical, mental and emotional self from this **Reaction**. And it can happen like flash lightning and pure devil red mist. A **Devastating Dave Reaction** occurs often when your values have been undermined and you feel completely compromised, when your contribution to the world is negated. Sadly, this **Reaction** (pure attack, self-preservation mode) creates the most damage. You have to spend hours, days or weeks begging forgiveness, making tea, grovelling and talking to get yourself out of the doghouse and mend those broken relationships. Begging for forgiveness happens with people you care about as you will choose to reinvest in building bridges. This **Reaction** can cost hundreds and thousands of pounds in blood, sweat and tears. At worst, if it gets to the point of no return, it can cost a f*ck load in court wrangles, lawyers' fees and clear out your once buoyant bank balance.

When **Devastating Dave** occur with people who you don't value or care about, you can cut your losses and move on. However, when they occur with people who you value or love, this **Reaction** can have a whole lot more of a negative impact on your world. As a default position to **Events** that happen in your world, a **Devastating Dave** is most definitely a stay away from and not a recommended approach. No, I am not being ironic. Avoid, avoid, avoid at all costs. If you do this regularly you will literally go through friends and acquaintances like water. It is an expensive and exhausting hobby, not one to highlight on your CV. Not to mention, it can be a very lonely existence.

Because Y♥u Matter
Chelle Verite

What Devastating Daves?

♥ **How often do you react to Events with a Devastating Dave?**

☐ As a default

☐ A lot

☐ Often

☐ Sometimes

☐ Occasionally

☐ Never

♥ **What Devastating Dave Reactions have you had in your life recently and what / who triggered them?**

♥ **On a scale of 1-10 what was the impact of each Devastating Dave Reaction?**
10 means off the scale never to return destruction (aka expensive).
1 means the relationship was retrievable.

Because You Matter

Chelle Verite

♥ **What was the impact of Reacting with a Devastating Dave?**

♥ **What did you lose?**

♥ **What did you gain?**

Because Y♡u Matter

Chelle Verite

♥ **Was it worth it?**

♥ **What did you do to get out of the reaction, and get an outcome that was more favourable?**

PING DEVASTATING DAVE

Now you've seen the impact of reacting with a **Devastating Dave**. The ideal **Response** is never to use him. However, realistically that's not going to happen, even for those of you who are kind and considerate. You will still have experienced at least one **Devastating Dave** in your life. (If your name is Dave, you are wonderful, of course. Do not bite my leg off.) For those of you who are the stroppy, self-absorbed, *I'm right you're wrong, I don't want to and won't listen f*cker* type of personality, then the likelihood is you will experience a heck of a lot more **Devastating Dave** initial **Reactions** in your life. So, if you are the type of personality who implodes and has an automatic tendency to go straight to a **Devastating Dave**, do the ping test.

STEP 1. PING TEST

Upon immediately finding yourself in the **Devastating Dave Reaction** imagine that you have a band of barbed wire around your wrist. Now imagine pinging it seriously hard into your skin to shock your system. If no barbed wire is available, nip yourself really hard to shock yourself into not being a nasty, selfish, self-centred bastard. Now get back on with your life. No one, not even your arch enemy is worth the destruction that having a **Devastating Dave** will cause.

You will have a mere handful of these moments in your life, and if they have reached the ready heights of a 7/10 score, or above, that really is the annihilation stage of your world.

STEP 2. GET INTO ADULT

Urgh, I know. Adult. A D U L T and focused on the prize of not winning or chopping your nemesis' head off. Let's take a moment to think as we know this response is seriously bad for your health.

> ♥ **What will you do to ensure that you stop Reacting with a Devastating Dave and instead head up towards the Meltdown Mary or Catastrophising Chris?**
> (Until you can get back to the Motivating Matt
> Yes Get In! positive, hope focused moments instead?)

One step is better than none. So, if you're struggling here think of the first step, then the second, and third... you get the picture.

Until yay! You made it back to **Motivating Matt**.

This is about choosing to **BE REAL... SHOW UP... BE SEEN...** Lip service won't work, and you ultimately signed up to fight for a life you love, remember?

CHOOSING LIFE RESPONSES

So, there you have it. **Motivating Matt** is the goody.

Catastrophising Chris, **Meltdown Mary** and our nuclear war **Devastating Dave** are all **Reactions** that will cause you negativity.

Choose life. Yours. For ease, your response explanations are below. I know that wine will have been required for the last exercise which may mean that you need a little additional nightcap… I mean recap, of all of the life characters we just met.

MOTIVATING MATT = Yes, Get In! WHOOP

You regard life events as positive.

You feel hopeful and solutions focused.

CATASTROPHISING CHRIS = OMG No! OH F*CK

Your brain explodes. BMW (Bitching, Moaning, Whining) starts.

Focusing on what could go wrong. Logical head strain.

MELTDOWN MARY = URGHHHH! F*CK NO

Emotional meltdown.

Tears and tantrums occur.

DEVASTATING DAVE = NO WAY! F*CK YOU

My way.

Or the highway!"

Because You Matter

Chelle Verite

So, what will you do to have...

💜 **Fewer Devastating Dave Reactions?**

💜 **Fewer Meltdown Mary Reactions?**

💜 **Fewer Catastrophising Chris Reactions?**

And yes, a huge bar of chocolate and glass of wine at each stage helps. Alternatively phone a friend if you need, or better still book a coaching session with yours truly.

♥ **Instead, which things will you actively choose to respond to and action, so you can welcome more Motivating Matt into your world?**
I will have more Motivating Matt by...

1.	
2.	
3.	

There you have it.

You're consciously choosing to have more **Motivating Matt Responses** in your world. All I ask now is that you choose to suspend the **Devastating Dave** nastiness from annihilating you, stop **Meltdown Mary Moments** from consuming you, and prevent **Catastrophising Chris** from cornering you.

Stop -> Breathe -> Think -> Focus

Welcome to the dark and bright side of life. The names Matt, Chris, Mary and Dave have now taken on a brand-new meaning in your world. (Apologies if you are a Chris, Mary or Dave. You are lovely people).

And why **React** with fewer **Catastrophising Chris**, **Meltdown Mary** and **Devastating Dave** moments?

Why decide to cherish and choose to create more **Motivating Matt Responses** instead?

Simple.

Because Y♡u Matter

This existence isn't about learning to 'accept' reality; but rather remembering the power to create it.

MICHAEL CUMMINGS

LIFE LESSON

10

Choice, power, change

WHAT'S IN A NAME?

Because You Matter

Chelle Verite

'What's in a name?' As Shakespeare would answer, 'That which we call a rose by any other name would smell as sweet.' So, what is in a name? Well, it's usually the first thing we know about a person. (That and what they do for a living!)

Talking about names reminded me about working with a wonderful coaching client, Michelle. She shortens her name, like me, except she spells it *Shell* rather than *Chelle*. There is one thing about names that everyone dislikes. if someone spells or pronounces your name wrong it's like touch paper being lit. At her request during a coaching session, we were thinking about challenging her mindset, driving motivation and innovation, and we were blocked on a way forward. We came up with the great idea of using third person. Shell found it so much easier when we weren't actually talking about her. Well, we were, but in her mind we weren't. Our conversation went something like this…

Topic of coaching conversation. Life pressure and life challenges (remember, this is in third person and not first person).

'Well, if I was Chelle, what would Chelle do, Shell?' says Shell to Shell (in her head and then out loud to me). 'Hmmm' says Shell out loud to herself, 'Well, Shell needs to really think about this. What would Chelle do, Shell? What would Chelle really do in this situation if Shell was Chelle? Yes, what would Chelle do? Well, Shell, what would Shell do if she were Chelle… and what do you think about what's just been said that Shell should do, Chelle?!'

Oh, how we cracked smiles. Tongue twister-esk it was. Shell thought it was excellent and got to the answer she wanted. My head, on the other hand, did get a little full trying to keep track of Chelle or Shell, and whether Chelle was thinking out loud or inside, or was that Chelle or Shell? See, head full! Actually, more than full, it was f*cking bursting at the seams! Nothing a nice slice of cake and a lovely cup of tea couldn't sort. Simple pleasures.

USE THE THIRD PERSON

TO FIND SOLUTIONS

However, joking aside, talking through a challenge using the Third Person can be very powerful. It has helped many of my coaching clients get to grips with how amazing and wonderful they actually are. Isn't it wonderful how the mind works. Of course, the techniques don't take long but the being amazing and wonderful lasting effects of them do. The results from my empowerment coaching sessions do too. They last a very long time, if you let it them into your world that is.

My offering is to use the Third Person technique for a maximum of about 5-10 minutes, otherwise it will end up taking you too far away from the problem and the solution that you want to create. It is, however, a really handy technique to use to explore if you need a different context. So is the helicopter 'let's see it from above' technique, so you can physically move away from being in the problem. Instead of being in the problem, you assess the situation and generate solutions while looking down at yourself and whomever else is involved.

Remember nothing is impossible. It is *I'm possible.* If it had of been impossible you would not have achieved all that you have, including breathing, getting out of bed. And if it had been impossible you would not have chosen to step one foot in front of the other. In short, '*I am inadequate*' is not permitted. Inadequate for what exactly? You are awesome. However, the real mileage here is when you embed the feeling that you are good enough. I repeat. **You are good enough.** Know that you are amazing and you are fully equipped and capable of carving a reality that truly makes a difference to yourself and your world. A difference that makes you feel good at the same time.

Because Y♡u Matter
Chelle Verite

That dawning realisation that it is actually yourself you're talking about...that's your *show me the money* moment.

Now, let me take you to the whole reason of this Life Lesson. So, what is in a name? Finding out what someone is called, and their similarities or differences to you (like *Chelle* and *Shell*) can lean you in a positive direction or a negative direction about that person. Not only that, we also make assumptions based on people we've known before by that name, our experience of cultures, what the name sounds like, and what perceptions, images and unconscious biases it brings up for us. All of which can help or hinder our causes, and how we react to them. All because of a name! A collection of letters. Crazy really, isn't it?

If you've had children, you'll know how long you spent choosing your son or daughter's name. Pages and pages and pages of baby names. And the time spent deliberating. For me, I deliberated over my son's

---

Because You Matter
Chelle Verite

name for months. That 'little' 9lbs 8oz bundle of joy was meant to be Sebastian before he was born until, for some unbeknown reason, I got it into my head that Sebastian meant 'big nose'. It all changed on the big day when Oliver, as he was named, finally appeared two weeks late, after twenty two hours of labour, nine inches dilation, a shit load of gas and air, an epidural and an emergency c section (he was having way too much fun as a bun in the oven to come out and meet the real world). Yet, there he was, scrunchy as only new-borns are, and Oliver simply didn't have a big nose, so that put paid to Sebastian as a name. He did, however, have bright ginger hair. I did think about calling my new son Girders from Irn-Bru fizzy pop, but that seemed a little weird and a lot wrong. Not quite as out there as the name Ziggy, now that is a brilliant name! I absolutely loved that name. It would have been so cool. Muppets eat your heart out. I'm damn sure that a Ziggy would, and could, have easily made it to Prime Minister level if any of the names and people we've had recently at Ten Downing Street are anything to go by.

Okay, before we get side-tracked, I also need to introduce you to my beautiful new daughter. Annabelle is my eighteen year old step-daughter and knows everything there is to know about the world as only a young adult does. She said that for those of you who don't know me yet, she wanted you to be clear on the story of my name. So here it is.

What's in a name? It's really powerful shit.

My chosen role name is now Positive Disruptor. My 'Name' is Chelle. The latter I'll explain more in a second, the former I have TEDx to thank for the inspirational change.

Positive Disruptor.

Because You Matter

Chelle Verite

Being a relatively new change, I still see the quizzical looks of *what the f*ck?!* on people's faces when I say that phrase and they go, 'Positive Disruptor? What exactly does that mean, Chelle?!'

It actually grew out of my childhood nicknames of Whirlwind, Tigger and (later) Storm and instead of bouncing, overenthusiastic destruction, I now get to Positively Disrupt people's mindset status quo, not to mention their businesses' status quo. Yes, yes, yes! How beyond exciting is that? It's where greatness comes from. Being proud of what and who you are and expressing it.

So, let's get thinking about the positive **Reaction** you want to create when you say your name and role. Because your name and what you represent really does matter. Not only that, deciding why and what you stand for will boost your confidence too. Double powered it is then. Hello new world, nice to meet you.

Hi, my name is Chelle. Chelle not Chilly, Shelly, Vermicelli, Melly, Kelly or any other similar sounding words you can think of. It's not a shortened version of Michelle either, although when choosing my name five years ago, Michelle did have something to do with it (and I will proudly explain our journey throughout this book). So, to the fabulous (even if I do think so myself) choice of name. Chelle. It's pronounced Shell, just like the seaside, except in my case with a 'Ch' and to signify you've been *'BOMBCHELLED!'* Then to my surname. Verite. That too was a new choice. My choice of identity. Having lived with my previous name for forty one years, it was time for a change. If you have ever gotten bored or want a change, I can highly recommend it. (At the time I changed my name for just £15 via deed poll, now I think it's about forty quid so not exactly going to break the bank). To clarify, no, I am not running from the law, but wouldn't it be so much fun if I was!

Because Y🖤u Matter

Chelle Verite

After I changed my name, so many people would cock their heads to one side and say,

'Ooooohhh, you changed your name?! What, your whole name?'

'Yup,' I'd reply. 'My whole name.'

'Are you in trouble with the police?' they'd ask.

Ah, I could have had so much fun with the tales I could have told. I mean you could imagine the look on my live webinar delegate's faces. The quiet words and then me being escorted off the premises mid-sentence. Great for a bit of a giggle but not so great for my career to be fair. I have such a dry sense of humour, but I also have bills to pay.

Whatever you do, remember what your new name is otherwise you're in for a shock when you get to the airport and attempt to fly out of the country. Instead of boarding the plane to your chosen destination, you'll be escorted to customs and excise never to be seen again.

Life Lesson 10

CHOOSE TO CHANGE

STEP 1. NAME CHANGE

Take a good look around you (or if there is no one with you and you are in your *quiet I'm reading and being grown up* space, then think about some others). Think about the people you know. How many of them have changed their names? Did they change their name because of marriage?

More interestingly, if it's a man who's changed his name then take a deeper look under the bonnet (you'll be in for a nice surprise if he's a true Scot donning a wee kilt!). What's their story? (No, not under the kilt, I mean the cause of the name change?)

And yes, I realise not everyone is a spy (or are they all just spies? Hmmmm, okay, that's probably my overactive imagination again) but if your name is Brian we need to talk, especially about the meaning of life, it's definitely more than forty two. (You'll read all about that in Life Lesson 19 **Making 'It' Happen**).

Why name change? For me, my name change was triggered because certain life changes happened. Some to do with me wanting to write a book of my own. (Ta-da! Here it is. If you're reading this then I have done it. Little celebratory dance of victory is happening around my dining room as we speak.) Another reason for the name change was

Because You Matter

Chelle Verite

that I'd discovered my original identity after being adopted at the ripe old age of six months (more about that story later). Just after my fortieth birthday, I met my birth mum and found out I had been named Michelle at birth, which was changed to Rachel for the remainder of my life. So it was to do with my own personal journey of exploration and not just a midlife crisis, honest.

I think the midlife crisis happened when my beautiful son, Oliver, was born. Jeez, becoming a mother and a parent, and even a grandparent, is a challenge, isn't it? I also got divorced. Knowing that I was going to write a book, I didn't want it on the shelves of Waterstones and other amazing places like Amazon under my ex-husband's name. Getting divorced… urgh, that's a story in itself, however I'll leave that one for another rainy day. Suffice to say, all you lovely women out there who have gone through that phase in your life will understand. You know, the one that goes something like…

'Yay! I'll lose my name and take my husband's in the excitement of getting married…'

And the, 'Ooh, I just have to say yes to the dress and simply have to have that fabulous party venue and ludicrously expensive / exclusive honeymoon of the century and credit card to boot' organising of new fabulous life, daaaaahling.

To then go back to, 'Oh F*ck, darn it, that didn't quite go according to plan. I need to change my name back again' when the romantic ideals of married life are smashed and the bubble bursts. Then, for the pleasure of it not working out and already feeling a total failure, you get to become a 'Ms' rather than a 'Miss'. I mean, come on people! It's the 21st century not the Victorian ages. Seriously, how is that fair?! Men stay as they are but women can no longer be a 'Miss' if they are divorced? Labelled for all the world to see. Rant. Rant. Rant. Yup, it begins. Now, where is my bra? Oh, that's right, I've burnt it.

Because Y♡u Matter
Chelle Verite

So, there I was. Online. It was October 2016 and there I was, all prepared to name change. To be clear, I did at the time have a glass of wine in my hand in front of the computer, which is indeed a very dangerous thing. So, I did okay with the first name bit. Combination of Michelle and Rachel wasn't that difficult. However, the first option of 'Rachel-Michelle' was a bit of a mouthful. 'Rachel-Michelle, Rachel-Michelle, Rachel-Michelle' doesn't exactly roll off the tongue now, does it? In the end I got to the combination of 'Chelle'. Easy. I did think about 'Rachelle' but everyone who already knew me would have probably thought I'd just drunk too much wine.

As some of you already know, I'm not exactly the type of personality to do things by halves, so why stop there? First name done, let's give the surname a go. Verite. A step away from the gifted or here-you-go-take-it surnames from my previous incumbents of Grantham, Hilditch and Phillips. (Yes, I do like wedding dresses. To be fair, I have also dabbled in events management, so it helps knowing all aspects of weddings from experiencing them and running them, don't you think?) Okay, back to the new surname. Verite, and thankfully now my very own choice of identity. There I was, on a chilly, frosty and wet windy October, obligatory glass of wine in hand, at the dining room table, poised to choose and allocate my new name and forgot that I needed Verite to end with an 'e' sound and was meant to put a French grave or acute sign on it. Oooops, note to self. Do your homework. Besides, it's a f*cking ball ache (welcome back Scottish Tourettes) of a way to write your name for everyone else. I mean, they'd constantly have to find a new alphabet key on their phone for the 'e' sign and imagine how challenging addressing an email would be. Verité.

Instead, I made it easy. I wrote 'Verite' spelt V E R I T E. At least I thought it would be easy. In my head it was. Just like those fabulous presentation speeches we make; we think it comes out exactly as

Because You Matter
Chelle Verite

we hear it in our heads! Or when we sing along to our favourite song and then the signal drops out and we have to continue with the right words. Well, that was my name. Verite. Pronounced 'Ver-it-eee' and not 'Ver-eight' like most salespeople do. 'Hi, can I speak to Chelly Vereight?' At least I know if the person ringing me is actually real, related, or knows who on earth I am!

As for the meaning of Verite, well, I'll let you ponder that one for a moment. Let's just say it's close to integrity, and I cannot lie, I love that my surname choice aligns with my first values, truth and integrity. I also love the fact that there is only one of me on this planet with the same name and the same spelling. Yes, I am original, but I think you guessed that already, didn't you? The only downside is that having a surname that means truth, implies that I can't have a day off, otherwise that would be hypocritical and, well, just a little bit shit. I can't exactly be a Positive Disruptor and Empowerment Coach resident life changing development expert if I tell fibs and lies now, can I? Damn. Yes, your bum does look big in that! (Life is tough when we don't work in fluffy marshmallow, rainbows and unicorn land, isn't it?) Congratulations though, you got out of bed and made a decision. It may only have been to put the kettle on and make a nice cup of tea and read this book, however, you still did it! YES.

For me, defining and choosing my own name was really important. Getting a new name was a decision that helped generate calm. **Just BREATHE**, as you know from Life Lesson 8, helps too. Oooooh and prosecco, and cakes and… Chelle! FFS, concentrate!

So, to my new name. It was about do what I say and do what I do too and being honest about it. I do believe in telling the truth. Even on days when it's difficult. And trust me, there have been some f*cking awful rock and hard place days that have literally been a deal breaker

Because Y♡u Matter

Chelle Verite

with the devil himself when facing my own reflection. It's more than the walk of shame; it's the walk of death and you cannot look yourself in the eye if you choose to lie to the world, yourself and everyone in it. Do not lie. Do NOT lie. Go away, Henry. Truth. Truth. Truth. But by f*ck it's hard.

So here I am now. Chelle Verite (C Truth). Telling it like it is, even when I want to have a **Meltdown Mary Moment**, or run and hide in a cupboard and forget that the world exists.

Seriously though, putting my *wee blether* to the side, put some thought into it. Start thinking about what you want for your life, what you want to create. What do you consciously want to be called for your 'Name' and for your 'Role Name'? The latter took me a number of years to find. Positive Disruptor and Empowerment Coach and now I simply wouldn't be without them.

♥ **What do you want for your 'Role Name'?**

Because You Matter

Chelle Verite

♥ **What do you really want to be known as? Think outside the box. What could you choose to be called for your 'Role Name'?**
(If you're like my brother, he opted for 'Evangelist' rather than 'Sales Person.')

♥ **More importantly, what do you want for your 'Name'?**

A name is such a powerful thing. What you get called and how you represent yourself can change the dynamics in your world dramatically.

Take my awesome new lockdown friend Joanne. Well, actually, she's Jo to me and she has just this situation going on for her. The HR specialist 'Role Name' she's known by is 'Joanne' yet for her wellness brand she's known as her 'Name' which is 'Jo'. Never the twain shall

Because You Matter

Chelle Verite

meet! 'Joanne' and 'Jo' are two very different versions of herself in her psyche.

Every name we decide to take on will bring with it an association. Positive. Negative. Amazing. Useless. Reliable. Or a bit meh. Your word is your bond. Your name is your bond. You are your bond.

So, what is it that you will choose for you? Start thinking.

♥ My 'Name' that I choose is to be known as is...

I know you won't take that much time here to think because you'll be like *there's more to read*, but still, make a start in your head. Just think about what happens when you think of nicknames you had when you were a child. It's like a timestamp or a song, you can often place where you were at that time.

For example, I was nicknamed Bear when I was a little girl. Upon reflection, I'm rather hoping it was because I was cute, and not that I was brown. Ironically, that's now come back full circle as Annabelle (or Belle as she much prefers to be called) calls me Mama-Bear. It's strange to think there are some very important people in my world that have only known me as Chelle, or Chelle-Bear, like my husband, James. Yet my son, Oliver (or Oli as he prefers to be called), has known me as Rachel, WaWa (his mum nickname for me), Chelle-Bear, and Mama-Bear. All of which give me a warm internal glow.

Because Y♡u Matter

Chelle Verite

My parents have known me as Rachel and Chelle (sadly, they still can't consistently honour me with the latter, despite my adopted father's name being Maurice and he gets called Michael). To top it off, my birth mum has known me as Michelle, Rachel and Chelle. As for changing both first and last names, I've only met one other person who has changed their whole name. Ironically, he was a man so it wasn't because of marriage. When we talked about it, it turned out he loved his name change and did it so that became the chosen one. His choice of identity. To be fair, that's a lot to do with my reasoning too. So, if you fancy it, I can hand on heart totally recommend it.

Like I said, it only takes a few online clicks to change your 'Name' by Deed Poll. You can have pretty much anything that you want, except Lord and Lady and acronyms. However, if you do **Take the Leap**, be aware that some people might not like it. At the time, my parents were absolutely disgusted with me for making the change, despite the honouring name change for both Michelle and Rachel and my adoption story, and I was my own person and forty one when I did it. So, you may be surprised at just what type of ownership boundaries come up for the people around you, and in your life. Same goes for your **Reactions.** Just recall the last time someone spelt your name wrong or mispronounced it. Remember, you will get protective over the strangest and smallest of things, so start noticing and being more conscious about what you like, what you dislike, and what makes you, you.

Because Y♡u Matter
Chelle Verite

STEP 2. MAKING YOUR 'NAME' DECISION

♥ **What have you chosen for your 'Name'?**

♥ **Why did you opt for this choice?**
(It may be confirming it's the same, or it may be different, like my name change of Rachel to Chelle).

Because You Matter

Chelle Verite

♥ **Why is this so important to you?**

♥ **What have you chosen for your work / life / me 'Role Name(s)'?** (Positive Disruptor, Empowerment Coach and Mama-Bear are mine, what's yours?)

♥ **Why is it so important to be known as this?**

Because Y♡u Matter

Chelle Verite

♥ **What positive Outcome will it bring to your world to be known as this?**

♥ **What is it that you truly want to notice and others to notice about your name and its association?**

♥ **What is it about your 'Name' and Your 'Role Name(s)' that will honour you for you?**

Because You Matter
Chelle Verite

♥ **How do you want your 'Name' and your 'Role Name(s)' to be recognised by others?**

♥ **How do you want to create your world, so you can BE REAL... SHOW UP... BE SEEN... and where you can truly BE YOU?**

Because You Matter

Chelle Verite

You have so much to offer the world.

Remember, when you can create it, you can f*cking make it.

So, I ask you, 'What's in a name?'

As Shakespeare would answer, 'That which we call a rose, by any other name would smell as sweet.'

What's in a name? Well that my friend, is down to you.

Why do it?

Why decide on what you want to be known as and how you want to **BE YOU**?

Simple.

Because You Matter

Sometimes you have to be your own hero. Put on your cape and go save the world.

DEB SOEFIELD

LiveLifeBE

BE REAL... SHOW UP... BE SEEN...

LIFE LESSON

11

BE your own Superhero

THE DAY REALITY SHATTERED

Because You Matter

Chelle Verite

'Be me?! Because I Matter? Really, do I have to?' I hear you say. More to the point, are you actually ready to find out what you're all about? To recognise that you do actually matter. Yes, you. Hello there. I'm talking to you, pay attention. Tough one, isn't it? I had a dream. A dream that I could make things simple, accessible and available to people. I had a dream where people didn't worry about how good they were. I had a dream where people could do anything.

Even me.

I could be awesome if only I allowed myself the freedom of expression to truly look at who I was and what that actually meant. I recall the first time I realised that I was different from everyone else. Not the same, not accepted, not normal. Except not normal in a bad way.

I was six.

Because You Matter

Chelle Verite

It wasn't because of my boisterous, happy-go-lucky personality. My mum later told me that even when I was a young sproglet (or *bairn* as we say in Scotland) in my buggy (or pushchair / pram in case I'm getting too Scottish colloquial), long before I could walk, I'd be the one chit chatting away to every single person we met on our travels, introducing my mum to them rather than the other way around. It didn't matter who they were. Young, old, man or woman, or indeed where we were going. I didn't mind, I wasn't fussy in the slightest who we talked to. Needless to say, that brash confidence of *I rule the world and don't give two hoots, mini-celebrity status* didn't stay forever. However, now I look back I put it down to a joyous lack of awareness and critical mind that only a child could have (those were the days) and me being generally just f*cking nosey. (On a good note, I didn't actually learn how to swear until I was thirteen years old, so it's good to know I'm making up for lost time.)

As well as chatting, I was always in and about things. A typical tomboy. Likely this had a lot to do with the fact that I was brought up in the Shetland Isles with no TV, so for amusement I'd dig stuff and plant vegetables in the vegetable patch to test if the hardened weather would actually let anything grow. I'd cut peat to burn on the fire and help my mum cook (she cooked everything from scratch and it was delicious). I'd help my dad with woodwork and leather work. I'd even make Viking leather belts for Up-Helly-Aa (the annual Viking fire festival tradition, it's a bit like Fight Club in that you have to know someone up high to get an invite). Oooh, and I even made wine. Elderflower, I recall. Although these days I tend to stick to drinking Chilean Sauvignon, or five litre French boxes. Winemaking was a lot of fun, and legal (so long as I didn't drink it), even at the ripe old age of three, four, five and six years old. (If you are working for or are connected to Social Services, the time has passed, and I didn't drink that much of it... honest!)

Because You Matter
Chelle Verite

So, there I was. I had not long turned six. I was having another busy day, chatting and interacting in my usual *let's explore the world and find out more* mode at breakfast time but I had a burning question on my mind. I looked up at my parents with my big brown eyes, whilst eating my no-added sugar healthy muesli and my wholemeal homemade toast, and I innocently asked.

'Mummy, why am I different?'

Time stopped.

A horrendous tumbleweed moment when both of my parents looked at each other and internally groaned. I mean, they did their best. The way they explained it should really have been beautiful. Case book, really. After gently putting down their cereal spoons and toast and moving their cups of tea to one side, they gathered me to them and quietly explained.

'Well, we couldn't have children of our own, you see. You really were the lucky one. You were the best gift ever. We got you on Christmas Eve. Our baby. You were beautiful, so beautiful to us.'

Yet as their lips moved and the words were said, I knew that my whole world was collapsing. The meaning behind what they said to me was such an earth-shattering, defining moment that destroyed and detonated any chance of self-worth that I had found on my small travels of life experience. The day I was told, 'You are lucky to be different.'

That was a day I will never forget.

Lucky that at six months old I was adopted and handed over to complete strangers? Lucky that I got to leave the arms of my birth

Because You Matter
Chelle Verite

mother at three days old? Lucky to be given up because I wasn't white enough to join the family of a newly wedded husband and wife? Lucky to enjoy six months of foster care? Lucky to be adopted in the 1970s with race discrimination legislation only just in force? Lucky to be on the northern, most Scottish island in the middle of the North Sea, two hundred and sixty three miles from the mainland of the UK, as the only non-white, brown face in a sea of 23,000 white ones?

Lucky? Let's just think about that for a few moments.

Lucky to be told I was so lucky? So lucky to be unwanted by my birth mum for being the wrong colour, and given up three days after I was born, because that meant that although my birth mum didn't accept me, my 'new' parents did want me? Like a prize in a raffle or something to be auctioned off to the highest bidder? Well, actually, just a bidder.

To be fair, this news revelation was a bit of a head f*ck, especially for a little, innocent six-year-old. I tried to process the information, which was before concrete personality or identity systems were in place, but it simply wasn't possible. I mean all joking aside, I even had to miss a day of school and boy, did I love school.

That day I found out I had no link whatsoever to any family heritage. That day I realised I had no baby photos of me or reference to my birth or existence, except one photo of my birth mum, heavily pregnant with me, marrying a man who wasn't my father. He was one of the main reasons I wasn't kept or accepted when I was born. My 'coffee coloured skin', as the social workers described, 'Wasn't normal enough' (ah, the irony) to be passed off as his. That day I was left to figure out what on earth was my identity, and to seek clarity. To find out why, every day when I looked in the mirror at my face, my reflection, my skin, if I was wanted so much, that I mattered so much, why was I given away because of it?

Because You Matter
Chelle Verite

That day I realised I was different to all those around me. That I didn't fit in. That day I looked in the mirror and failed to understand what I truly represented and what I actually stood for. That very day, when I was six and asked, *'Mummy why am I different?'* and had to miss a day of school for the first time in my life. That very day, I believe my innocence was shattered, and the sense of loss overwhelmed me.

Up until that point I had been happy. Happy little Rachel had been a bundle of carefree thoughts. *I can do anything. I can be anyone. I can conquer the whole world.* I ran around the garden with my jacket above my head thinking I was a Superhero. I bounced so high on my yellow trampoline I should have been sure to break something, however, I just didn't, since the world was my oyster and everyone was my friend. It was at the age of six that I realised I was different because I was brown, rather than white like my parents, and with that came the realisation that I had been rejected because of it. But I just didn't see it. I knew I was different and I also knew that deep down I wasn't normal. The feeling of loss, of difference, of confusion that I didn't matter hit me so hard I just lost myself completely and my life energy drained away like Superman touching kryptonite. That day was mine. The day my Superhero confidence and positive outlook on life left me. The day my kryptonite hit. The day the otherwise indestructible little Rachel formed a hole in her soul and a void in her heart.

From that day on, my smile simply didn't reach my eyes.

Since that day I started searching for my meaning in this life, so I could shake the feeling of being in a place where I never truly felt that I mattered, or that I fitted in or that I added value. Since that day I learned so many tricks of the trade to keep me safe, to keep me in a place where I could walk with my head held high and survive. Where I wasn't disregarded, bullied, rejected, or disowned because I was different.

Life Lesson 11

Because You Matter
Chelle Verite

I was born in 1975. In 1981, when I was six, we were still in the era of apartheid in South Africa. News was in papers only; mobile phones didn't exist. We were on speed dial only because the one telephone we had (you know the type you have to actually dial with your fingers for each number, and that had a cord) was only four numbers. 3337. I remember it to this day. Little did I know that I would be training people on the Power of three and Magic seven one day. (I'll save those theories for my next book.) Back then, Shetland consisted of 23,000 white people and me, the only non-white, little person. I didn't really have a chance. A bit like the fact that in the Shetland Isles there aren't any trees. It's just too windy to have anything higher than a bush, so the landscape, albeit beautiful, is very low. It consists of sheep, dry stone dykes (walls) and heather, mostly. Well, there was one exception to the rule. I did see a solitary tree once but it was so weak, so little, so bent over, so wind-swept and so bashed and bruised by the harsh yet beautiful conditions. (Shetland truly is beautiful, like the Caribbean only a f*ck lot colder!) This little tree had snapped branches, not many leaves, and was bashed up by the environment so much so it had a hard time standing upright. But there it was, for all to see, to be marvelled at, judged, commented on, ridiculed, ignored, pointed at, laughed at, discussed, but sometimes supported and attempted to be understood by others. All the while its main focus, the main focus for that little tree, its source of struggle, was simply to stay alive.

I was that tree.

But what is normal? What defines us?

As I looked at my parents' white faces, my dad's Jewish heritage, my whole surroundings, I tried to figure out questions about how to, well, BE. *How do I conduct myself? How do I gauge myself with no role models of cultural fit? How does that all work?* I swear my brain was pre-programmed to be interested in the psychology of human

Because You Matter
Chelle Verite

behaviour long before I even knew what Positive Psychology was all about and actually started working in this field. Now I recognise that for days I used to sit and think. Think and think and think. I'd try so hard to figure shit out. *How do I be me?* Some questions have never left me. *How do we work? How do we define ourselves? How do we get the balance right of our critical mind? How do we stay in control of how we perceive the world and still be okay?*

These questions, and many more, have rumbled around in my head and my heart for years. I said at the beginning of our journey together that it was the curse of the normality worry fear monster. However, it's not just about normality, is it? This is about being you, showing up in whatever way you desire with the right outcome for you, on your journey, because you've chosen to walk the walk. Not because someone else has pushed you or tugged you or dragged you there. But because you decided.

Being you. To **BE REAL... SHOW UP... BE SEEN...** Seen in a way that makes you glow and stop and go, 'I've got this, and it feels good.' That feeling of contentment. That feeling of indestructible power and strength. Since that day, when I was six years old, I have wanted to tell my story. Not to have pity or recognition, but so you can take solace that you are not alone in your struggles. And that despite it all, you can be whatever you wish for, regardless of the amount of demons you may carry in your life. To know that life is just that... life. A place where we do our very best to find our way in it (and even, at times, a way out of it).

Despite all my attempts to self-sabotage and rip my guts out in my professional career and as a mother, wife and friend, I am in control of my own self, most days. Most days I can breathe and everything is alright with the world. Most days I am content to walk the walk of life and enjoy the journey.

Because Y♡u Matter

Chelle Verite

Most days (even despite my newly diagnosed Borderline Personality Disorder) I am able to love the life I live AND live the life I love, and that my friends, is a very big thing.

I am not normal.

Thank God.

I am not normal.

Thank f*ck.

I am **NOT** normal.

Absof*ckinglootly!

And neither are you.

Life is filled with so many awful, kryptonite strength zapping, life crippling moments.

Moments that, if we aren't careful, will define us, what we achieve, and how we feel about ourselves for a very long time. Quite frankly, that's f*cking shit. Trust me, I've been there.

So, to all of the people that made me feel like my little tree didn't matter, I say FU. And to all of you who cherished me, I say I love you, and thank you.

I've created my time. Now my friends, it's time for you to realise yours too.

Life Lesson 11

BE YOUR OWN SUPERHERO

STEP 1. HOW READY ARE YOU?

Take a moment to think, really think...on a scale of 1-10, how ready are you, to **BE YOU**?

♥ **How ready are you to be you and NOT be normal?**
[/10]

♥ **How ready are you to stand proud and stand tall?**
(Even when you feel like the world has bruised and bashed you like a little tree.)
[/10]

Because You Matter
Chelle Verite

♥ **How ready are you to take that leap, be your change and realise your empowerment?**
[/10]

♥ **How ready are you to BE you?**

☐ Yes

☐ No

☐ Maybe

And yes, that may mean opening Pandora's box and acknowledging feeling terrified, disappointed, confused, scared, beaten down or nervous. But this is it. Your Life. So, I will ask you again...

♥ **How ready and willing are you to be the 'Superhero You'?**
[/10]

Because You Matter
Chelle Verite

If you're faltering, just know that today my own number isn't 10. Today my number is at least 103 (sometimes it even ranks at 163), however, there were reality shattering days where my number was so far on the minus scale that it didn't even register. If that's you, you are not alone. I promise.

Regardless of how exhausted you are, regardless of how lost, unsure or even gut wrenchingly scared you might be on your life rollercoaster, even when you are utterly terrified, even when you think you can't, even when it seems impossible, the word itself says what it is. I'm possible. The real life lesson here is that how you feel, how you experience this world, how you live your life (or not), is down to you and what mindset you choose.

In light of that, we will be discovering how to **Take the Leap** in the next Life Lesson.

Let's take a moment now to **Superhero** and realise your empowerment. Whoop, kryptonite can take a big run and jump off a very short pier! Empowerment. The ability to do, recognise and realise your needs, wants, opinions, beliefs and feelings. Oh, and while you're at it, your glass (or mug) must need a refill. **Superheroes** always need fuel.

STEP 2. SUPERHERO YES YOU!

I want you to make a decision. And yes, it's an easy decision before you get 'OMG, Chelle, this is so hard, you've made me think loads already… blah… blah.' It's an easy decision, okay? You in? Good. I want you to cast your mind back to what life was like when you were a youngster. When you were five, six, seven or so. When you were carefree, full of energy and into learning and exploring everything. Like climbing trees or learning to roller-skate for example.

Because You Matter
Chelle Verite

I remember roller-skating on the road just outside my house. We lived in Shetland, remember? There weren't many cars so road play was safe. It was also a time when your mum said go out and play and come back for tea when you got hungry / when it started getting dark (select as appropriate). So, I'd go out to play and you'd find me roller-skating on the road or playing with my friends at the Mart building, which I might add, I thought was so cool. It was a big warehouse of a building with huge metal scales that were about the length of a car, and wooden gallery seats that me and my friends used to jump around on and run all over. It wasn't until later in life that I actually found out it was called the Mart because it was a market for cattle to get sold and slaughtered. (Ah, the innocence of youth). On sunny days, bear in mind this was Shetland and it's like the North Pole and so rainy that it rained horizontally (I actually did think rain was like that, horizontal rather than vertical). You'd find me and my friends Louise, Alison and Kim, running around with coats over our heads, with my Mickey Mouse Fraggle Rock hair do, playing hide and seek and battle games at Clickamin Broch (a 600bc three storey stone dwelling surrounded by water).

Because You Matter

Chelle Verite

Remember, I didn't have a TV so I had a lot of time on my hands! However, for those of you who did have a TV, comic books and access to films, I'm sure you can recall your favourite TV programme and favourite **Superhero**. Powerful, invincible, and they had bucket loads of adventurous fun.

So, here's the easy decision...

♥ **Who was your favourite Superhero when you were younger?**

♥ **Which Superheroes couldn't you get enough of?**

♥ What Superhero powers did they have that you loved?

And here's where the real, Life Lesson starts.

STEP 3. SUPERHERO ME

Realising your empowerment is about figuring out how you experience this world. It's about choosing how you fight, and how to equip yourself with the right tools to empower your choices. In short, your '**Superhero me**' moment. Contender, ready? Gladiator... I mean **Superhero**, ready?

♥ If you were a Superhero, what Superhero would you be, and why?

Because Y♥u Matter
Chelle Verite

♥ **If you could choose three Superhero powers for your own life, what powers would they be?**

1.

2.

3.

♥ **What Superhero 'strengths' do you have that makes you, you?** (In other words what do you offer that you are proud of and positively impacts on your world.)

Strengths I have now are	Strengths I would like more of are

Because You Matter

Chelle Verite

♥ **What Superhero behaviours, actions, thoughts and feelings do you choose to pay attention to and use that positively empower your world?**

♥ **What are the behaviours, actions, thoughts and feelings that you choose to pay attention to or implement in your life that are your kryptonite, and up until now, have devastatingly weakened and shattered your world?**

(And what will you now do when, or if, they arise again?)

Because You Matter
Chelle Verite

♥ **What is it in your life that you value about you?**
What values are true to you and that you simply won't
leave home without?

♥ **What is your calling? What is it in your life that really,**
truly makes you get out of bed to be the Superhero you?
Why be you?

There you have it. Now you know what to focus on. It will take a few moments of wine/cup of tea drinking to answer all these questions. In fact, come to think of it, you may even need a slice of cake too.

Recap

While you eat and drink, let's put our learning together and decide on your main points. Use the recap grid provided to collate your answers.

My Superhero is	
My powers are	
My strengths are	
My kyrptonite was (which is now replaced with)	
My values are	
My why I am a Superhero (aka my calling) is	

Because Y♡u Matter
Chelle Verite

Yes, get in! Ooooh, look at you go. Coat around your head, you are invincible. To infinity and beyond.

Now you know when the going gets tough and you know exactly where to go and what to call upon to realise your empowerment. Now you know it's not just big girl pants or Yorkie chocolate bar boxers, it's a **Superhero** costume! (What an awesome excuse to get the dressing up box out, either that or get online and order the onesie version).

Events will happen and you will **React**. However, it's not about the **Reaction** (that will happen regardless), it's about how you choose to **Respond** to get the positive **Outcome** you need. It's about choosing to focus your attention on you. Choosing to **Focus** on your hopes rather than your fears. Choosing to **Focus** on your **Desire** to overcome your kryptonite and choosing to empower you. It's all about you making choices to help and not hinder you. It's about releasing and quietly and self-assuredly realising you.

Your **Focus**.

Your **Desire**.

It's not just willpower, this is *I will power* and sticking to exactly what you know to be true about you. What you believe, you will achieve. It's about seeing and believing in you in a way that makes you grow and glow and think. *I've got this and it feels good.* No one else defines you. No one else gets to take that power away from you. You get to have that. That feeling of contentment. That feeling of indestructible power. That feeling of **Superhero** strength. That feeling of *yes, get in!* So, here's to you **BEing YOU**. Here's to you, **Superhero** and here's to your **Go Be**, 'realise and empowering me' moments.

You've got this!

Because You Matter

Chelle Verite

And why do it?

Why grow?

Why put yourself first?

Why **BE your change**?

Why re-programme your **Reactions** to consciously choose **Responses** and get positive **Outcomes**?

Why empower yourself to **BE your own Superhero?**

Simple.

Because You Matter

You really, really do.

"

Getting over a
painful experience
is much like
crossing monkey
bars. You have to
let go at some
point in order to
move forward."

C. S. LEWIS

LIFE LESSON

12

Take the leap

DECIDE, BAKE AND EAT

Because You Matter
Chelle Verite

My father once told me success in life isn't down to luck. It's down to hard work, dedication and being prepared, coupled with opportunity. As they say in Scotland, 'What's for ye wilnea go by ye.' (What's for you won't go by you.) Except I'll add in another bit to the saying. 'What's fer ye wilnea go by ye, so long as yer looking fer it.' No, that's not the furry animal ferret variety; if you put on your best Scottish accent, translated it means 'for it'. (What's for you won't go by you, so long as you're looking for it.) Being ok with what you do and being brave enough to **Take the Leap**, is a lot like being on a trapeze. You've got to hold on tight but let go of what you do know to trust you'll reach the other side. It's about leaving what you do know, leaving what's comfortable, and going for something that can be shit scary to get to on the other side. Yes, even when you can't see what is on the other side.

In other words, you've got to be prepared to work for it. **Success** and a life that you love won't just come and say, 'Ta-da, here you go, it's all yours!' Then all you need lands itself in your lap. As if! The innocence of youth.

That brings me back to my college days and I remember my first boyfriend, Jo. Well, it was actually Josef, or Zef for short. I was in my first year at college, fresh out of leaving home, all of eighteen, and in a very clear bubble of non-streetwise existence, bless my cotton socks. Jo was a white hip hop DJ who I met while he was doing light jockeying out on a college night out. (Back then I didn't even know there was such a thing as light jockeying, putting disco light shows in night clubs to music.)

Stepping out of my comfort zone and the belief that things will land in my lap, I recall one time I asked him, 'Jo, what do you want from life? What do you want to be when you grow up?'

Because You Matter
Chelle Verite

Those questions hung in the air for a bit then he cocked his head to the side, looked at me earnestly and said, 'Well, that's easy. To be a househusband, of course. You're working. You can provide. I mean, no need to be sexist, after all we are in the 1990s, are we not?'

No need to be sexist?

Househusband?

I'll just focus on what you do and what you can provide!

Breathe, breathe, breathe. Do not freak out.

Then there was this one time, at band camp, as we were continuing to discuss life and the fact that Jo didn't ever want to get off his backside to do anything, except perhaps make a cup of coffee from a kettle that of course he hadn't actually contributed to. He said, 'Also, we needed a microwave, right? Well, my sister is throwing her old one out, so we've now got one. Along with some of her old kitchen stuff too.'

He literally beamed with pride, obviously thinking that I would be chuffed to bits to be with a bedroom DJ all my life after graduating university and going out to work. Hey, at least we could get a microwave and some wooden spoons to land in our laps. There we had it. The difference between us.

Once I reached my early twenties, I was in my fourth year at university, studying my socks off, while Jo was sitting on his backside waiting for life to happen, and for everyone else to do the hard work. Still bedroom DJing. Whereas I worked two jobs (one in a bar and the other as a function silver service waitress), wanting the chance to learn and break out of what would have otherwise been my destiny.

Because You Matter
Chelle Verite

You see, I'm from working-class stock. Albeit adopted into white middle class. Fighting those nature vs nurture demons. It could have been a very different life choice for me. Limited education. Government benefits. Council house. No college or university. Low paid job or no paid job. Waiting for life to just jump into my lap with the expectation that I would eventually get help. **Taking the leap** wasn't even on the radar. Instead, it was a given that the state would provide.

Sadly though, or maybe it was an unconscious relief, two weeks before my finals I found out that Jo hadn't actually sat his backside on the sofa and waited for life to land on its feet. No, sadly, the only drive he had was to get one of the girls in our circle of friends pregnant. F*cking brilliant. Not. She was only nineteen. The same age my birth mum was when she fell pregnant and I was given up for adoption. Ohhh, yippee, life ghosts and demons here we come. Needless to say, it was a very fast two stones that I lost in that two week run up to my finals.

It's ironic too, as the only reason I found out that particular day was because Jo had just found out the girl (Danielle was her name) had lost the baby, and I just knew. Call it female intuition or call it the culmination of many, many, many **Red Flags**. Danielle had been bedroom DJ star struck, just as I suppose I had been at her age. To be fair, I was kind and I asked after her and said that it was best that Jo left immediately to spend some time with her and look after her. He left his keys behind and he also left me. I was a wailing wreck behind closed doors.

By literally saying, 'F*ck it!' and taking the leap, albeit the wrong one, Jo lost his home, his means of income and his pride. I lost my pride too but found strength I didn't know was possible. I found freedom in the knowledge I was no longer with a cheat or a sponger. I found strength to **Take the Leap**, despite my utter devastation (I had by this time been with Jo for almost six years; almost a third of my life). I finished my studies and achieved my Psychology Honours Degree. I didn't get a first, but I did get a 2.1. I don't remember sitting my actual final exams about two weeks after that fateful day as that time was a bit of a blur. However, the paperwork a few weeks later told me I f*cking did it! I got my degree and my pride returned. Everything happens for a reason. If that situation hadn't happened, I wouldn't be here, writing this for you today. Love hurts, duh! So too does ignoring what you need for you.

Ignore your **Red Flags** at your peril. Do you even notice them in your world or are you too busy discrediting what the back of your mind is saying, like I did? Or ignoring when your gut is shouting, even sometimes screaming, 'Hellllooooooo, **Red Flag** here! Oi, pay attention to me, I'm talking!' The thing is, a **Red Flag** usually tells you a personal boundary has been crossed. A core value has been disrespected. Your emotional, intellectual or physical safety is in jeopardy. If you noticed someone you loved or respected was in danger, no matter how big or small, you sure as hell wouldn't just walk away now, would you? So how come it's acceptable to ignore your own **Red Flags**?

Looking back at that relationship with Jo, there were so many **Red Flags** and yet I let them slip away from myself. **Red Flags** on values. **Red Flags** on behaviours. **Red Flags** on outlook. **Red Flags** on expectations. **Red Flags** on respect. In fact, the list is literally endless. The sad thing is that I didn't trust myself enough to listen to what I had to say to me. Perhaps I didn't want to know. Perhaps I genuinely couldn't see. Both of which are huge denial **Reactions**.

Now, I'm not here to wax lyrical or to tell you woe is me stories about my life, or maybe I am so that you don't do what I did. Investigate what's going on for you, recognise the signs, and trust there is a Life Lesson appearing that can be acknowledged without failure, so instead of reacting you can choose conscious **Responses** and get a different **Outcome**. Love hurts. Worse than that, you and your life will hurt you if you don't recognise and acknowledge those **Red Flags**.

Life Lesson 12

RED FLAGS AND TAKING THE LEAP

What about the **Red Flags** that have appeared in your life, your past situations? (There may not have been many but let's be brave and take a look.)

Think back over your life and work situations, choose a **Red Flag** that your intuition and gut told you about and answer the following questions

Because You Matter

Chelle Verite

♥ When have Red Flags appeared in your life?
(People, situations, decisions...)

♥ What were those Red Flags telling you?

♥ What could you have done about them?

Because You Matter
Chelle Verite

♥ **What will you do about them that will enhance your world now?**

♥ **What are your (limitless) options that would add value to your life?**

♥ **What will you do more of or less of that will add value to your life?**

Because Y♡u Matter

Chelle Verite

There, well done you. Those questions and answers will definitely help you learn to identify the impact of **Red Flags** so they become less prevalent in your world. It's about adding value, enhancing what we can create and **Take the Leap**. As for **Responses** and choices, I am going to say, on a slightly lighter note, that if you're reading this book, then I know what I am, I learned from my situations, and I decided to **Taking the Leap** even when I thought it was a scary proposition and write this book! So, will you **Take the Leap**? Are you a person who will take action to empower your life and get off your arse, and go forth and conquer, even when it scares the living daylights out of you?

Then again, maybe you're a **Backside Sofa**? One of those people who doesn't want to take the leap. When you're having a bad *I just can't be arsed* day and you've got your backside firmly plonked on the sofa eating a shit load of crisps and biscuits stating, 'Nope, I'm not up for it today.' Or 'My world is utterly shit.'

Or perhaps you're a **Woe-is-me Walker** who believes that everyone owes you the world. Perhaps you wallow in self-pity about how hard done to you are and thinks *I'll wait until it lands on me.* 'Why should I do it when someone else will?' *(And if it doesn't the infamous microwave moment will happen eventually.)*

Or are you a **Talker Exhauster**? The type of person who wants to break free of expectation but you are like 'Ooooh, yes please, shall we have a nice little talk about it first?' You talk and talk and talk and talk and T A L K! About doing the same things over and over again. So much so that people start avoiding you and the activities and tasks that simply never happen. (Max, I sincerely hope that your family garden shed is now up?)

Because Y♡u Matter

Chelle Verite

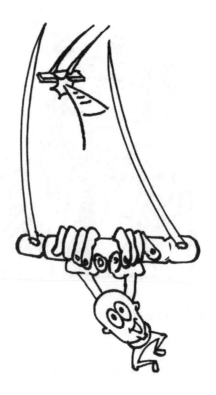

Or maybe on a good day you're a full-on **Trapeze Leaper** when you face your reflection, make conscious choices, even when you're scared you still go for it and **Take the Leap**, and do it anyway. Yes Get In! Hello **Superhero** me. The world is your oyster and you can conquer the world.

Well which one are you? BE honest!!

For a lot of us it's the **Talker Exhauster**, isn't it? Reminds me of baking a cake. In fact, tonight as I sit here to write this Life Lesson, James has baked the most divine lemon drizzle cake. It was yummy, although to be fair, I'm not sure my waistline is as thankful.

Because You Matter
Chelle Verite

The **Talker Exhauster** approach is like saying you're going to bake a cake, but you've not been to the supermarket and have no intention of getting off the sofa to get the actual ingredients. (No, COVID lockdown is not an excuse anymore).

Excuses mean whatever you're waxing lyrical about is actually a pipe dream. Yet you truly believe it. You might even go online to look at all the fabulous cakes you could make, or even eat a shit load because that's what you do to taste test, right?! Then you might waste hours of your time reminiscing about the cakes you had as a child. 'Oooooh, banoffee pie / chocolate brownie / syrup sponge / chocolate gateaux…' There you go again, cake, cake, cake (so many favourites!). You get so easily distracted with the 'Ooooh yes, I wish…' game. It's not real, people! It's a pretend look at what you could have won. There you are saying you'll bake a cake. You finally decide between two favourites and just as you think you might actually go to the supermarket to get the ingredients, you realise you need those pink bowls (or man spatula tools) because, well, the art of cake baking simply wouldn't be complete if you didn't have all the gadgets and shiny things to make it now, would it? Before you know it, you're down at least fifty quid on Amazon. Of course, it's on Prime, so at least the delivery is at no extra cost. Not to mention the fact it's all arriving in separate orders (in those brown packages we love), but it all feels totally real, you are actually making a cake!

Ace, you're baking. Yup. You tell all your family and friends. Imagine that. Then, lo and behold, an amazing outer body experience happens. You are now on MasterChef (you're the next Gordon Ramsay, or perhaps you'd prefer to be the new Jamie or Nigella?). All the while, your amazing cake is merely a twinkle in your eye and still not baked.

Because You Matter

Chelle Verite

Now, isn't this interesting? Replace 'cake making' with pretty much anything you want to do / could do / wish that you could do and you have a typical human response to how you wish your life to be. It's far easier to wish for something, talk about it and busy yourself with the idea of it, than it is to actually go and get it.

That requires the **C** and **R** words.

Commitment and **Responsibility**.

Not to mention **A** for **Action**.

Urghhhh! Now why on earth, even if all aspects of your life are utterly pants, would you want to take a dose of *grow the f*ck up?*

Oh dear. I did say this wasn't an easy read. Or did I omit that part?

Well, hello there sailor, it's not an easy read, so deal with it.

Now here you are making the decision to bake a cake. You've looked up the recipe, bought the whole of Amazon, maybe even made the obligatory trip to IKEA. Not to mention you are the MasterChef of the 21st century. You're R E A D Y! Except in reality, you're so not. You're not ready at all. You aren't even close. Not until you decide. Until you decide to take the leap and commit to it. To be prepared and actually get your ass to the supermarket, or just get it off the sodding sofa. You have to decide to take the first step.

Life Lesson 12

And it's true. You've got to give it a go, otherwise your wish just stays that, a wish.

A prayer, a hope, a maybe, a possibility. Until you decide and *really* decide, it's not real. If it's not a reality, then what's the f*cking point? You may as well put on your pink velour jogging pants and sit watching every TV soap there is, because you aren't going to get the life that you really want. Come on, people, you are worth so much more.

So how are you going to **BE REAL**? How are you going to prepare? Well, the first thing that you need to do is to make a decision. You need to decide what it is that you actually want. I made a decision to **Take the Leap** and write this book. To make it available to as many people as possible, so that you can have a chance at Living the Life you Love AND Loving the Life you Live. And I mean *love* it. Properly. Not wishy washy I'll-put-up-with-a-DJ-boyfriend-microwave-landing-cheating-nonsense shit.

So, decide. It's today's decision and it can always be changed tomorrow. For today, make your decision like your life depended on it. What do you decide for today? What do you actually want (and not what you don't want)? And it has to be real. Happiness does not count; you'll get that in bucket loads as a by-product. You have to decide to take the leap and decide on something that you actually want!

HOW DO YOU SEE YOU
TAKING THE LEAP?

Well? How do you actually see the prospect of **Taking the Leap**? Which approach will you take? 'Impossible', where you don't actually want to take the risk? Or 'I'm possible', where you will **Take the Leap**? What approach to life will your decisions be made on? What do you actually want? Not what you don't want (we aren't talking Henry here).

To make a wish list into a reality list you need to know what you actually want and how to approach that particular task, coupled with the fact that you need to get your backside off the sofa, stop being a **Woe-is-me Walker** or a **Talker Exhauster** and actually **Take the Leap**! Focusing on what you actually want means being clear on what's potentially blocking and stopping your progress in the first place. Those blockers, stoppers, actions, behaviours and thoughts that have (up until now) gotten in the way. These things stop you from 'showing up' and making the most of yourself. The *Impossible Mindset*. Once you know what's blocking you then you can think about how you really want to show up. *The I'm possible Mindset*. The enhancers and advancers, the little things you could and will do more of (or less of) to get you the positive outcome that you want.

Ahhh, hello **God ERR☺ME**, you're back again. It's choosing your **Response**, rather than relying on your automatic **Reaction**.

In short, there are, and will continue to be, lots of things that prevent you from **Taking the Leap**. Mostly barriers that you put in the way of yourself. Some to keep you safe, others because you're lazy, and even some that are so ingrained, like Pavlov's dog, you don't even realise you are reacting to them.

So, before you **Take the Leap**, we need to find out more about how you approach your wants, and how to positively disrupt your initial thought patterns so we can be that fabulous go getter, facing fear, creating awesomeness in your world **Trapeze Leaper**.

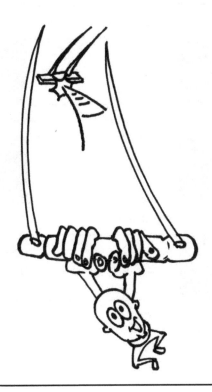

STEP 1. IMPOSSIBLE OR I'M POSSIBLE?

What's your approach to the world? Let's find out.

Answer the following statements below by circling the number on the continuum that best represents your approach to life and the things that you want.

When approaching the world, are you more focused on...

Scarcity? (Not much)	1 2 3 4 5 6 7 8 9 10	Abundance? (Lots avail)

When challenge comes along are you more...

Fearful? (Timid)	1 2 3 4 5 6 7 8 9 10	Fearless? (Brave)

When being asked to do a task is your initial response more...

No?	1 2 3 4 5 6 7 8 9 10	Yes?

When doing tasks are you more...

Reactive?	1 2 3 4 5 6 7 8 9 10	Proactive?

Total your scores /40

Because Y♡u Matter

Chelle Verite

The higher your number to a score of 40 = the more you are an **I'm possible mindset**.

The lower your number to 10 = the more you have an **Impossible mindset** approach to the world, goals and tasks.

People with an **Impossible mindset** focus more on blockers, stoppers, restrictions, worries and problems in a situation. For those of you who have higher numbers (28 and above), you tend to approach life activities with an **I'm possible mindset** focused on advancers, enhancers, ways forward and solutions.

❤ **What do you notice about your approach?**

❤ **What differences are there between your work / career / home and family life approaches?**

STEP 2. WHAT DO YOU ACTUALLY WANT?

This is about being the courageous and brave **Trapeze Leaper**. What decisions will you make? What do you actually want? Not what you don't want. It's about what you actually do want.

> ♥ **I want to Take the Leap to do...**
> (Think of all the things you actually want, that you haven't, up until now, been brave enough to list. If it's easier, split this into career, home, family and finances or any categories of your choosing.)

> ♥ **I want to do them because...**
> (Really think about what your why is, what do you **Desire**?)

Because You Matter

Chelle Verite

♥ **What will potentially block and stop you achieving these?**
(Be honest here. Think about the behaviours, thoughts,
patterns and habits you may have that get in the way
or have stopped you taking the leap before. This is your
Impossible mindset.)

♥ **What little things could you do more of (or less of)
that will help remove your blockers and stoppers to
Taking the Leap and your success?**
(This is your **I'm possible mindset**.)

I will do more of	I will do less of

Because You Matter

Chelle Verite

♥ **My first step to this is...**

♥ **What I could get distracted by is...**

♥ **I will keep myself on track with this by...**

♥ **This will make a positive difference to my world because...**

STEP 3. SHOWING UP

Remember, being ready, able and willing to **Take the Leap** isn't about slacking. It's about choosing what you want and choosing to show up to actually get it. It's about getting your backside off the sofa and actually choosing to **Take the Leap** in the first place.

♥ What 3 things will you do to ensure that you actually SHOW UP and are ready, able and willing to Take the Leap?
I will...
1.
2.
3.

You won't get what you want if all you do is eat someone else's cake or wait for them to get it for you. Instead, this is about empowering you to get what you actually want. Name it, create it, bake that cake and **Take the Leap** for yourself. Most importantly, stay away from waiting for that sodding microwave! Life is for living, baking and creating, not waiting and deliberating.

Because You Matter

Chelle Verite

Oh, and just in case you didn't know what to bake, I've created a **Take the Leap chocolate muffin cake recipe** especially for you (it's in the Appendix in the back of the book). Why did I do that? Well, you know I love cake, so I thought I'd be kind and break you in gently to the world of baking. I've designed the recipe so that it only contains good fat and the muffins are under one hundred calories each. Once you have a batch, we can all have them for breakfast to stimulate our brains while we decide what we actually want in our lives. You'll be pleased to hear that the cake needs Amazon purchases of different types of flour and even a Kitchen Aid mixer that'll set you back at least five hundred quid. If you're on a budget and don't want to spend that much, the pink spatula (or man baking tools as they are often referred to) is way more affordable.

In other words, no f*cking excuses.

Take the Leap, eat and enjoy.

Why do it?

Yup, you know why.

Because You Matter

> ❝

Attract what you expect. Reflect what you desire. Become what you respect. Mirror what you admire.

AUDREY HEPBURN

LIFE LESSON

13

Valuing LOVE and HATE

MIRROR, MIRROR

Because You Matter

Chelle Verite

"Mirror, mirror on the wall, who's the fairest of them all?" Well for a start, I stand corrected. It's 'magic mirror', not 'mirror, mirror' or so I'm absolutely told by Belle, my lovely teenage daughter. And my husband, James, of course (who knows more facts about life than is possible with his Mensa brain), when having a rather heated discussion round our pine farmhouse kitchen table. (I love that table and chair set and the fact that it is the place where we whittle our family time away on many an after-dinner conversation.) I googled Disney and the 'Mirror, mirror' quote. Lo and behold, there it was, even the online interweb phrase book even said so. Magic mirror it is. It must be real then, because we all know that the interweb is so truthful, especially the facts that we find on TikTok. "Duh", said Belle (she is eighteen you know). "Of course TikTok is a valid source of factual information about everything. It's TikTok!" She looked at me with the innocent, twinkly eyes that only a young adult influenced by the latest iPhone and access to Wi-Fi has.

Because You Matter
Chelle Verite

Anyway, I digress, which I seem to do a lot of these days. I must just be having too much fun writing this, or drinking wine. It's actually both! Right, so. 'Magic mirror on the wall, who was the fattest, I mean fairest, of them all?' Snow White, of course. All pure and innocent and within the realms of normality and social acceptance. However, this leads me on to the reflection part and the whole point of me quoting this to you in the first place. One should cherish the magic mirror reflection of oneself. Urghhh! A mirror. 'Urghhhh! Cherish my reflection?' I hear you cry. Is that before or after I am dragged through a hedge backwards, attempting to get out of bed and battle with everyday life, all the while still breathing? 'The reflection of ourselves? We should cherish what is in front of us, Chelle, really?!'

'Yes,' I say. 'Face it.' Miss Bossy Knickers is in the room. Get in front of that long mirror. Head and shoulders aren't enough. Full length please. Go on. Yes, that will mean taking the leap, getting your backside off the sofa and locating that mirror in your house or hotel room. When I wrote this particular Life Lesson, pre-COVID-19 lockdown, I was sitting in a Premier Inn in Glasgow about to deliver leadership training to a great bunch of people on talking to the team. Even that room had a full-length mirror, albeit in true Glaswegian style it was nailed to the wall. Gotta love Glasgow. *It smiles better.* Anyway, now I come to think of it, just use whatever mirror you can get your hands on. Even a picture of yourself looking into your flipped mobile phone camera will do.

Yes. Be brave. Face it.

Life Lesson 13

HELLO LOVE AND HATE

STEP 1. BE BRAVE AND MAKE A START

Say hello. This is saying hello to you. In your mirror, whichever one you ended up getting your paws on, big or small (remember size doesn't matter, honest), have a look at your reflection and say, 'Hello.' Yes, I know it's strange.

'Hello.'

'Hello you, it's me.'

Now I want you to look at your reflection again. When you do, ask yourself the following questions one at a time and write down one thing about what you see in that reflection of yourself looking back.

❤ Look at me, what do I see?

Because You Matter

Chelle Verite

♥ **Look at me, what do I think is good about me?**
(Be kind)

♥ **Look at me, what do I hate about me?**
(No more than three things)

♥ **Look at me, what do I believe about me?**
(Positive things only)

Because You Matter

Chelle Verite

♥ **Look at me, what do I value of the me that I can see?**
(Positive things only)

♥ **Look at me, what things do I accept about me?**
(Yes, accept)

♥ **Look at me, what do I love about me?**
(Go on, I know its un-British to say but give it a go)

Because Y♡u Matter
Chelle Verite

Oooooh, that got you thinking, didn't it? How did you get on? Which of the questions did you find easy? Which did you find hard? There may even have been some that you just gave up on. Or perhaps it was the question about your value that got you, or the hate question.

I know this Life Lesson is going to be tough going for some of you. Taking some time out to look at you? Most days we usually look at ourselves to style our hair, put our war paint makeup on (and that's just the boys), or to see if we pass as presentable. However, this is about starting to say hello to you, not just look at you. Look so you can actually see you, for you, and what you bring to the world. It's about understanding how to value you, how to be you.

Remember, I said to you at the beginning some of the Life Lessons you'll love and you'll hate? Well, there's a fifty fifty chance of you liking this one. Actually, knowing the human three to one rule tendency to make everything negative, the odds are likely stacked against you to be jumping from the rooftops in adoration, and instead be totally disgusted. What I will say? Well, my shout is, 'Stick with it.' You've got this. Remember I made a promise. I won't ever ask you to do something I haven't done myself, and there is a good reason why the energy of this Life Lesson is focusing on you.

STEP 2. REALLY SAY HELLO

Now you know why you are here. It's about really seeing and valuing you. Let's have another go. Get that snazzy mirror at the ready.

Be brave.

> Look.
>
> Really, really, really, loooooook in your mirror.
>
> (There are three 'reallys' here,
> so it must be important for you to do it.)
>
> LOOK AT YOU.
>
> Look at all of you.
>
> Really look at you.
>
> Look at what looks back at you.
>
> Look at what this world has gifted and created you as.
>
> What do you see?
>
> What do you really see?

The reflection that has been created by you is what you have made it, whether you love it, or whether you hate it.

Because You Matter

Chelle Verite

Let me just slow that one down for you…

Listen to these words.

Look at your reflection.

That reflection is you.

Look at your reflection.

You have created it.

It is created by you.

It is what YOU have made it.

Whether you love it or whether you hate it.

Boo! Yup, it's you!

The same person that has been staring back at you since as long as you could remember.

Look at your reflection.

♥ What do you truly value about you?

Now I know I asked you that in the last set of questions, however, you would have whizzed over that so fast I can guarantee you didn't really sit with yourself and recognise you at your core now, did you? You may not have even remembered doing that exercise as the squirm factor of having to give yourself time and energy may have been too much. So, let's draw breath now and truly look at your reflection.

Because You Matter

Chelle Verite

♥ **What do you value about you? Is it...**

LOVE?

or

HATE?

that you are experiencing when you look at your reflection?

♥ **When you look at your reflection...**
Do you LOVE you most / least?
Do you HATE you most / least?

Either way, it's you. If you haven't noticed, you can't hide from your own reflection, no matter how hard you try. You are still there.

How much do I LOVE / HATE me?

Look at your reflection of you and who you are.

♥ **How much do you LOVE what you see and the reflection of who you are?**

1 = 10%

10 = 100%

I LOVE ME score here [   ]

Because Y♥u Matter
Chelle Verite

♥ **How much do you HATE what you see and the reflection of who you are?**
1 = 10%
10 = 100%
I HATE ME score here [   ]

As I say this, I need to clarify certain things, important things. Being typically British (and yes, I know I'm Scottish, but even we fall into this camp at this time) and more reserved, and lacking American-esque self-awareness, we have a huge tendency to veer away from saying we love something (especially ourselves). Even worse, I've now been educated in the language of Yorkshire. In response to something good in the world I would say, "That's f*cking brilliant." James would say, "It's not bad." I used to hit the roof. "Not bad. Not bad? WTF is that?!" He explained in Yorkshire terms that means it's bloody marvelous. Phew, panic over then. It is not, however, the same when my dad used to say something was, "Quite good." Quite good? Can't you just say it's great?

You'll now have *I HATE me* scale and an *I LOVE me* scale.

♥ **Look at your LOVE and HATE scores, what do you notice?**

Because You Matter
Chelle Verite

Interesting. My LOVE score before I started this journey was a meagre 2 (sad face) and a whopping 9 for hating myself (even sadder face). Now, I'm no mathematician, but it was very clear that hate outstripped the love by a f*cking long chalk. I couldn't even bring myself to say the word love. It wasn't love. It was begrudging acknowledgement that I existed and totally nothing about my reflection was good. Nothing in my whole existence or what I saw looking back at me was actually about self-value, self-love or actually self-anything. In fact, when I did this first time around, I actually scribbled out the world *LOVE* and changed it to *like*. Nope that's a lie. It wasn't even *like*. Who am I trying to kid? It was *tolerate*. I merely ~~loved, liked~~, *tolerated* 2 things about myself. I certainly didn't love myself. The mere thought of it would have made me want to throw up. In fact, up to very recently, I really struggled with the whole concept of loving who I am. Valuing self. It was even the name of my company back in 2007. SelfValue. Oh the irony. And this is me, Mrs Empowerment Coach, Positive Disruptor.

However, we are all human, remember. How we act towards ourselves will define how we are, how we exist. Yet I was dealing with an internal battle of *why the f*ck would I want to blow my own trumpet and do that?* I mean, by the very nature of my beginning, I was unwanted and put up for adoption and then at three days old put into care.

'Why was I put up for adoption?' I asked my birth mother on our first ever face to face,

'Ah yes,' replied my birth mum, 'why?...'

'Well...'

(long pause)

'Well...'

'You were that black bastard baby.'

Because You Matter

Chelle Verite

Seriously.

I mean, I know my birth mum left school at fifteen but f*ck that was a bit of a blow, and that was said in a public place. Just matter of fact.

To put it into context, we were in a pub, a Wetherspoons I recall, in a booth for our first face to face meeting. Oli was with me (he was nearly one) and my now ex-husband, and my birth mother and her partner Brian completed the party. Needless to say, thirty-six years of patching myself up to gather my own SelfValue simply disintegrated the second she said that phrase.

As the words were released, they hit me like vomit. I had to politely hand Oliver over. I ran from that pub table in a blur of utter devastation to the pub toilets. I was there for a while, sobbing my heart out and trying to breathe. I didn't do very well. Even when it was explained, after I finally came back to sit down at the table with my mascara running, that no, my birth mum didn't actually mean it like that. What she meant to say was (and I quote).

'I didn't keep you because I didn't want to be known as the whore with the black bastard baby.'

Oh, COME ON! That's f*cking twice.

Knowing that makes it all so much better then, that it wasn't my hatred of self, just another person's hatred of what I represented. It was a bit of a blur to be fair, but by the end of the conversation I did understand that yet again I was 'lucky' as the social workers said, 'What a shame. She's too dark to pass off as her mother and new husbands, so she'll have to be put into the social care system and see if anyone else wants a baby like her.'

It was the 1970s, people.

Because You Matter
Chelle Verite

Well f*ck me, that's a bit of a tough call so you'll have to excuse me if I'm not all, 'OMG, O. M. G., I totally love, love, LOVE my awesome 'brown' reflection of myself, and what this means about how I feel inside.'

So how could I value self?

The thing is, thankfully, it isn't your experience of the world that makes or breaks you. If you grew up in a world of positive love reinforcement and **LOVE ME** value system, then your love score will be higher than your hate score. And vice versa. If, like me, you grew up desperately clawing at life and never feeling like you fitted in, or not being held or told that you are valued or loved for what you are and how you are, then the **HATE ME** score will be higher than your love score.

It's that simple.

We are in control of our own destiny. It is indeed our minds that can screw up. We should have signs up on every mirror that reads. *I'm good with what I see, and I truly value me.*

Anyone want to help me mass produce mirrors with those words embossed on it?

Is your reflection healthy? I mean, is it really?

The stronger we value self, the better we run, and the more productive we are. This is the **I LOVE ME** bit. Yet the **I HATE ME** bit, well, that means we often self-destruct, and chronic resentment, anger, impulsivity or abuse of self or others becomes part of our daily routine. Remember, we are facing the mirror, people. We are fighting our internal battles continuously.

LOVE. HATE. LOVE. HATE.

To value self. to not value self.

Because You Matter

Chelle Verite

To love me. To love me not.

Here's the small print (aka the next challenge). Facing up to your reflection, figuring out what is real and what is not, what you want for your life, what you say and how you see yourself, will be what your life plays out. You get to be in control of how you see you and how you are real.

STEP 3. WHAT DO YOU WANT?

♥ **What do you want?**

♥ **What do you really, really, really, really want?!**

Do you want to be filled with light and LOVE?

or

Do you want to go to the Dark Side and HATE?

Because You Matter
Chelle Verite

No one has the capability to control your life, and how you, or I, feel. That, my friends, is down to us. We are in the driving seat. Even as early as the age of seven we know what our personality is, what motivates us and what makes us feel good. The me, myself and I.

It's me that puts me in the *I deserve to be loved* category or the *I am loved* category or the *I'm under valuing me and I hate myself as a result*, whether or not I want to see that I am truly lovable. Whether or not I want to stop the hate consuming my every move and every breath and look at things with different eyes and a different heart. Eyes that are clear and not clouded with points of view that are simply not true, and a heart that is warm, open and loving.

I can do it for everyone else so it's about time that I did it for me too.

Isn't it time you did the same?

No, it doesn't happen overnight, this is not an American, happy clappy, your world is amazing in a blink of an eye. Or laser eye treatment restoring your once screwed up vision to 20-20 with a fabulous new mirror that does not play tricks on you, and a heart that is just pumping with the Oxytocin / MDMA 'love' drug.

I am not the miracle giver. It is way, way easier than that. A miracle is not required. This is simply about making a choice. It's about waking up and shaking things up and giving you the opportunity to notice what's going on and helping you choose some different options. When you notice, you can **Focus**. When you **Focus**, you can choose. Choices, choices, choices. Look into the light. Choose life not drugs. (That's the wrong analogy, Chelle, this is not Trainspotting.) Choose **LOVE** not **HATE** and look into the light. Although, don't stare at the f*cking sun or place the mirror right in the sunlight, otherwise you'll be seeing white spots in front of your vision for a very, very long time. In short, go easy on yourself. Allow yourself time to notice and give yourself permission to do things differently.

STEP 4. ACCEPTANCE NOW AND FROM

These two phrases will give you permission to do things differently.

Up until now

and

From now on

For example.

'**Up until now**... I focused on hating who I was.'

'**From now on**... I will focus on loving what makes me, me.'

Yes, it really is that simple. I promise you

So, let's give it a go.

♥ **Up until now...** (What did you do that you can ditch?)

Because Y♡u Matter

Chelle Verite

♥ **From now on...**
(What will you do to replace the behaviour you want to ditch that will make a positive difference to your world?)

From this point onwards, you have the chance to look at your reflection and say with dawning realisation, 'Hey, I'm here and I have choice.' You no longer have the chance to look at your reflection and go, 'Nah, not today.' From now on you have the choice to **Respond** rather than to automatically **React**, and choices that you actually give a shit about to acknowledge. From now on you have the choice to accept that despite the fact you've been around the block enough to feel bruised, exposed, used, exploited, confused, broken, demented, small, hurt, vulnerable, disgusted, alarmed and trapped in a world where none of it makes sense, just maybe, for today, there is a ray of hope. A ray of sunshine where you can feel a little bit excited and maybe even exhilarated that your goodness and the value that you put on you is something to be proud of.

From now on I will honour acceptance.

- ✓ **Acceptance for you.**
- ✓ **Acceptance for your world.**
- ✓ **Acceptance for the past. It's passed.**

Because Y♡u Matter

Chelle Verite

- ✓ **Acceptance for you to live in the present today.**
  (Just as you are).
- ✓ **Acceptance for the future that is yet to come.**
- ✓ **Acceptance for all that you are.**
  (And all that you will become).

Just one thing before you have that internal battle and wrangle...

♥ **What will you LOVE for being you today?**
(Go on I know you want to)

Remember, I'm here with you through your personal journey, to hold your hand, scream, shout, rant and turn the corner with you. In fact, if you want a proper rant and release, head over to Life Lesson 17 to **HALT Emotional Turmoil** and learn all about how to handle your **Anger**. Oooh yes, now I do like the sound of that, another adventure!

In the meantime, let's get our **Self LOVE** in order.

Repeat after me...

Because You Matter
Chelle Verite

Up until now hatred of me ruled my world

Now that's gone

From now on love will be my new world

Up until now hatred ruled the world

Now that's gone

From now on love will be my new world

I value all that I am and all that I will be

From now on until eternity

Like Wimbledon.

LOVE one, **HATE** nil.

And if I can do it, you sure as f*ck can too.

Tennis racquets at the ready, people.

LOVE, game, set and match.

And why do it?

Why value, love and accept you?

Simple.

Because You Matter

"

Trust your inner
creator and let go
of your inner critic.

J R INCER

LIFE LESSON

14

Kick your
Critical Mind

SDM VERSUS PAM

Because You Matter

Chelle Verite

'You're useless, you're stupid, you do that...'

'Don't think so, you'll forget, you'll fail...'

'Don't even bother.'

'What the f*ck were you thinking?'

'You'll screw it up.'

'DUH, as if.'

'You're boring.'

'Why would anyone listen to you?'

'You'll forget.'

'God, you're thick as mince.'

'You, no way, you'll never be able to do that.'

'Who do you think you are?'

'You're shit.'

'You? You'll never make it.'

And the sad thing is, no that's not what people say. That's you!

That's just some of the things our own **MindF*ck** of a critical mind says to us on a daily basis. The thing is, we all have it. That internal voice that goes round and around in our head. Spend a day in the life of Chelle and you'll be introduced to my critical **Sabotaging Devil Mindset (SDM).** It's Scottish and doesn't just shout, doesn't just scream, it does both and rants at the same time. It's like Billy Connolly on speed and crack cocaine, a lethal concoction of humorous pain, bucket loads of hurt and sadly no gain.

That inner critical voice can be so loud sometimes it literally shouts. At times, not only does it shout, it screams, it rants and when it stops that it just cruelly whispers. Our **SDM** makes us falter. It makes us

Because Y♡u Matter

Chelle Verite

believe we can't when we can. It means we stall and put things off, or worse still, it stops us dead in our tracks. It brings in dread and annihilation of our supportive and encouraging thoughts, and instead opens the floodgates to our worry rubble and **Fear Monsters**, which then consume us. Our **SDM** can knock our self-confidence so much it depletes our amazingness and our self-confidence in an instant.

We should have bucket loads of confidence and feel-good factor instilled in us. Some days we have it in abundance. That feeling of self-belief and self-reliance and self-trust in what we do, and will create, and the belief that we are amazing. Yet there are other days when self-confidence and self-belief plays hide and seek, and worse still, disintegrates to let the negative self in instead. It's like that voice and our critical **MindF*ck** state is a real nasty piece of work. A huge bully that goes for our throats, leaving us winded and in a messy puddle of despair, with a shredded sense of self-worth and annihilation of any self-achievement possibilities. Except, instead of fighting back, we follow the bully's instruction and willingly beat ourselves up. We take the role of **Reacting** in ways that disintegrate any sense of possible achievement, or praise, or even self-acceptance.

It's like we are blindsided. We throw away any concept of trusting ourselves and we push aside any notion that we can achieve anything worth doing, saying or being. When that happens, crippling self-doubt, debilitating **Worry-woe-is-me**, thoughts of past regret, procrastination and/or lack of (or stopping of) going for and achieving goals kicks in. We begin to disappear inwards and stop glowing. We worry about everything. We stop being who we want to be and shy away from putting our heads above the parapet. We might even get to the point of finally achieving something magnificent but it doesn't even register or we don't feel happy to have achieved it. Worse still, we get there but our **SDM** keeps telling us over and over that it just wasn't quite perfect enough, or we didn't work hard enough, or we're just not good enough.

Because You Matter
Chelle Verite

Urghhhhhhh, the noise!

Maybe, just maybe, you're one of the lucky ones and already have your **Pioneering Angel Mindset (PAM)** all sorted. If so, please can you bake the rest of us some **Take the Leap chocolate muffin cakes**, because we could do with one to celebrate when we get to that amazing point too (and we will, people, we will).

So, when exactly does that negative **SDM** actually hit us? When do we become aware of it all? For most of us, we begin to recognise the things that make us feel good, and the things that make us feel bad, when we are young. In fact, there are kids as young as five years old that I'm coaching, using the *'Lets Get BOMBCHELLED!'* Motivational Life Toolkits, that tell me 'Chelle, a voice inside of me makes me do bad things, and that voice makes me feel bad. I just want to feel good. I never feel happy enough with me, I never feel good enough.' Seriously?! That's young, and that's plain wrong. It makes me want to bundle them up in a positive duvet of life and say, 'You're safe.' I know if you have kids you would want to do the same. As Billy Connolly would say, '**SDM** get te fe.' As I would say in my language, 'F*ck you, critical mind.' Or, on a slightly less aggressive day, 'Do one, ya bas.'

All of us; children, adolescents, adults alike, deserve to feel good and to be kind to ourselves. What age were you when you realised you had an internal voice? Maybe it was as a young child? Maybe it was at school, college, university, your first job? Perhaps it's right now that you've gone, 'Oh yes, I've never noticed that before, but there it is.' Maybe, up until now, you've never even thought about it.

For me, it was when I was six. The worst voice was my own. The one in my head. The one that said I wasn't good enough or I didn't do well enough. That my bronze medal in swimming wasn't enough. That my silver medal wasn't either. That my horse riding wasn't as good as

Because Y♡u Matter

Chelle Verite

everyone else's. Even when I won Chase-me-Charlie (that's jumping really high in competitions, all you lovely, horsey mad people will know). Nope, my little six-year-old brain said I only won because everyone else dropped out, because it was luck and I was really rubbish!

Hands up if when you're about to do something your **SDM** says.

'Oi! stop right there...'

'You'll never do it.'

For me, it was writing this book, or delivering a '*Lets Get BOMBCHELLED!*' seminar or virtual conference to hundreds of people.

That self-limiting, irritating chitter-chatter noise of self-critical doubt in your head. It's there, isn't it? That relentless noise. But, and it's a huge BUT, that all calms when you're in flow. When you're doing the things you love, with the people you love, and being your authentic self, then it's all angelic rainbows, pink fluffy marshmallows and lovely, squidgy unicorns. Ahhhh yes, that is when the gorgeous, ever supportive, empowering **Pioneering Angel Mindset (PAM)** kicks in (and how we all love her). For some of us, our inner voice and our **Pioneering Angel** chitter chatter is that nice angelic one. In Scotland we'd say, 'It's braw.' (Which means brilliant.) **PAM** says, 'Aww, aren't you great?' Even better than that she'll say, 'Wow, look at you go. You're awesome.' She's a friend, and a really good one at that. **PAM** that lovely, gorgeous, and supportive guardian. She's someone you can rely on to guide you and keep you sane, constantly supporting and smiling down on you. Your **Pioneering Angel Mindset** keeps you warm, makes you smile inwardly and helps you walk tall with that *Ready Brek* cereal glow.

Because You Matter
Chelle Verite

Well, that's like your mind. It depends how you process the world and how you see it. It depends on what you consciously choose to do with it that makes a difference. Your critical **Sabotaging Devil Mindset** has a warped sense of humour. It sits on your shoulder pretending to be the best friend. Be warned, people, **SDM** is not your friend. It is a wolf in sheep's clothing and regardless of how it is dressed up, a wanker is still, well, a wanker. **Sabotaging Devil Mindset** is still that inner voice that screams, shouts and tells you off for.

- ✕ all the things you did wrong.
- ✕ all the things you should have done.
- ✕ all the things you could have done better, or forgot, or did badly at that precise moment after you did that particular task.

As a result, you feel utterly deflated, defeated and crap about yourself. It's the voice that tells you, 'You're a total loser, what on earth were you thinking?' It says, 'Don't even bother to do that because you're shit anyway.' Then self-doubt kicks in, along with a huge bucket of procrastination. It's the irritating noise that pushes the timelines back on your tasks and means you put off what you have to do until it gets so urgent that you end up doing a crap job anyway. That then fulfills the critical mind's intention which is, 'Urgh, I should never have done it in the first place because it made me feel shit and the result was crap.'

Ah the joys of being a grown up and having to take responsibility. Funny how us humans work, isn't it? Often against us, then for us, then against us, then for us. I'll be seasick if we carry on with the back and forth. Reminds me of that sodding **Worry Woe-is-me** rocking chair, which we do not need in our lives, people! **Dissolve. Dissolve**.

Because You Matter
Chelle Verite

Instead, I propose we get a handle on our worries and our **SDM** and start promoting our awesome **PAM** instead. I bet (and I'll make you a promise) if we think about our mindset differently, we will feel differently. If we feel differently, we will experience the world differently. If we experience the world differently, we will be different. By conscious choice, not just by automatic pilot default. **PAM** is most definitely a friend of that man in a kilt.

Hello **God ERR☺ME**, we love you.

Because You Matter

Chelle Verite

For the majority of us, whether we are manager, parent, CEO, graduate, apprentice, life explorer (love the phrase 'life explorer', it's like we should don safari hats and shorts and point our binoculars to smashing beliefs that the world is indeed round not flat) or pioneers (yes, that's exactly it, pioneers!), we need to stretch out of our comfort zones. When we kick that **Sabotaging Devil Mindset** into touch and equip our minds with catapulting encouragement and positive motivational disruption, so we can fling ourselves enthusiastically into our new and once scary but now exciting adventures. Yes, let that emotional and success rollercoaster begin!

Become that authentic and confident life explorer or pioneer flinging yourself into positive action by creating, providing and solidifying ways to get through life. Find ways of making life work for you whilst doing the things you need to and want to, and even the things you don't want to. Here's the best bit. what if, while all of this 'pioneering' was going on, you actually felt good about yourself along the way?! Is that actually possible? Yes! It might scare the shit out of you but you can do it. You have choices, choices, choices, you can take the hard route or the easy route and still feel awesome. *Top of the morning to you* instead of *OMG, no, it's morning already!* Regardless of what adventure route you take.

Some of us, however, like things to be difficult. We actually enjoy the hardship of utter balls of shitness that our lives gifts us. Remember Aunty M and her washing that never gets dry? If I was to gift her goal achievement and she actually enjoyed it, I think she would have probably keeled over and had a heart attack on the spot. I mean, what on earth would she moan about if she got everything that she actually wanted and life was easy? For others of us, it's the satisfaction that we worked damn hard to get here. Working harder not smarter to prove our worth, to tell the world just how difficult it was.

Because You Matter
Chelle Verite

When we don't actually meet the goal we have been aspiring towards being a **Backside Sofa**, continuing to be a **Talker Exhauster**, justifying all the reasons why we never did it, or couldn't (who, me? As if…), we're hiding behind our self-sabotaging patterns of self. For many of us though, I'm sure we'd actually like the easy route, the path of least resistance, where the least amount of energy is expelled to reach success. If we can do that plan, then great. If not, well, it's not that we're lazy, it's just we couldn't actually be arsed. I mean something way more pressing came into our line of sight that simply had to be done, right? Either that or our **SDM** convinced us to waste our energy on beating ourselves up, instead of actually choosing what to do, how to be, and what Positive **Outcome** we actually wanted. This leads to either the **Worry-woe-is-me** or a whole heap of procrastination-beat-ourselves-upness.

It makes no difference why you find yourself here, reading this book. What does matter is that you will now have options you can choose to pack in your 'life explorer' rucksack that will empower you to positively disrupt and start banishing that **SDM.** It'll also mean that you can start to explore how wonderfully expressive and empowering your **PAM** can be, how to action it and feel good along the way.

Life Lesson **14**

WHICH ARE YOU?

ANGEL OR DEVIL?

This is what I like to call your search for your pioneer mind state. It's a happy, angelic place that empowers your state of mind and your abilities, and positively disrupt your life, rather than a negative, sabotaging devil place that takes pride in negatively and devastatingly impacting on your world. Firstly, let's figure out what type of pioneer mind you have.

Are you a ...

PAM (Pioneering Angel Mindset)?

or a SDM (Sabotaging Devil Mindset)?

Because Y♡u Matter
Chelle Verite

STEP 1. WHAT DOES YOUR MIND THINK ABOUT YOU?

Think of a fairly challenging task you are about to do (or have done recently). For me, it would be writing a development proposal for a senior leadership executive team. Or even last night loading the dishwasher. (The former caused me mental strain, the latter caused me relationship strain, but I'll come back to my dishwasher chats later.) Ooh, and probably writing this book!

♥ What challenging tasks have you done recently?

Because You Matter

Chelle Verite

♥ **Regarding the challenging tasks you have listed what did your critical mind/inner voice think and say?**

a) **Before you did the task?**

b) **While you were doing the task?**

c) **After you completed the task?**

Life Lesson 14

If you can't recall, go back to where you were and redo the challenging task in your mind. What did (or does) your mind tell and say to you?

For example.

Are you **PAM Pioneering Angel Mindset** saying, 'Yes, I'm ace, I'm going to do brilliantly, I am awesome!' Pink marshmallows, fluffy unicorns, I can conquer the world and be loved nice mindset?

Or are you **SDM Sabotaging Devil Mindset** saying, 'I'm rubbish and incapable, I can't do it, I won't do it, I'll fail, it'll be crap!' strength and will zapping, I will trample on you and spit you out nasty critical mindset?

♥ **Which one were you?**
PAM Angel?
or
SDM Devil?

♥ **How did they appear?**

STEP 2. LET'S SCALE IT UP

Now you have an idea of where your mind takes you on a particular task, I want you to widen the net, and your thought processes, and think about what your mind is like generally when you go about your day to day. Whether that be a big task, a small task, a hard task or an easy task (or even, in some cases, just a breathing and getting out of bed task).

❤ **On a scale of 1 to 10, think of the number that represents your inner voice and Critical Mind...**

1 - your mind is a **Pioneering Angel** to you. Like a best friend, it tells you you're ace and is quietly soothing and cooing. It loves your company, just sitting down and chilling, drinking a cool beer or fizz, and eating snacks or the best cake in the world. It says, 'You're amazeballs.'

Or

10 - your mind is a **Sabotaging Devil**. It tells you you're bad and rubbish and is loudly screaming, shouting and ranting at you. It tells you what you can't or shouldn't do. Like a boot camp sergeant major, it makes you run up a hill when every part of your body is screaming in agony. It makes you feel sick and consistently says, 'You're a loser.'

The number between 1 and 10 represents how kind or evil your Critical Mind is.

Write it here.

Because Y♡u Matter
Chelle Verite

This is a snapshot of what you are thinking now, about you, in this moment.

It's also part of your **LiveLifeBE** 'life explorer' rucksack.

Now you have your score we are going to work on your **Critical Mind**.

STEP 3. WHERE DOES YOUR CRITICAL MIND SCORE?

Score your **Critical Mind** on the task table below.

My mind is...

(Circle your answers and then answer the questions below)

	Pioneering Angel									Sabotaging Devil
On a good day	1	2	3	4	5	6	7	8	9	10
On a bad day	1	2	3	4	5	6	7	8	9	10
Easy Task	1	2	3	4	5	6	7	8	9	10
New Task	1	2	3	4	5	6	7	8	9	10
Familiar Task	1	2	3	4	5	6	7	8	9	10
Challenging Task	1	2	3	4	5	6	7	8	9	10

Take a look at your results and write your thoughts on the next page.

Because Yõu Matter

Chelle Verite

♥ **What do you notice?**

♥ **Where does your Critical Mind go to first?**
(Are you more **Angel** or more **Devil**, and why do you
Think that is?)

♥ **What's the difference between your mindset on a
good day and a bad day?**

Because You Matter

Chelle Verite

❤ What's the difference depending on activity / task level?

❤ What patterns exist in your mindset?

Fingers crossed, I'm making you think here. In other words, are you a nasty git to yourself or a wee sweetie?

Other things to consider too...

Because You Matter

Chelle Verite

♥ **Was there a time in your life when these scores would have been different?**

(If so, when and why?)

♥ **How does this relate to you and what you want now?**

♥ **What do you want your Critical Mind to be like and feel like?**

Because You Matter

Chelle Verite

In case you haven't noticed, this adventure is all about creating a new and empowered you.

I selfishly, and for ease of life, want you to have 1s and 2s and even 3s **(PAM Pioneering Angelic Mindset)** which will mean you are way happier too. Ohhh, wait a minute, I think I may just have done myself out of a job, Oh well. I'd much rather help you celebrate achieving a **Motivating Matt Pioneering Angel Mindset** revolution, instead of letting those **Sabotaging Devil Mindset** and **Dark Side** moments win. You feeling happy, authentic and empowered? Yes, I'll sign up to that.

'So, how do we get rid of our **Critical Mind** then, Chelle?' I hear you ask. And just like Blue Peter, here's one I made earlier (yes, I do have a Blue Peter badge).

STEP 4. KICK YOUR CRITICAL SABOTAGING DEVIL MINDSET

This is when you get to think and instead of **Reacting**, you get to choose your **Responses** to the world.

In your mind's eye, picture the world as a globe.

I had a globe on a stand. Except it lit up like a lamp. Must have been a 1980s trend. How I loved that globe. It was blue and made my bedroom glow like the deep blue sea. So calming. Sadly, by the time I left home at eighteen and went to college the lamp was no more. It had long since died from being twirled too much and switched on and off thousands of times. However, I did crave a different ambient light for my student bedroom. I recall I was at Fife College, studying

Communications and living above a betting shop in Kirkcaldy. If you know the town it isn't exactly a bustling metropolitan city, and it was also a while back so Home Bargains and B&M had yet to take over the world. So there I was in a town that had shops and electricity (unlike Shetland) but the shops by my little flat only stocked white lightbulbs. Bright white, cool white and soft white, however, still f*cking white. Until, clever me, I spotted something different packed away behind the white coloured bulbs. A box that was covered in dust. Inside there was a red one. A red lightbulb. One meant for the element in fires, but still a red one. I was proud as punch... except I was now an eighteen-year-old-girl living in a first floor flat above a bookies, with lighting in her bedroom in a hue of red. Duh!! Thank you Shetland for protecting my innocence.

Anyway, I digress, back to the globe.

STEP 5. KICK YOUR CRITICAL SABOTAGING DEVIL MINDSET (WITHOUT THE DIGRESSION)

Give it a spin.

Spin the globe in your hand (or your mind). Now think of a destination that you would never ever want to visit (or visit again) and stop the globe there. It might be somewhere hot, somewhere cold, somewhere water locked, somewhere land locked, somewhere war torn. In fact, I asked someone this the other day and they said they stopped their globe at their mother-in-law's house! Ermmm, no. You might land on a holiday destination that you didn't enjoy, but that's fine too. However, I do draw the line at you choosing ex-family, ex-friends, ex-husbands, ex-wives, ex-boyfriends, ex-girlfriends... or any people for that matter. Choose a destination, a place, not a person or a house.

Because Y♡u Matter
Chelle Verite

Write here the destination that you don't ever want to visit / never return to	Next, recall and write here your Critical Mind number *(That was the score between 1 & 10 that you wrote in Step 2)*

Now, I want you to check on something. The nearer your **Critical Mind** number was to 1 (aka your **PAM Pioneering Angel Mindset**), the closer your globe destination can be. For example, if you had a score of 3 or less then you could have your destination within a hundred mile radius of where you live. However, if you had a score of 4, 5 or 6 you need to make sure the destination requires a train, boat or plane journey to get there (for the purposes of this exercise we are ignoring COVID rules and are permitted to travel). If it's 7 or more you need to choose a destination that requires packing for long haul! In other words, the noisier your critical **SDM Sabotaging Devil Mindset** is, the further away your chosen destination is required to be.

My destination, by the way, is Paris. I hate that place. I nearly got wiped out by two huge lorries driving on the motorway system there. French city drivers are evil. Parisians are soooo rude. Did you know you aren't even allowed to sit on the grass in a park? You have to sit on chairs. Seriously, what is wrong with those people? The romance of Paris is to sit on a gingham patterned rug next to the River Seine, with a picnic hamper, drinking champagne and eating strawberries covered in chocolate, while admiring the Eiffel Tower. You cannot do that perched on a chair that is stuck to the ground. Yup, my **never go to / return to destination** is definitely Paris!

So, you've got your **Critical Mind Number** (the one you decided up until now it is) and you've also got your **never go to / return to destination.** Now the fun starts.

We are going to kick your critical **Sabotaging Devil Mindset** to that destination.

STEP 6. POWER KICK YOUR SDM

Say hello to your **SDM** (this is your gun in holster, wide legged, cigar smoking, Cuban gangster moment. 'Say hello to my liddle friend.') Then watch it as it climbs in the car, boat, train or plane and arrives at its **never go to / never return to destination**. Or, if you have a more violent personality, boot it hard out of the window and watch it land in your **never go to / never return to destination**. Now it's there to stay, spending its time playing dodge the bombs in Azerbaijan, freezing it's nads off at the North Pole, or burning in the Sahara.

Now your **SDM** is in its **never go to / never return to destination**, you can concentrate on doing what's going to be good for you. From now on you can kick your critical **SDM** into touch. In fact, I don't just want to you to kick it out of the window. While you are getting used to the power that you can create, I want you to grab a rugby ball (imaginary or real) and go out to your garden / green space / park. I want you to listen to the sabotaging crap that god awful, wanker-esque, **SDM** is saying to you about that job, activity, thought, task, or belief in your body, mind or soul. I want you to pick up all of those sayings, words and thoughts with both hands and transport them into the rugby ball. All that noise. All that pain. All the turmoil and the emotional rollercoaster of utter shitness that is busy screaming and shouting at you, stuff it into the ball.

Because Y♡u Matter

Chelle Verite

Now imagine in your mind your **never go to / never return to destination.** Once clear in your mind, I want you to kick the rugby ball. As you do, I want you to say, 'FU you, you critical **Sabotaging Devil Mindset!**' I want you to watch it disappear with great glee high into the sky and follow it in your mind's eye until it comes crashing down in your no-go location of choice.

For me, it's that green space in Paris and when mine lands it smashes all those stupid stuck fast chairs in the park all over the place. Bang! The **Critical Mind** noise is gone, not to mention half of Paris Champ de Mars Park too.

This is your 'And the dirt is gone moment'. Clean slate. Yes Get In! However, this clean slate will not happen overnight. In short, you will need to practice, practice, practice. Practice kicking your **SDM** into touch many, many times before you get the hang of it. This may mean looking like a person who needs to be put in a straitjacket and carried away to somewhere special, as you practice kicking your imaginary rugby ball in your garden / local park / in your head while talking to yourself. But who gives a f*ck what you look like, right?

You don't care now, do you?

Course you don't, right?!

Aha, that was a trick.

Hello **SDM**. Yup, it just appeared, didn't it? That happened despite all the work we've just done to get that rugby ball ready. Your critical **Sabotaging Devil Mindset** is there bleating negatively at you. This is where we say STOP! And it's time for a good old dose of **God ERR☺ME. E + R + R = ☺ ME.**

Because You Matter
Chelle Verite

E = Event happens. Followed by your automatic **Reaction**, aka the critical **Sabotaging Devil Mindset**. Except you are no longer paying any attention to your fight-flight-freeze reactions. No, no, no. You are instead choosing to engage in a different **Response**. This is the perfect opportunity for you to actually choose your positive **Response** (now and in the future). Hello **PAM Pioneer Angel Mindset**. Yes, this will mean practising your kicks and even looking like a person that needs to be put in a mental asylum. However, my lovely *'Lets Get BOMBCHELLED!'* friend, Jo, has been in her local park kicking her imaginary rugby ball into touch many, many times over, and she has not yet been picked up by the police. Believe me, she's power-kicked a load of balls over the last few months.

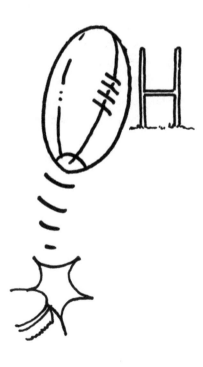

STEP 7. KEEPING YOU IN THE ROOM

You now know that your **SDM** has been power-kicked to your **never go to / never return to destination** far, far away. It cannot be reached. However, your little (or big) devil will lurk, its voice will appear from time to time, which may mean you have to pick it up and kick it into touch like that rugby ball flying over the big H score, or give it a football to the goolies (aka *bollocks* or *baw sack*, as us Scots would say), or something just as violent from your own pick and mix of getting rid of your **SDM**. When it comes back, keep doing it (something has to be done twenty two to sixty six times to make it a habit, remember).

Whichever option you go for, once the critical **Sabotaging Devil Mindset** is no longer in the building, it will get replaced with **PAM**, your angelic, lovely, pink, fluffy, marshmallow, rainbow, unicorn quiet space, full of calmness and compassion. If she's not available because you haven't hit the zen button of a full-on Buddhist life, you will at least be able to reduce your number from an evil 10, 9 or 8 to a softer 5, 4 or 3, or at least get to a place in your mind where you can notice your score, do stuff to reduce it (which, luckily for you, is in the next Life Lesson) and find a way to positively feedback to yourself.

Love it when a plan comes together.

And why do it?

Why kick your critical **SDM** into touch?

Why create space for **PAM** instead?

Simple.

Because You Matter

> The deepest
> principle in
> human nature is
> the craving to
> be appreciated.

WILLIAM JAMES

LIFE LESSON

15

Feeding back
to self

THE 'BUNCHES' WAY

Because You Matter
Chelle Verite

We're interesting, aren't we? **Human BEings**. Riddled with expectation. But it's the do's and don'ts in life that confuse us most. When we're told, 'Well done, you did XYZ, great!' we have a knack of not hearing that. Instead, we hear, 'Oh you could have done better.' I mean, how exactly do we feel good about ourselves in a world that has so much noise? But we can mute the noise. Yes, we can stop the bombardment with our Bell Jar technique (you'll be introduced to this very soon in my next book). However, for now let's concentrate on how often do we actually listen properly? Out of ten things, one of them may not quite be right, just one. That's 10% wrong and 90% right, and what do we focus on? Yup, you got it, the 10% wrong! We beat ourselves up, giving our critical **SDM** an absolute field day and then bam! we are right back into the whole *I'm rubbish* scenario and our **Critical MindF*ck** takes control again.

Up until now.

You are learning how to recognise when your **SDM** appears so you can choose your never go to / never return to destination to send it to. You are also learning to recognise that you can choose to engage your **PAM**, that will positively support you, along with your **Motivating Matts**.

Oh, we have many things to thank **God ERR☺ME** for.

In addition, it's important that you journey into the world of appreciation. I speak to so many of my coachees who say things like, 'I want to please people so much.' And the flipside of the coin is, 'Why am I never valued enough by others?' It harps back to that **Crown of Acceptance**, doesn't it? Putting all your feel-good eggs into someone else's basket. Here's the thing, when you learn to appreciate yourself, other people's thoughts and opinions stop having such a huge impact on your world. The waiting game stops and your self-worth,

---

Because You Matter

Chelle Verite

appreciation and own feedback to self become the only things that matter. Put simply (and it's one of the major reasons for this book), it's *Because YOU Matter*, and you realise that your view of you truly does matter. Gaining the approval and accolade of others is always nice, however, when you appreciate yourself and what you offer, the approval of others becomes more like the icing on the cake, rather than the cake itself.

Knowing your worth and recognising and acknowledging your worth is so important. As Michel De Montaigne said, 'The greatest thing in the world is to know how to belong to oneself.' Except we're often not programmed that way, are we? We spend so much of our time exhausted by the activities of constantly seeking approval and acceptance from others. Developing a mindset of kindness and appreciation is important. As Buddha once said, 'The mind is like water. When it's turbulent it's difficult to see. When it's calm everything becomes clear.' Ah, clarity, calmness and appreciation, that sounds like a very nice grown-up world to be in.

Now, I know I'm asking you to grow up and take responsibility for empowering the good things in life, but that doesn't mean we can't have some fun along the way, does it? With that in mind, let me introduce you to what I've named **BUNCHES**, the Walt Disney cartoon mouse shape of feedback models. Before I reveal what that is (and I know it will make you smile), here's a wee Life Lesson about developing an appreciative mindset.

Because Y♡u Matter

Chelle Verite

Life Lesson 15

CHOOSE TO BE APPRECIATIVE

THE BUNCHES WAY

This is about choosing to accept. Let go to let in. Your habits form through practice (twenty two to sixty six times). So, here are some simple and easy ways to practise being appreciative.

STEP 1. CHOOSE TO DECIDE
YOU ARE WORTHY

Choose to decide that you are worthy just by being alive! Sounds simple. Yet way back in Life Lesson 8 when we focused on **Just BREATHE**, you'd not even noticed that your heart keeps beating, oxygen reaches your system, and you function just by opening your eyes. Your body is amazing, and so are you. Breathe in and notice, breathe out and relax into acceptance. Taking time to notice and appreciate how good your life is. Appreciate the choices you have made. Appreciate the kindness you have shown. Appreciate the challenges you have faced and overcome. Appreciate the fact you are worthy by just being alive.

STEP 2. DITCH AND REFRAME

Ditch and kick your critical **Sabotaging Devil Mindset** and reframe. Some people are way better at the appreciation stuff than others. It takes time to be kind to you. The key to success, as you now know, is kicking your **SDM** into touch and actively engaging your **PAM** with the language that you use on a day-to-day basis. This means really thinking about the words and phrases you use and encouraging an active reframe, so they flip from **SDM** to **PAM** instead.

Let's play the reframe game...

- ♥ *You're stupid. -> I know what I need to know, and if I don't know I'll go learn.*
- ♥ *You'll never do that. -> I'm ready to learn how to do that.*
- ♥ *I'm a mess. -> I'm human.*
- ♥ *I'm a failure. -> I'm learning.*
- ♥ *Why is this happening? -> What is this teaching me?*

So much opportunity to be appreciative and feedback good things to yourself.

Have a go.

Because Yờu Matter

Chelle Verite

My 'up until now' SDM ☹ phrases were...

Reframe to 'from now on' PAM ☺ phrases are...

STEP 3. REMEMBER ALL THAT
YOU HAVE ACCOMPLISHED

I'm about to introduce you to a great way to do this in detail with the **BUNCHES** technique. For now though, take a moment to stop and realise all that you have accomplished this far in your life journey. I can assure you there will be shit loads of great, amazing and pride inducing things on your list.

Give yourself sixty seconds and write down 10 accomplishments that spring to mind (getting out of bed every day is already on the list). List the small stuff as well as the big stuff.

Contender, ready? Go!

1.   **Getting out of bed and facing the world**

2.   _____

3.   _____

4.   _____

5.   _____

6.   _____

7.   _____

8.   _____

9.   _____

10. _____

See, you did it! (If you didn't list all 10 achievements in your eagerness to get on and read the rest of this Life Lesson, you likely did at least 3.) It's all about focusing on your achievements, the things you do on a daily basis, at work, at home, for your friends, your family and colleagues. Recognising and acknowledging your achievements and the good feelings that you generate will, funnily enough, make you feel good. Ah, the world of feeling good. Validate your own efforts, stop looking for others to do it, and develop habits of positive self-talk.

A big hello to another new character and life methodology called **BUNCHES**. Welcome, welcome, popcorn at the ready. No, it's not really Walt Disney's but you do draw the model like Mickey Mouse, well, probably more like my hair in bunches when I was a wee bairn. You know, the two balls on the head situation, and not just bunches, I mean a big, huge, f*ck off afro stuck right on top of my head and shaped into round ball bunches. Picture three round circles like Walt Disney's Mickey Mouse head and ears, and me with my huge bunches on my head, and compare.

Because Y♡u Matter
Chelle Verite

I mean, what on earth were my parents thinking?! Cute yes, but sticking an adopted, brown, Afro-Caribbean child amongst 23,000 white, Viking Nordic people, in bunches? Bunches!!! Dear Lord, way to go. I would have needed some hefty protection mechanisms in place to avoid utter ridicule from pretty much anyone and everyone. Although, at the time, we did have an Airedale Terrier dog called Ben, who was tan and black with curly hair, so kind of similar to wiry, Afro-Caribbean hair. Ben was the grumpiest dog I ever did meet. Thinking back, I would imagine it didn't help having a rather loud and boisterous little girl running around after him all of the time (I did leave his tail alone, some of the time). It didn't help my parents either as they aren't the loudest of people. I used to think that if they had actually had a biological child of their own, s/he would have been studious and worked in a library. Except ta-da! Here's Chelle, the whirlwind, the bomb set to go off at any minute, surprise! Or Rachel, as I was known back then. Oh well.

We've already had Life Lesson 1 '**I am NOT normal (Absof*ckinglootly)**, and if you recall I am NOT normal. The good news is neither are you. You are you. Unique and special and a lovely **Human BEing YOU.**

Anyway, I digress. Back to **BUNCHES**. Great way of using three circles too. Two balls on my head. I've just realised that being Scottish there are so many things that I could do with that metaphor. 'Oh man, whit on earth was that yin thinking, she's got a bawhbag for a heeeed.' Translated that means, 'What on earth was that one thinking, she has a (I'll let you fill in the blank here) for a head.' Yes, I really do need to get out more.

Right, rant over. That reminds me, we'll be heading off to putting a **HALT** to our **Anger** and **Emotional Turmoil** very soon.

Because Y♡u Matter

Chelle Verite

Welcome to **BUNCHES**. Your feedback model on life and feeding back to self.

Getting to know your BUNCHES

When you think about something, say a task you've done, regardless of how noisy your **SDM** is, you spend time focusing on the negatives. That 10% out of 100%. That one item out of ten that you didn't get quite right that you end up trashing and bashing your whole-self up about, like a dog destroying their favourite cuddly toy. (Inevitably it's the expensive one that gets shredded, the toy not the dog!).

Feeding back to self.
Your turn without the hairdo!

So, to feeling good about you and a methodology involving those **BUNCHES**.

Take a moment to think about some work, home or life tasks that you've done recently. A report, a presentation, a customer sales pitch or a project, or even dishwasher loading, that huge basket of ironing that you have been meaning to do for at least three weeks, or that bucket load of washing in the corner of the utility room.

Write your tasks down here.

Now look at these tasks. Where exactly do you go with them? No, not to do the washing and ironing in the utility room, I mean where do you go if you are in the brave place of actually critiquing them? Well, I say brave enough. Usually the critiquing, or rock spitting as I call it, happens the instant the task is done, and the critical Sergeant Major of your critical **SDM** starts back on that boot camp 'you're a loser' expedition. Nasty bastard, isn't he? Well, he is until you kick him into touch.

How many of you (when you thought about one of your tasks and analysed how you go on with it) actually had your Pioneering Angel Mindset? The best friend. Well, if you hadn't completed the previous life lessons, I can imagine a lot more of you wouldn't have known that **PAM** even existed. If you know all about your **Pioneering Angel Mindset**, then I'm utterly impressed. You have learnt well. If not, then you simply need more practice picking up that **Sabotaging Devil Mindset** and kicking it like the rugby ball it is (twenty two to sixty six times for a habit, remember? If you don't pop back to the last Life Lesson for a wee refresher).

In addition to **PAM**, here's new, fun, **BUNCHES** methodology to the rescue. Instead of never giving yourself that well-earned feedback loop, **BUNCHES** will not only help you gift it to yourself, but in such a way that you're **Superhero** at the ready. Being your own **Superhero**. Like when you were little in the primary school playground, running down the hill to catch the wind with your coat over your head, ready to take flight while feeling invincible. Translated into adult terms, instead of thinking of all the terrible things you should have / could have done, here you get to use the 'Little Rachel in Shetland' **BUNCHES** model instead. For those of you who hate implementing models from books or are just downright lazy (like most of the human race), this one is sooooo easy and fun. So much so I even used it with a white-collar financial services sales team, and a team of solicitors, to boost learning of brand-new sales processes. If I can use it in those industries and pass it off as productive (the teams loved it), I can sure as hell use it for your world. Before I do, let me introduce you to how you draw **BUNCHES**. Draw the following on a big piece of paper (or your journal... Amazon here we come).

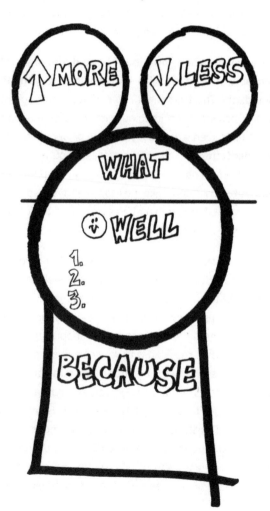

Because You Matter

Chelle Verite

One big circle (the head) divided into **What** the activity is that you want to be appreciative about and the things that have gone **Well**. Three things is a good number to focus on here and be specific. Then draw a rectangle (the body) underneath the head. This represents the **Because**. Write down the reasons as to why things have gone well. Then draw two balls, (I mean bunches), on top of the head. These are for your next steps that will enable you to grow. The left one is for what you need to do **More of**, the right one is what you need to do **Less of**.

That's it. Simple, isn't it? However, to ensure that you are successful you have to consciously filter out the shit.

Normally, when we think about tasks we have done, we spend all of our time thinking about the **Unchangeable Past**. 'I wish I'd not done this' and the noise of 'I'm rubbish' or 'I didn't do it right, better, or best.' Whereas with the **BUNCHES** model, you can only (and I mean only) focus on the stuff that you did well.

Positive habit formation here we come.

BUNCHES 1. EASY PEASY LEMON SQUEEZY

For your first go at **BUNCHES**, choose an activity or task that's easy or mundane, like loading the dishwasher or doing the laundry. A simple task that means you're unlikely to get entwined and entangled in your critical **Sabotaging Devil Mindset**.

So lets get started. Here's to us focusing on empowering the good stuff in our world.

I'll talk you through an example of mine.

> **Step 1. First we identify WHAT the task was**
>
> **For me it was loading our new dishwasher.**
> (Yes, I know it's simple but it was new tech!)
>
> We write this in the **'WHAT'** section in the **BUNCHES** drawing.

> **Step 2. Then we identify 3 things (or more) about what went WELL with that task**
>
> Loading our new dishwasher and washing the dishes.
> (These go in the **'WELL'** section in the **BUNCHES** drawing).
>
> 1. **I managed to choose the right programme and switch the dishwasher on.**
>
> 2. **All the glasses got cleaned without me having to rinse them out before or afterwards.**
>
> 3. **The big pots fitted in too and got clean!**

Step 3. Then we think about the why.
The dishwasher loading and washing task went well
BECAUSE...

(This is the why and where most of your learning will come from, and goes in the **BECAUSE** body section of the **BUNCHES** diagram).

- ♥ **I read the instruction manual properly.**
- ♥ **I untied the holding string from the sprayers at the top so the washing arm was actually able to work.**
- ♥ **I flattened the plate wrack at the bottom so the pots would fit on one side, as well as the plates.**

Now we have our learnings we can go onto if we are to do the task again.

This is where the Step 4. more of and Step 5. less of **BUNCHES** on the head of the diagram come in.

Step 4. What will I do MORE of for next time?

♥ **Reading more of the manual and reading it properly.**
(As it turns out dishwashers need rinse aid and salt
as well as a cleaning tablet to help it work!)

♥ **Putting the pots in first as it stabilises the bottom tray.**
(Putting plates at the back works so I can stack the front).

♥ **Separate the cutlery more.**

Step 5. What will I do LESS of for next time?

× **A little less get on and do.**

× **Less rushing and just shoving the pots in at any angle.**

See, **BUNCHES**, it works. Generating a logical and emotional connection to think about the things you achieve, no matter how little that task, we feel good with our accomplishment. We learn, we conquer, which means we can do again, and tweak it so our success is even better. Given some practice I may even put myself as dishwasher loader extraordinaire. Ah, thank you **BUNCHES** for those simple pleasures, and sod off critical **SDM**.

We might even be able to encourage Aunty M to give it a go...

For example.

(My Aunty M will like this, actually she probably won't but I'll use my washing as an example anyway).

WHAT was the task?
I hung my washing out on the line.

What 3 things went WELL with the task?
1. **My washing stayed on the line.** 2. **It dried quickly.** 3. **It smelt nice when it was dry.**

Why did these things go well?
They went well **BECAUSE...** 1. **I used new pegs (pink of course).** 2. **It was sunny and windy.** 3. **I took the washing out of the washing machine after the cycle had finished.**

Because You Matter

Chelle Verite

I need to do MORE...
♥ **Putting the washing out on the line early morning.**

I need to do LESS...
× **Worrying if it will rain.**
× **Stopping procrastinating and Bitching, Moaning, and Whining about the lack of decent weather.**

You get the picture. Easy, see? (Unless you like permanently being in the Bitching, Moaning, and Whining space, that my friends is now something you're aware of.) I suggest having a nice cup of tea and giving the **BUNCHES** technique a go. You never know you might even enjoy it.

Your turn.

Now you have a go.

Think of your own example and draw your own **BUNCHES** visual (or use the one on the next page).

Because You Matter

Chelle Verite

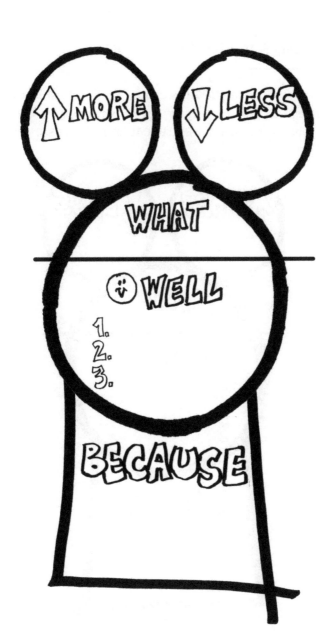

BUNCHES 2. LET'S GET IT ON

For your second go at **BUNCHES**, choose a personal task that was a bit harder, a bit more challenging and real, rather than the mundane task! Same process. **WHAT, WELL, BECAUSE, MORE, LESS.**

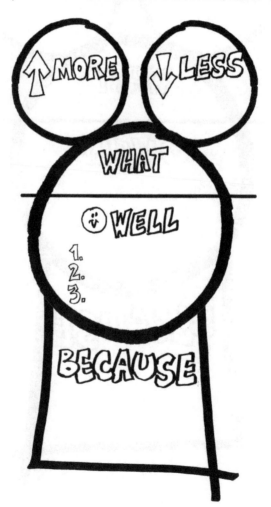

BUNCHES 3. WORK IT BABY

Now for your third go.

They say three is the magic number and you'll remember it as you're becoming a Master of the Universe! (well, at least having a **Superhero** 'I have the Power!' He-Man or She-Ra moment).

Choose a task related to your world of work, whether that be…

- ♥ as a busy parent screeching around playing Dad / Mum taxi
- ♥ in your corporate 'home' office world managing, or playing God
- ♥ as a life adventurer, daring to climb those heady heights

Choose a task that made you think, that really challenged and stretched you.

(Warning! There is potential for your **SDM** to want to join in here. Remember, only **Focus** on the good stuff. Appreciate the good stuff = feel good! **Focus, Focus, Focus.**)

Again, draw your **BUNCHES**, and fill in:

- ♥ **WHAT**
- ♥ **WELL**
- ♥ **BECAUSE**
- ♥ **MORE**
- ♥ **LESS**

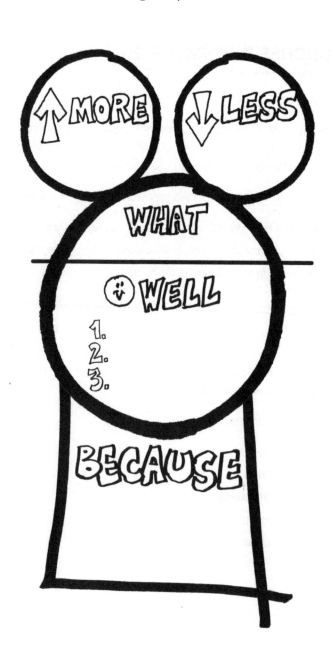

Excellent. Well done. Now you're a master at feeding back the good stuff using **BUNCHES**, and you didn't even have to grow or style your hair. It's important to cultivate an *I appreciate and feel good about me* spiral rather than *I am shit and rubbish at everything* spiral. Therefore, taking a moment to draw little me shaped **BUNCHES** and filling in the blanks has got to be good for the soul, hasn't it? Not only that, when you've written about what the task was, and what went well and why, you get into the habit of positively processing the rationale behind and reasons for your actions. You even get to productively shape your capability levels for next time through the more of and less of thoughts. It's a great way to encourage kids too (big kids as well as little kids) as they love any excuse to draw things. Just be mindful that as an adult, if you draw on the walls the little people in your world will have the green light to do the same. That's great if you want to change the wallpaper and repaint but not so great if it doesn't rub off.

BUNCHES
MAGIC COMMITMENT QUESTIONS

Right, you've sorted your **BUNCHES** and fed back to yourself with the task, the reasons because, and the more of and less of. This is great progress. Although, what really makes the difference and gains commitment are the 3 magic questions. Using these will mean you are way more likely to hold true to your word of actually using your new-found learnings when you do that task again.

You're now well versed in using the **BUNCHES** model

In relation to my task called 'XYZ'...
that worked because of 'ABC'...
and when I do it again, I will do more of 'OPQ'... and less of 'UVW'...

And now the rabbit out of the hat. The 3 magic commitment questionsto ask yourself. **1. WHAT**, **2. WHEN**, **3. KNOW**.

Because You Matter
Chelle Verite

1. **WHAT = What exactly are my next steps to enhance my XYZ task for next time?**

   (You'll get that from your **MORE** of and **LESS** of sections, and also reflecting back on the **TASK** with your new found knowledge of **WHAT**, **WELL**, and **BECAUSE**).

2. **WHEN = By when? (date / time)**

3. **KNOW = How will I know?**

   (What will be different, what will I see or hear as a result of making this change? Key to measuring success).

Because You Matter
Chelle Verite

You'll find by writing the answers to the **WHAT**, **WHEN**, **KNOW** **Magic Commitment Questions** down in black in white they become way more ingrained in your brain. Give this a go by choosing one (or more) of the three tasks you did in your earlier **BUNCHES** drawings and complete your questions below:

WHAT will I do to enhance the success of the task next time?	WHEN will I do that? (time and date)	KNOW How will I know my change in behaviour happened?

Because You Matter
Chelle Verite

Whoop, whoop, you did it! You were kind to you. Well done. And if you cheated by skipping to this bit at the end, go back to jail, do not pass go and definitely do not collect £200. Come on! Take a few minutes of you time to give yourself some well-earned feedback. (After all, it takes between twenty two to sixty six times to make a new habit and I'm only suggesting three things in your life so you can feel good about your achievements.) For all of you stubborn personalities out there, be mindful, you first have to let go of your old shit to let in new stuff. Even then it'll take time to forge this as a new habit. I know you can do it.

You've got this!

And for all of you wonderful people who actually did the **BUNCHES** practice, I'm super proud of you.

FEEDING BACK TO SELF REFLECTION

Let's take a moment to reflect on your **BUNCHES** practice and completing the feeding back to self Life Lesson.

♥ What was the name of task that you were asked to do?

Because You Matter

Chelle Verite

♥ **What went well when you were filling out the BUNCHES practice?**

♥ **What could you do more of, or less of, that will make this task better for next time?**

And BAM! Did you see what I did there? Yes, of course you did. It's the **BUNCHES Feeding Back to Self** technique. This is about learning how to **Focus** on what is actually going well in your world, rather than what isn't. This is about **Focusing** on the good, rather than the bad. This is the first step towards consciously giving your mind something better to do than trip you up with that critical **Sabotaging Devil Mindset**. That, my friends, is how easily it's done. The only things missing in my reflection questions were the 3 magic **WHAT**, **WHEN** and **HOW Magic Commitment Questions** and the drawing of the actual **BUNCHES**. However, if I'd put them in, that would have been way too obvious.

Because You Matter

Chelle Verite

See, I told you it was easy, and just imagine how much fun you can have with people when you show them the model. I do it with all my customers, and you can too. You have the perfect excuse.

- ♥ We are NOT normal.
- ♥ Learning is supposed to be fun.
- ♥ If it isn't fun, what the f*ck are you going to do to make it fun?

Ah, yes. Learning, fun and a bit of Scottish Tourette's thrown in for good measure. I think it's time for a nice cup of tea and a piece of cake. Ooooh, is it too early for wine or prosecco yet?

And why do it?

No, not the prosecco, no excuses needed for that.

Why **Feedback to Self** in a kind way?

Why get your **BUNCHES** at the ready and appreciate you in a way that makes you glow?

Do I really need to say it, or have you got it yet?

Because You Matter

Of course!

That and I'd love to see your hair in **BUNCHES**. You never know, if COVID starts misbehaving again hairdressers might be on another lockdown ban and we will all be sporting wonderful hair and beard dos. Has the kettle boiled yet? Ooooh, yes a wee cup of tea, lovely.

> ❝

If you are depressed, you are living in the past. If you are anxious, you are living in the future. If you are at peace, you are living in the present.

LAO TZO

LIFE LESSON

16

Ridding UP and IF

IDENTIFYING EMOTIONAL IMPACT

Because You Matter
Chelle Verite

Ahhh, you've had a nice cuppa. That's refreshing. However, there are times in your world when you aren't refreshed. When you let people take too much from you. Where you simply run out of energy. I liken it to gifting away an apple pie. You've baked it, you made it and you definitely want to eat it. It'll give you sustenance and physical energy when you eat it, as well as emotional and mental energy because you know how much hard work went into creating it. Except, your best friend comes along and says, 'Oooooh, apple pie! I'd love some, thanks.' Then your son or daughter comes up and goes, 'Oooooh, apple pie! Yes please.' Then your husband, wife or partner says, 'Thanks, love. That looks good.' Then they blatantly whisk it out of your hands like an expectant child who knows they'll get fed. Before you know it, guess what? All of your apple pie is gone and there is nothing left to feed and replenish you because the sustenance you created is now someone else's fuel.

Life is like that. We often give away so much of ourselves in the hope that other people will gift it back or recognise that we have given it. We offer the apple pie, our energy and our enthusiasm. We offer ourselves too. If you're like my husband, James, you're actually kind and nice and want to gift people things. I want to gift people things too but I want them to learn how to make the apple pie, not just take the apple pie. I liken it to that old adage of *Give a man a fish, he'll eat for a day. Teach a man how to fish, and he'll eat forever.* Still, here's the thing (and back to making and eating the apple pie), we often give too much away because we care. We often give too much away, not just because we want to, but because we are conditioned to. Sometimes we are so conditioned to do it, we don't even realise we are doing it. We give ourselves away and do things we say we wouldn't, even after the boundary is set. We know we shouldn't, we haven't really got the time, the energy or the finances, yet we still give it away.

Life Lesson 16

Because You Matter

Chelle Verite

AND here's the biggie...

Despite giving it away, we don't often get it back. That energy remains with all the other people we give it to. So why on earth don't we get it back? Well, ultimately, us humans are as selfish as f*ck. Yup, I said it. We aren't built to be selfless; we are ultimately selfish. Even to the point where all we want is to take, take, take. Sometimes we are completely selfish without even realising it.

Yet how come when there are so many people taking it, we don't end up taking it for ourselves? We want the apple pie for ourselves. We want to keep our energy and use it on what we want. Yet we don't. We make it and then we give it away to the point that we are running dangerously low on energy. Then we become labelled as the unapproachable ones. The grumpy ones due to impatience. The ones that other people don't want to be around. We become so drained in our emotional or mental energy to the point that our physical energy can, and does, sap us away from ourselves. Like a weeping sore of anxiety, or self-destruction, or just plain *I'm absolutely knackered*. So knackered our health gives way, and I don't just mean physical health, I mean emotional health, mental health and the looking after 'me' health. We are absolutely nothing without it. We need it to function.

Because You Matter
Chelle Verite

I was working with a great client of mine recently. Funnily enough her name is a reminder of my old name Rachel and new name Chelle as hers is Rachelle. So, Rachelle told me that she was three months into what she thought was her dream job, but it was very quickly turning sour. She was also dealing with a recent bereavement of a very close family relative and struggling with health issues that could change her whole outlook on the next twenty years in regards to having a family. The anxiety and emotion of which had been spilling into her previously idyllic life and putting pressure on her relationship. She called me in what I would call a *tizz state* life crisis moment. She said, 'Chelle, I'm still in my duvet and I can't face work today. I need to talk to someone who understands. Someone who actually won't take sides, and who will listen to me rant without taking something from me or trying to appease me.'

Because You Matter
Chelle Verite

Hands up how many of you have had that type of day? Where you simply cannot get out of bed and face the world (today might even be one of them)? The *Yup, I'm up. Nope, I'm f*cking not. I don't want to do today* kind of day? Where you call in sick to work because you're totally exhausted and in need of a recharge day (well more like a recharge year), and want to stop the bus just because you can? And then add in a pandemic on top too. Ooooh, now where is that duvet?

Instead of hiding from the world, who's up for learning how to **HALT** negative internal **Emotional Turmoil** and positively wake up to living a life you love? **HALT** is for when you feel exhausted / tired / drained / at a loss / confused / upset (circle as appropriate, and just so you know, it's okay to be human and circle all of them). Those life situations when you have given away all of your apple pie and you need, just like Rachelle did, a duvet recharge. Having an *I need to get a handle on my life* day then learning how to successfully put a **HALT** on your internal emotional rollercoaster is most definitely up there on the *please make it my reality* want list instead.

Before we start, I do need to clarify a bit about emotions. Emotions are something that we all have. When I say emotions, I don't mean being a moody bastard. (Moods are different. They last longer; days, weeks, even months.) Emotions are intense, short lived and ultimately the driving force behind our motivation. Our get up and go. Emotions drive how we experience the world. They drive our behaviour and our decisions. However, it's not the experience of emotions or moods (remember, we are human) that cause us problems in our world, it's the fact that for some of us we opt to act them out. Emotions, depending on how we experience or act on them, can (and regularly do) consume us and blindside us, like a red mist rage, sending us spiralling quick as a flash into our pals **Devastating Dave, Meltdown Mary** and **Catastrophising Chris**. That stomach lurch, to the full-

Because You Matter
Chelle Verite

blown solar plexus knockout pain that emotions can cause, is unreal. On the positive front, if we are lucky, we get a huge exhilarating, 'Life is utterly amazeballs.' However, for the most part, we experience the complete opposite, and we are literally left gasping for air and facing disaster.

It does very much depend on how we process information and life experiences. Emotions are subjective. We all experience them differently. Not one of us will experience happiness or sadness, fear or excitement in the same way. Also, if you are a logical left brain type, then it's unlikely you'll hit the depths of highs and lows that will stop you in your tracks. If, however, you are the type of person who carries a washing machine on spin cycle for a stomach (like I am), then emotions can be your greatest friend as well as your biggest enemy.

When we do experience emotions, regardless of how they appear, all of us will have a physiological **Reaction**. Our sympathetic nervous system will kick in and we will get all sorts of things going on like heart palpitations, sweaty palms, loss of breath, shakes and flushes. In fact, a whole range of automatic fight or flight **Reaction**. When that happens in your body, how does your physiology experience it? Are you a flighter? A passive runner-awayer? A bury your head in the sand, shut down type of personality? Alternatively, are you more of a fighter? An aggressive, attack everything and everyone that moves type of personality? Either way, if our **Reaction** to emotions go on for too long it is inevitable that we will become overloaded and a longer lasting experience, aka **Emotional Turmoil** (**ET** as I like to call it and no, not that Extra-Terrestrial, however we do want to find a way to return it back 'home' to where it came from), will occur.

Because Y♥u Matter
Chelle Verite

Emotional Turmoil is defined as. *A state of great commotion, confusion or disturbance; tumult; agitation; disquiet. mental turmoil caused by difficult decisions.*

Or as American author and philosopher, Alan Robert Neal, eloquently stated.

'**Emotional Turmoil** is rooted in what we miss, deny or forget about ourselves or others.'

Let's focus on you here. (The 'others' we will focus on in the next book). For now, that state of **Emotional Turmoil** 'what we miss, deny or forget about ourselves' is what you will focus your energy on eliminating. Getting a handle on your internal noise is exactly what you need. I'm all for all of us generating internal peace.

Big sigh, inhale in, shoulders up, exhale out, shoulders drop, shake your hands and wiggle your toes.

Ahhh, those lovely breathing exercises are great, aren't they? And rellllllaaaaaax.

Up until now, you may have been far too busy distracting yourself with other things or focusing on the wrong things, like what should have, could have, or will be that you won't be able to cope with, or just not taking the time for self-care and looking after number one. Hold on, that sounds a little bit like what happens in Rachelle's *I'm in a tizz* state of life, doesn't it? And you all recognise those days. However, even when life is soooo busy, when you forget to breathe and everything appears to be spiralling out of control, you still deserve to feel good. **BUNCHES** at the ready. You also made a pact at the start of this book and life journey that you would focus on yourself and be part of our **BYM Fight Club**, so you really do owe it to yourself to feel good.

Because You Matter

Chelle Verite

So, what is stopping you from feeling good and focusing on yourself? I've bottomed it out and noticed that it's about **UP** and **IF**.

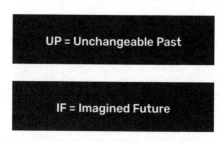

UP = Unchangeable Past

IF = Imagined Future

'**UP**' and '**IF**'. Ah those. Yes, we are all guilty of focusing on those aspects, aren't we? The thing is, when we are dealing with **Emotional Turmoil**, we tend to spend so much time choosing to act out and react to our **UP (Unchangeable Past)** and **IF (Imagined Future)** that we can very easily exhaust ourselves to tears, for all the wrong reasons. That's even before we attempt to figure out what we need to do in the present. I know. I know. Being a grown up and taking responsibility for our well-being is hard! That back-and-forth exhaustion tactic fills us with anger, fear and despair.

I have experienced this first-hand in my life, spending hours driving after a Sunday-evening-child-share-drop-off, bawling my eyes out in full **Meltdown Mary** mode (ah, the joys of divorce). When I was in my single mum world, I beat myself 'up' about the **Unchangeable Past** elements. The things I could have done, should have done, and wish I'd done. Then to the flip side, to the **Imagined Future**. *What if this happens? What if that happens? What if I can't find a way? What if I can't cope or deal with it?* All of a sudden, the emotions start to flood in, such as anger, disappointment, rage, fear.

I have previously taken advantage of and been consumed by my own **Crown of Acceptance** situations choking me, using my 'F*ck You, world' **Devastating Dave** reactions as a default, screaming and

Because Y♡u Matter

Chelle Verite

ranting like a **Catastrophising Chris**, to the point where my voice is scratchy (definitely not sexy). I have cried so hard, been so bleary eyed, weak and tired out with life that I am beyond surprised I didn't crash into the back of a lorry, and that I was still able to see the road and drive. God, those were some exhausting car journeys.

We all have days like that. Not necessarily being a single parent and having **Meltdown Mary** moments, or having **ET** tear streaming, rage filled car journeys. However, we all have days when we find ourselves plunging into the depths of pure exhaustion, fear, anger and the desperate back and forth on the rollercoaster of the *I wish…* **Unchangeable Past** or the *What if?* **Imagined Future**, where we are utterly consumed by emotion or simply can't get our heads straight. We are consumed by what we feel and we act it out, and I mean really act it out. That huge TNT blow up the world and destroy it (and ourselves) mentality.

It reminds me of the wolf story. which wolf will you feed, the good one or the bad one? Which wolf will win? If you haven't read the story, here it is for you.

Because Y♡u Matter
Chelle Verite

The story of two wolves

An old Cherokee is teaching his grandson about life.
'A fight is going on inside me,' he said to the boy.
'It is a terrible fight, and it is between two wolves.'

'One is evil. He is anger, envy, sorrow, regret, greed, arrogance,
self-pity, guilt, resentment, inferiority, lies, false pride,
superiority and ego.'

'The other is good. He is joy, peace, love, hope, serenity, humility,
kindness, benevolence, empathy, generosity, truth,
compassion and faith.'

'The same fight is going on inside you... and inside every
other person too.' The grandson thought about it for a minute
and then asked his grandfather. 'Which wolf will win?'
The old Cherokee simply replied,
'The one you feed.'

Because You Matter

Chelle Verite

The moral of the story is simple. The wolf we feed will win, of course. Which wolf of yours will you feed?

When you feed the bad wolf, you will create a life around the bad stuff, acting out those negative emotions. If you focus on and feed the good stuff, you will create positive emotions, and **Motivational Matt** and **BUNCHES** moments. In other words, you will get to feel good. Not rocket science, is it?! Stop feeding the bad wolf. Give that up. Replace automatic, negative **Reactions** to emotions with chosen, positive **Responses** instead. Feed the good wolf. Pay attention to the positive emotions. Notice, **Focus** and choose happiness.

However, happiness is only possible if you learn to cope with your negative emotions. The key here is to remember that emotions are calling you to action. It just depends on what type of actions you can create; ones that will make you smile and create a positive **Response** in your world rather than destructive, negative ones. Now you know this and knowledge is power. (Little dance around the room, yay, yay, yay!) Except hold on, before you get too carried away. Although you now know that **Focusing** on negative emotions will be debilitating and **Focusing** on positive emotions will be empowering, knowledge alone does not mean that you can actually change how you are and how you want to experience life. You still need to know how the f*ck to **Make 'It' Happen**.

Relax. I made a promise, remember? This isn't just a book that gives you ways to positively disrupt your world so you can make different choices and create positive action. *Because YOU Matter.*

Because You Matter
Chelle Verite

With that in mind, the following will help.

Breathe, people, breathe.

Remember, you've got this.

Big breath in. Inhale the future.

Big breath out. Exhale the past.

Big Sigh.

Shoulders up to your ears.

Push your shoulders down hard.

Big shake of your arms, body, wiggle your toes and fingers.

Be sure to shake and flick that negative energy far, far away.

Life Lesson 16

UNDERSTANDING ET

(EMOTIONAL TURMOIL)

Excellent. You've breathed. Welcome to understanding **ET**. Great for when you are having an off day. Think about the following questions.

> ❤ **How often do you feel / have you felt Emotional Turmoil?**
>
> (Be honest here. If it's easier, think back to your last few days, weeks or months and count uo how many times you have felt it).
>
> I feel/have felt **ET** episodes
> (insert amount)
>
> _____
>
> In number of hours / days / weeks / months
>
> _____

If it's a f*load, and easier than counting the number of ET episodes you've had recently, just tick here ☐

Because You Matter

Chelle Verite

> ♥ **Thinking back, what are the most debilitating / negatively impacting emotions that come up for you in your life / world when you are experiencing these episodes?** (Tick all that apply).

☐ Self-doubt	☐ Anxiety	☐ Rage
☐ Self-pity	☐ Anger	☐ Disgust
☐ Fear	☐ Sadness	☐ Loss
☐ Angst	☐ Uncertainty	☐ Weariness
☐ Feeling jittery	☐ Feeling judged	☐ Jealousy
☐ Disappointment	☐ Feeling spiteful	☐ Disgust
☐ Irritation	☐ Defensiveness	☐ Confusion
☐ Worry	☐ Feeling vulnerable	☐ Guilt
☐ Other		

So, which ones did you get? (If it was me, it would have been all of them! So if this is the case for you, you are not alone).

Because You Matter

Chelle Verite

♥ **Looking at your ticked list, what's the strongest emotion(s) that you experience?**

(It's often easier here to rate the emotions you have ticked out of 10. 1 being the least negatively impactful, 10 being the most negatively impactful). That way you can see what patterns emerge. It also means you get to doodle on your book again with those fabulous pens you got from Amazon. (If you're yet to buy them, I find the fine tipped coloured Staedtler pens are excellent. This is almost a product placement moment; I hope they're kind enough to consider me for commission!)

Because Y♡u Matter
Chelle Verite

♥ **What do you notice about the negative impact of these emotions?**
(Which one is strongest? Is there a pattern?)

♥ **What causes or triggers your Emotional Turmoil?**
(Ooooh, this is getting a bit deeper now, isn't it? Remember to breathe. Inhale in, exhale out, and relax. You know you best. We are doing this so you feel better about you and have ways to consciously choose to empower yourself, rather than the pressures of life just *happening* to you.)
For ease, I've provided a list below that will help.

☐ Work	☐ Friends
☐ Relationships	☐ Ex-partner
☐ Being disrespected	☐ Bad manners
☐ Family	☐ Finances
☐ Other	

Because You Matter

Chelle Verite

♥ **Look at what you identified as triggers.**
What do you notice?

♥ **What do you think are the real reasons why you**
experience this Emotional Turmoil?
(The reasons that are truly under the surface.)

Thinking about the real reasons may mean you need to stop and think for a moment or two. That thinking time may require a change in brain waves, so to help with kicking in your left brain and right brain, let's get your accelerated learning whole brain thinking involved. To kick start your brain, stand up and take a walk for at least a hundred paces, counting as you go. It may be a jaunt around the garden, a wee trip to the loo, a casual stroll to pop the kettle on for a nice cup of tea.

Because You Matter
Chelle Verite

(In my case it would mean letting the dogs out for a wee and going for a little daunder with them, while encouraging our Newphiedoodle Boo to hurry up and do her business so I can get back in from the baltic cold).

Thinking about the real reasons why you are experiencing your **Emotional Turmoil** can be tough. If you can't quite figure it out (or reach a conclusion), phone a friend and ask them. Or don't really phone a friend but instead imagine your bestie by your side to help you, the person who you love, trust and respect the most in this world (you know, **PAM** your **Pioneering Angel Mindset**). What would they say to you?

♥ **What did your bestie and / or PAM say are the real reasons for the Emotional Turmoil in your world?**

Now we have established that **ET** actually exists in your world. Hellooo! Firstly, if you don't have any **ET** then you wouldn't be reading this book. Secondly, if you haven't previously experienced **ET**, then you are either Mother Teresa or Buddha. Most of us, at some point, will experience **ET** as we are human, awesome and fallible.

7 STEPS TO ELIMINATING ET

On the next page are 7 steps to eliminating **ET**. (Not ET although we love that big bug-eyed creature, I am of course referring to eliminating **Emotional Turmoil** and instead choosing **Empowering Positive Feeling**.)

Take a moment to think back to the last time you were in **Emotional Turmoil** (you may still be in the turmoil as we speak) and answer the following questions. Be honest!

Because You Matter

Chelle Verite

**Eliminating Emotional Turmoil
and Empowering Positive Feeling
When I am in Emotional Turmoil...**

1. What am I feeling? (How would you describe it?)

2. What shape or colour does it create?

3. Where do I feel it in my body?

4. If it could talk, really talk, what would it be saying to me?

5. What might it be teaching me?

6. What do I need right now that will make me feel better, calmer and more present?

7. What tiny step(s) can I take today to meet my need?

Life Lesson 16

Because Y♥u Matter
Chelle Verite

Oooooh wow! Now that's a powerful way to put yourself firmly back into the present, isn't it? What would **God ERR☺ME** say right now?

Ditch, Forget and Choose

The **Event** has happened, the **Reaction** has happened (aka **Emotional Turmoil**), and it's likely that **Catastrophising Chris**, **Meltdown Mary** and/or **Devastating Dave** have appeared. Well, I hear you ask, 'What the f*ck am I going to do to encourage less negative reactions and more lovely, positive feelings and **Motivating Matt**?'

1.   Firstly, ditch the Unchangeable Past (What is done is done.)
2.   Second, forget the Imagined Future (It is yet to come.)
3.   Thirdly, and most importantly, choose to focus on the Present (What do I need here and now?)

Let's have a go...

1. Ditch (Unchangeable Past)	2. Forget (Imagined Future)	3. Choose (Be Present)
The past is past! What do I need to ditch immediately that focused on the past and was stopping me from feeling good?	*It's not here yet! What do I need to stop thinking about that is focused on the future and is causing me* **Emotional Turmoil?**	*How will I choose to truly show up and be present? How will I focus on my 'here and now' so I feel emotionally calmer?*

Because You Matter
Chelle Verite

Yes, get in! You are consciously on the way to acknowledging what you need and empowering yourself with a present mindset. Next, we are going to look at how to **HALT** that **Emotional Turmoil** even further, but in the meantime, lets reset you.

> **Reset you**
>
> **Big breath in.**
>
> **Inhale in the future, exhale out the past.**
>
> **Big breath out.**
>
> **Big loud Sigh.**
>
> **Shoulders up to your ears and push your shoulders down hard.**
>
> **Big shake of your arms and body.**
>
> **Wiggle your toes, shake your hands.**
>
> **Consciously channel that negative energy far, far, away.**
>
> **And relax ...**
>
> **(Repeat as many times as is necessary).**

Brilliant! Ya wee dancer! You are well on your way to getting in the mode of listening to what you need, and consciously choosing to focus on positive 'good wolf' emotional impact.

Getting a handle on your **Emotional Turmoil** requires you being present and focusing on generating a feel-good factor in your world. It means staying in the here and now and ridding yourself of the **Unchangeable Past** and **Imagined Future.**

Because You Matter

Chelle Verite

Often, when we experience **ET**, we run on empty and deny ourselves sustenance. Either we simply missed it, didn't notice it or, worse still, decided we weren't worth the investment. Good wolf. Good wolf. Good wolf. Focus on that one. It's far nicer than the bad wolf. Also, let me tell you, if you're opting for the bad wolf, I will have to take you by the scruff of the neck and *dekneecapitate* you. That's my gentle, Scottish Tourettes, full-on personality protection towards your self-worth coming out, which in the grand scheme of things may seem a wee bit on the violent side. Choices, people, choices. Good wolf. Good wolf. Good wolf. You are so, so, so worth it.

And why do it?

Why **Focus** on the present?

Why rid yourself of **Emotional Turmoil**?

Why create **Empowering Positive Feelings** instead?

Simple.

Because You Matter

You own your
feelings.
You own your
thoughts.
No one has the
right to any of it.
To any of you,
without your
permission.

CARLOS WALLACE

LIFE LESSON

17

Introducing HALT

STOP YOUR EMOTIONAL ROLLERCOASTER

Because You Matter

Chelle Verite

Wouldn't it be great to be able to stop the impact of feeling overwhelmed with emotion? Wouldn't it be great to stop living our lives like a human emotional washing machine? To be able to identify what's going on and actually **HALT** that **Emotional Turmoil** in order to stop feeling like we've been dragged through a hedge backwards?

I wish I'd been taught how to deal with my emotions when I was younger. When I did suffer from **Emotional Turmoil** (to be fair, I had a fair few crises of confidence), I either destroyed things or bottled up my feelings until I exploded. I guess that's where **Devastating Dave** moments started for me. I also wish I'd been offered emotional support at home. However, I was brought up by parents who were very stoic. You know that stiff upper lip, British tendency towards

Because You Matter
Chelle Verite

'Emotions?! Goodness, no, we don't show those, that simply wouldn't be right, we just get on with it!' mentality. Keep it in and not talk about it rather than the more relaxed *let it all out and shake it all about emotional expression* that I, as a whirlwind personality, really craved and needed.

In my household when I was growing up, emotions were labelled as 'uncalled for, stroppy outbursts'. I wasn't seen as the flamboyant and expressive personality that I craved to be accepted and loved as. No, I was labelled as 'truculent' and 'unruly', neither of which were deemed acceptable. Ah hello **Crown of Acceptance**, I see where that waiting to be accepted game started. (Remember, our hands are untied. Except, being real here, it's kind of hard to untie your hands when you are only little though isn't it?) If you are anything like me, you would have craved acceptance from your parents, and that unconditional love. I certainly did.

Anyway, before I get too emotional, it's best we focus on learning to look after ourselves, and **BEing** attentive to our needs. That means getting a handle on our filters. It means shedding that *stroppy-child-throw-our-teddies-out-of-the-pram* and the *controlling-parent-do-as-we're-told-pointing-fingers-my-way-or-the-highway* tendencies. It requires a more gathered, together, logical, and adult approach to ensuring we get the emotional, physical, and mental sustenance we need to breathe easy and relax into recognising that we do matter and deserve to live a life we love.

However, **BEing** adult and choosing to logically respond to, rather than automatically **React** to, our emotions means we need to *say hello to our liddle friend* **God ERR☺ME** (**Event** + **Reaction** + **Response** = **Outcome** and a happy **ME**, remember?), and in doing so we need to choose to **Stop -> Breathe -> Think -> Focus**.

Using accessible and memorable ways of slowing down the negative impact of the **Emotional Turmoil** that we experience, isn't that easy? (Well, it wasn't until I wrote this book, thank you for giving me a reason.)

Now, we have identified that we all experience bouts of **Emotional Turmoil**. Logically, we get it. However, we need to add to our empowerment toolkit ways to provide sustenance. This will catapult us into positive action so we can chill the f*ck out and enjoy life without the clutter of the previous **Crown of Acceptance** worry and anxiety patterns getting in the way. Yay!

Without further ado, let me introduce you to the wonderful world of **H A L T** and getting a handle on your **Emotional Turmoil** rollercoaster.

Life Lesson **17**

HALT YOUR EMOTIONAL TURMOIL

H	Hungry
A	Angry
L	Lonely
T	Tired

H = HUNGRY

You'd think being **Hungry** would be a relatively easy one, wouldn't you? As easy as getting your backside off the sofa and sticking your head in the fridge surely? Yes, there is feeling **Physically Hungry** and we'll come to that element in just a moment, but there is also feeling **Emotionally Hungry**. feeding and nourishing the inner you.

Feeling **Physically Hungry** is often an easy fix. Getting a deliciously refreshing drink. Baking some **Take the Leap chocolate muffin cakes**. Eating some of your own apple pie. Locating, preparing and eating 'good' food. (Good food, people, not just junk food. Even though junk food may make you feel good in that instant, it will not bring you wholeness and longevity of nourishment. The nutrients and fuel just aren't there. Burgers or that Chinese takeaway always sound better than they actually ever are.) You need to choose to eat and refuel with physical food that will actually provide you with long-lasting energy. Yet sometimes you forget what they are. Sometimes you are so busy **DOing** that you forget you need sustenance and refuelling. Sometimes, you might not even know what you like to eat, let alone when! This is all about empowering and **BEing** and providing proper sustenance for your life.

Refuelling feeling Physically Hungry

Here's when we take a little moment to have food for thought, literally.

♥ **What do I like and, most importantly, need to eat that truly refuels and replenishes me?**
List the good food and drinks that will support your good wolf
List the junk / fast food and drinks that only create more of your bad wolf

This is not a junk food option, or a stress go-to option, this is something that enhances you and your world. Bear in mind that you need to actually want to eat the good foods. There is absolutely no point putting items down as good food if they taste like cardboard to you, so be real here when you think about what truly refuels you.

Because Y♡u Matter

Chelle Verite

Now you have a list of proper go to foods that will replenish feeling **Physically Hungry** when **Emotional Turmoil** hits. **ET** only leaves when you look after number one and have the right focus. High five to feeding your good wolf. Pink spatulas, kitchen aid and a nice cup of tea and those wholesome **Take the Leap chocolate muffin cakes** at the ready. Physical Hunger sorted. Tick. (It's a relatively easy one, if you keep reaching for the good foods that is.)

But what about feeling **Emotionally Hungry**?

Feeling **Emotionally Hungry** is the second element that can consume you. This is a bit tougher. If left unattended, feeling **Emotionally Hungry** can leave you empty, with low feelings of self-worth, and where real deprivation often kicks in. Linked to the amount of loneliness you can experience (I'll come to that element in a bit), **Emotional Hunger** is all about self-security and self-protection. That need for nourishment, closeness, support, self-intimacy, safety and nurturing all of your own wants and needs. It's about recognising and acknowledging what 'little you' needs to feel good. A healthy way to do this would be to spend some more time with you. It's about asking your inner child what s/he needs for nourishment, to feel wholesome, fulfilled, and present. Otherwise we run on empty and feel deprived. This is doubly difficult if you are constantly focusing on the needs of others, busying yourself with the pressures and expectations of life, or simply battling with the lack of self-love or self-worth mirror reflection. Urrgghh, **Focus**. Love one, hate nil (Wimbledon Tennis, remember?) Come on, you can do this. Who said **BEing Human** and an adult was easy? I wish. Oh, to be younger. No responsibility and all the freedom in the world. Not to mention creating those **Superhero**, coat-over-head, feeling invincible moments. Yes please.

You can and will do this.

FEELING EMOTIONALLY HUNGRY
ASK AND ANSWER

When you're feeling **Emotionally Hungry** this is what you can do.

Ask and Answer the following questions so that when it strikes next you know

   a)   **how to do it.**
   b)   **what it feels like when you do.**

STEP 1. ASK

Grab a pen, focus on the fact you are feeling Emotionally Hungry, and write the following with the hand you normally write with.

'Hello [me*] what are you Emotionally Hungry for?

*Choose an age, less than 10 years old works, and also the name / nickname you liked to be called at that age. In my world this would look like. *Hello 6-year-old Rachel Bear whirlwind, what are you hungry for?* (And my dominant hand is my right hand).

Choose your name, and age now (using your dominant hand) Write your Hello sentence below.

STEP 2. GET THE ANSWER

Now this is where the magic happens. With your other hand (the hand you don't normally write with), let your younger little you self come alive, write back to you and answer that question. *Hello [me], what are you hungry for little one?* Let YOU be heard. This will mean sitting for at least two whole minutes and letting your little self write back to you. No noise or interference from your adult self. Just your younger, inner little self speaking back to you.

Now one of two things will happen. One, you'll think I've lost my marbles (highly possible. Remember, I am NOT normal), and two you will probably feel a bit stupid asking your inner child a question. Doing something new, as you know, often comes with resistance from yourself. However, let me reiterate how important it is to listen to you. Habits take between twenty two to sixty six times to form. They can only be formed if you let go of old ways of doing things and let in new ways of **BEing YOU**. This is most definitely new! Depending on how stubborn you are (and you, my friend, I suspect are stubborn) means that you will likely be scoring in the high sixties rather than the low twenties of doing something new. Anyway, I'm just reiterating how important this is. **IT IS IMPORTANT!** (Yes, I know I am shouting). I want you to know that it's sooooooo important that you start listening to you. You are important. Remember, you matter. So much so we are learning how to do away with that emotionally turbulent life rollercoaster.

Feeling **Emotionally Hungry** ask and answer exercise is about tapping into your unconscious mind and heart to find those wishes, wants and needs that are so often denied and locked away due to being a **Human DOing** and thinking, *I'm way too busy to focus on*

Because You Matter

Chelle Verite

refuelling my own self-worth. Except we know **Emotional Turmoil** comes from what we 'deny, miss or forget about ourselves'. When was the last time you actually spent time consciously acknowledging you, all of you? When did you take the time to decide how to be real, show up and be seen? When did you actually decide to invest in you and gift you what you actually need and want to make you feel good? I can guarantee you don't do it that often. In fact, for some of you it will have been a very long time ago, or you may never have done it at all.

This time is for you.

Because YOU Matter, being *'BOMBCHELLED!'* and catapulting your world into positive action so you can **LiveLifeBE** is all about waking you up, shaking you up and positively disrupting your world so that you can be authentically present and create a calm, confident and contented world filled with positive (not negative) action. All for you. You deserve all the empowerment and goodness in the world. You really do. It also means doing things differently. **Take the Leap.** Say 'No' to being a **Backside Sofa**, a **Woe-is-me Walker** or a **Talker Exhauster**. Your **Take the Leap Trapeze** adventure awaits.

Ok, pep talk over.

Reach for that pen, put it in your hand and get writing!

Because Y🙂u Matter

Chelle Verite

Your ASK Question
(dominant hand)
Hello [me*] what are you hungry for?

(Write your question in here ...)

Your 'little inner child you' ANSWER
This is when you (using your other non-dominant hand answers the question. Keep your hand on the paper, and yes the writing will be squiggly). Remember, this is not your adult self, this is little you that is answering that question. Stay present. Wait patiently for an answer and when it comes write down whatever you say. No filtering (or saying 'what piffle' or 'utter shite'). Sit with it and let your little inner child you talk.

STEP 3. ANALYSING WHAT YOU NEED

♥ **Well, what did little inner child answer back to you?**

♥ **What emotional nourishment have you denied him / her?**

Because You Matter

Chelle Verite

♥ **What have you missed for them (and you) to be calm, confident and content?**

♥ **What did you forget you needed to feel good, and to stop feeling Emotionally Hungry?**

Because You Matter
Chelle Verite

Replenishing emotional nourishment is all about paying attention and gifting back the little things we need. It might be gentle self-talk. A lovely warm bath. A chance to 'skiddle' in the sink. (What I used to do when I was little, with plastic bottles and bubbles in the sink, just pouring water back and forth playing.) It might be a moment to look at how amazing you are. An intake of breath that fills you with hope and joy. It could be that the little you wants to play around (or **Stomp, Rant, Breathe Dance**) in the garden. It could just be a crazy, half-hour giggle fest and uncontrollable laughter session. Or, in my case, a KitKat (ooooh, chocolate) and a laugh-out-loud at just how much fun life can be. Perhaps it's just a cuddle and to be told you are enough. It's the small, yet massively big stuff. The stuff that, as adults, we forget because things suddenly got serious, and we got far too busy just getting through and **DOing** life.

Your little you *is* important. S/he needs to be recognised and acknowledged too. Whatever it is that your inner you says they need, you'll find **Emotional Turmoil** can be nourished by providing that inner child self-acknowledgement. When you acknowledge all of you, your adult self and little self, both parts of you are heard and the emotional turmoil washing machine calms, or even stops, at least for a while. You may even be pleasantly surprised at just how easy it is to enhance your world and provide sustenance feeling **Emotionally Hungry**, when you stop to ask and listen that is. **Ask and Answer** and taking positive action is about finding out what you need. It's about asking your little self what you truly need in the here and now. When you ask, the answer that comes back may be a big, inflatable bouncy castle but that doesn't necessarily mean you need to go out and buy or rent one this instant (although I did, and it was well worth it!)!

However, taking real time to stop, **Ask and Answer** does mean taking a moment to translate what that means for you in your adult self. This is about standing up for you. You are no longer denying, missing or forgetting yourself and causing **Emotional Turmoil**. Instead, you are acknowledging, creating, remembering and providing what you need, when you need it to feel good. Feeling **Physically** and **Emotionally Hungry** acknowledged. Tick. Lovely. Now we are cooking on gas. What then about our nourishment zapping frenemy feeling **Angry**?

A = ANGRY

Feeling **Angry** (despite its often negative impact) is a natural and inevitable reaction to frustration or stress. Experiencing anger and feeling **Angry** is often unpleasant, it varies in intensity from annoyance to rage, that strong, debilitating emotion we find ourselves experiencing. However, ironically, it's not the experience of feeling anger that causes the problem. It's whether our feelings towards that anger are rational and appropriate to the event and situation that occurs. Connected to physical problems and even chronic illness, such as stress, high blood pressure, breathing problems, and pancreatic, liver and digestive system problems. Anger is definitely the bad wolf. If our reactions negatively impact on us, our health, or the situations we find ourselves in, it's something we need to learn how to **HALT** the impact of.

Firstly, let me point out that

a) **Everyone, at some point, will experience anger and feel Angry.**

b) **Anger is subjective, like all emotions, and we do / will experience it differently.**

Everyone you know will experience, internalise, vocalise and react to feeling **Angry**. This is not about making you the same as everyone else or dimming it down. This is about you learning how to focus on how you choose to respond to feeling **Angry**, rather than reacting and being consumed by it.

We had better establish pretty quickly how you experience anger then, so we can put a **HALT** to the emotional car crash before it happens.

Because Yöu Matter
Chelle Verite

Feeling **Angry** can be categorised into two types.

A) **Internalised Anger**

B) **Externalised Anger**

Both of which we will all have experienced at some point in our lives and will continue to experience in the future.

Internalised Anger is frustration at self. That critical **SDM**. Those harsh words and actions directed at you. The self-hatred, **Worry-woe-is-me** ball of fire. 'I am useless.'

Externalised Anger is the opposite. It's where you project your frustration and spit rocks at everyone around you. Those **Devastating Dave** f*ck you moments. 'Life is shit, I am disgusted by the world and enraged by the mere fact you, and everything else, is in it.'

Anger, and feeling **Angry** can therefore stop us in dead in our tracks. That red mist of uncontrollable wrath can destroy ourselves and the relationships we have around us. To be fair, feeling both **Internalised** and **Externalised Anger** aren't exactly a calm, confident and contented **Human BEing** existence, are they?

Shall we see what we can do about it?

WHAT TYPE OF ANGER DO YOU FEEL?

Understanding how you feel **Angry**, how it affects you, and how it appears in your world is important. Taking a moment to find out how you experience it and what you can do about minimising the negative impact on your world is vital to you feeling good and also catapulting you into positive action. If you merely stay experiencing feeling **Angry**. It's going to stop you creating and making a world that you love and want to live in. Getting a handle on **Emotional Turmoil** and feeling angry will ensure that other people want to be in your world too.

♥ **On a scale of 1 to 10, how Angry a personality would you say you are?**

On a good day.

On a bad day.

On a particularly **Emotionally Turbulent** day.

Be honest!

(1 = calm and peaceful)

(10 = filled with pure anger and rage)

	No Anger									Extreme Anger
On a good day	1	2	3	4	5	6	7	8	9	10
On a bad day	1	2	3	4	5	6	7	8	9	10
On an ET day	1	2	3	4	5	6	7	8	9	10

(This will give you your range of feeling **Angry**).

Because You Matter

Chelle Verite

My lowest experience of feeling Angry is a score of

My highest experience of feeling Angry is a score of

What I notice about these scores is...

♥ **When feeling Angry when you are in Emotional Turmoil, how often is your Anger Internalised?**
(How often does your anger and it's negative energy wrath point inwards so it negatively affects you?)"

☐ All the time
☐ A lot of the time
☐ Most of the time
☐ Some of the time
☐ Occasionally
☐ Never

Because You Matter
Chelle Verite

> ♥ **How would rate the negative impact that your Internalised Anger has on your life, situation and world when you are experiencing Emotional Turmoil?**
>
> ☐ No noticeable impact
>
> ☐ Low negative impact
>
> ☐ Medium negative impact
>
> ☐ Highly negative impact
>
> ☐ Extremely high negative impact

How would you describe the effect Internalised Anger has on you physically, emotionally and mentally?

The Internalised Anger that I experience shows up as...

So, now you know if you have **Internalised Anger** in your life, the levels of negative impact you experience because of it, and how it shows up. As a result of **Internalised Anger**, you may have experienced tension, stress, headaches, hypertension, self-critical talk, self-hating feelings, depression, insomnia and worthlessness to name just a few! Not the best really, is it? **Internalised Anger** really is that bad wolf.

Because You Matter
Chelle Verite

What about how much **Externalised Anger** do you have? Let's take a moment to explore that aspect.

> ♥ **When experiencing Emotional Turmoil, how often do you find yourself filled with Externalised Anger?**
> (The negative energy gets fired and projected on to other people as a direct result of how you feel.)
>
> ☐ All the time
>
> ☐ A lot of the time
>
> ☐ Most of the time
>
> ☐ Some of the time
>
> ☐ Occasionally
>
> ☐ Never

> ♥ **How would you describe the negative impact your Externalised Anger has on your life, situation and world when you are experiencing Emotional Turmoil?**
>
> ☐ No noticeable impact
>
> ☐ Low negative impact
>
> ☐ Medium negative impact
>
> ☐ Highly negative impact
>
> ☐ Extremely high negative impact

Because You Matter

Chelle Verite

> ♥ **How would you describe the effect Externalised Anger has on you and others physically, emotionally and mentally?**
>
> **My Externalised Anger shows up as ...**

Externalised Anger is reacting to and acting out anger inappropriately. It is dysfunctional patterns of passive aggression, or withholding, or justification. Ooooh Chelle, that sounds serious! Well, let's face facts here. Feeling **Angry** appears in many forms, if not handled well, *is* really serious. Feeling **Angry** is wildly uncomfortable. It's hostile. It can be extremely intense in its wrath. A reaction to a perceived provocation, hurt or threat is often likened to that of a pressure cooker or a hurricane.

Have a look at the sorts of symptoms your **Externalised Anger** and how it shows up. Be brave and honest when you examine what you wrote above.

Because You Matter

Chelle Verite

♥ **How does Externalised Anger affect you, and those around you?**

♥ **How does it showing up affect you mentally and how does it show up physically?**

♥ **How does Externalised Anger affect your day-to-day life?**

> ♥ **How exactly does that Externalised Anger project itself?**
>
>
>
>
>
>
>
>

FEELING ANGRY
IS IT PASSIVE OR AGGRESSIVE?

Perhaps your behaviour is to provoke others for a **Reaction**, so you can blame, alienate or withdraw. Perhaps it is the persecutor in you that needs to justify and project your disdain at the moral wrongness of it all. Or perhaps it's to play the 'woe is me' victim card. Feeling **Angry** is that pressure cooker that sometimes explodes, sometimes just quietly and menacingly seethes, or often it's that hurricane that destroys everything and anything in its path. The Russian Roulette of passive aggressive behaviours including hurtfulness, dispassion, evasiveness, withdrawal, destruction, bullying, risk taking, grandiosity or plain threats. Many behaviours which I'm sure you will, when you're brutally honest, recognise that you have exhibited. We are all human after all.

Emotional Turmoil and exhibiting anger can, therefore, be catastrophic in terms of the damage you can inflict on your relationships with others, and your life. However, it's important to recognise and acknowledge which anger elements you tend to utilise. Once you can identify what's going on as your automatic **Reaction**, you can choose a different, more positive **Response**.

Because Y😵u Matter
Chelle Verite

Have a look at the list below and identify which anger elements you have, up until now, exhibited.

When having an Emotional Turmoil episode, what Externalised Anger elements do you recognise in you? *(Be honest, this is your book and no one else is looking.)*	
☐ Dispassion, cold shoulder, fake smile	☐ Threatening, insulting, shouting
☐ Expressing frustration at insignificant things	☐ Playing on people's weaknesses
☐ Obsessive behaviour, demanding perfection	☐ Talking over others
☐ Provoking aggression and then patronising	☐ Vulgar jokes
☐ Crocodile tears	☐ Breaking confidence
☐ Secretive behaviour	☐ Ignoring people's feelings
☐ Stockpiling resentment	☐ Pushing people for unwanted deeds
☐ Silent treatment	☐ Speaking or walking too fast
☐ Under breath mutterings	☐ Reckless spending
☐ Avoiding eye contact	☐ Ignoring other's needs, selfishness

Because You Matter

Chelle Verite

☐ Putting people down	☐ Not responding to requests for help
☐ Sexual provocation	☐ Finger pointing
☐ Apologising too often, self-blame	☐ Tailgating
☐ Being overly critical	☐ Slamming doors
☐ Inviting criticism	☐ Explosive rage
☐ Withdrawing socially	☐ Being over punishing, vengeance
☐ Sulking	☐ Making general accusations
☐ Heightened anxiety	☐ Destruction of objects or relationships
☐ Evasiveness, avoid conflict, turn your back	☐ Showing off or expressing mistrust
☐ Choosing unreliable people, defeatism	☐ Solving problems via kiss and make up
My Passive Anger score is	**My Aggressive Anger score is**
/20	/20

Because You Matter

Chelle Verite

♥ **What were your scores out of 20?**

♥ **What Externalised Anger features most in your world? (Passive or Aggressive, or are they both equally present?)**

♥ **What do your scores tell you? What do you notice?**

Remember, feeling **Angry** is like a pressure cooker. It can be debilitating. Not only just for you, but for the people and relationships surrounding you. It's likely that the **Devastating Dave** moments (aka the *F*ck you, and then some*) will appear when you are in that **ET** pressure cooker moment. But when you become aware of what your potentially damaging automatic **Reactions** are, you can choose to engage in different and more positive **Responses**. That, however, means you need to be able to re-channel your energy. Afterall, **Anger** is an expression of energy. Imagine what life will be like when you can choose something else to plough your energy and expressions into instead.

RECHANNEL YOUR EXTERNALISED ANGER

When feeling **Angry** consumes you, and you start to point the finger and engage in challenging conversations with others, follow the technique **Stop & Breathe -> Think & Focus -> Listen & Express.**

Stop & Breathe

This means using the **Sigh Breath** technique we learnt in Life Lesson 8 wiggle your hands, feet, shoulders. This will release tension, reduce your blood pressure, heart rate, adrenaline, and balance your energy hormones. Remember, this is about putting yourself in a position where you're able to choose your response rather than acting out your **Anger**. You also need to eliminate your fight-flight-freeze reactions. Breathe in, breathe out, and **Focus**. Be sure at this stage to 'Hold yer whishst' in other words don't talk, or even attempt to utter words from your mouth!

Because Y♥u Matter

Chelle Verite

Stop & Breathe -> Think & Focus

This step is about recognising that you may react. However, it's about choosing and deciding what you actually want. It is not about choosing what you don't want. (Stay away, Henry). Instead, you want to engage and choose **Responses** that create positive, wonderful **Motivating Matt** moments instead. (**God ERR☺ME**, we love you.) What is it that you want to **Respond** to (not **React** to) here? **Focus** on that and not **Reacting** automatically.

Stop & Breathe -> Think & Focus -> Listen & Express

Once you have recognised what you want, and what you need, be prepared to **Listen**. This will require you to be in an adult frame of mind. Yes, this will mean ditching the stroppy child or the controlling parent approach. It will also mean being brave. Contender, ready? Gladiator, ready? When the going gets tough, the tough gets going. Mute the noise. This may mean noise that your internal, **Angry** voice is creating, or the noise from the other person. Rather than only working from your *I want* agenda, **Focus** on being hopeful and solution-**Focused**, so that you will be more likely to collaborate with the other person involved. In short, it is all about **BEing** present and **Focusing** on the here and now. Listening out for the positives. **Responding** (not **Reacting**) to the facts. Stepping away from the problems, or fearful elements, of the situation. **Focusing** on the 'can do' solution.

For some of you, being brave, being adult, staying in the present and being **Focused** on the solution might prove tough. Hmmmm, just in case you're not quite there yet and are only ready to rant, I have the **Stomp, Rant, Breathe Dance** just for you. More on that in a moment and I will say it's great done in the garden, office, spare bedroom anywhere really, so long as you warn people that you will be a bit odd for a few minutes (how I love not being normal!) Once done, you will

---

have decluttered and calmed your mind so listening will be a breeze. It's also a lot of fun. So too is being able to truly **Listen** without feeling **Angry** or it consuming your every move. Sign up for a live masterclass if you'd rather have company in the world of stomp. Just shout.

Once you've listened then you need to **Express.** This is about clearly and logically stating how you feel, and what you need. More importantly, it's about being able to express clearly how your needs, the needs of the situation and the other person's needs can be met, so you can come to a positive resolution. Expressing understanding and communicating what you need, whilst still considering what the situation and the other person needs too, takes practice. It may also mean having to do the **Stomp, Rant, Breathe Dance** to gain clarity on what that looks like before you engage with this stage. And yes, it is okay to stomp and rant before you can gain clarity on how you want to engage with the situation or another person. You are, after all, a **Human BEing**!

It can be tougher than you think to stop your **Externalised Anger** taking over, especially when you have been used to being consumed by it. However, when you are caught in feeling **Angry**, thinking consciously about responses like

Stop & Breathe -> Think & Focus -> Listen & Express

Creating an outcome that will actually serve you well in the situation, will help a lot. So too does not being defined by your automatic **Reactions**. Although, for some of us, before we can be present or able to actively **Listen** and be productive in the situations with ourselves and with others, we need a way of rechannelling our **Internalised** and **Externalised Anger** elsewhere. This is where the **Stomp, Rant, Breathe Dance** proves very effective.

Ready?! Whoop, whoop. Yes, let's do this! Even if you're not quite ready to let go of your anger, remember this is **BYM Fight Club** and we are fighting for you. Use feeling **Angry** to your advantage and let those rants rip.

Stomp Rant Breathe Dance

Number your Anger level

I want you to decide what level of **Externalised Anger** you are currently experiencing.

(1 means low, 10 means off the scale.) Give it a number. It may even be higher than 10 depending on what type of day, week, year you've been having.

(That's okay. Just give it a number.)

My current Externalised Anger is [   ]

Because You Matter
Chelle Verite

The aim of this game is to reduce this level to something that is manageable. By focusing on the present, not acting out your emotions and getting to a place where **God ERR☺ME** can feature, you can choose your **Responses.**

Now Breathe

Complete your **Sigh Breathing** in Life Lesson 8 (Inhale, exhale, sigh, shake, wiggle).

Now Move

Now get your backside off the sofa and go to your garden, office or spare room.

Get yourself ready to think, focus and listen.

Let's Rant

Welcome to the **Stomp, Rant, Breathe Dance**!

This means picking your feet up to stomp like an African Tribe member or a person who is really pissed off and literally stomping **Externalised Anger** out of their system. It involves stomping as hard as you can all around your garden / office / spare room. Stomping so hard your feet will practically fall off.

Ready?! Get in position.
Here we go, feet at the ready to hit really hard on the ground...
(You may even find your hands want to fist shake too.)

Because You Matter

Chelle Verite

--- Start Dance ---

STOMP! STOMP! STOMP!

Shoulders Up. Shoulders Down.

STOMP! STOMP! STOMP!

Shake your hands out in front of you like a medicine man.

STOMP! STOMP! STOMP!

Shoulders Up. Shoulders Down.

STOMP! STOMP! STOMP!

You get the picture
(As always though, please check who's watching.
Those men with white coats are never too far away!)

While I remember, you have my permission to rant too.

Let rip all the things you are feeling pissed off about.

STOMP! STOMP! STOMP!

RANT. RANT. RANT.

This is where you get the chance to vocalise all
the things you are angry about

Because You Matter

Chelle Verite

(fill in the blanks)

'My RANT No.1 is _____ because _____'

'My RANT No.2 is _____ because _____'

'My RANT No.3 is _____ because _____'

STOMP! STOMP! STOMP!

Now you get the chance to vocalise what you actually want instead of just ranting.

'My RANT No.1 is _____ because _____
which means my WANT No.1 is _____'

'My RANT No.2 is _____ because _____
which means my WANT No.2 is _____'

'My RANT No.3 is _____ because _____
which means my WANT No.3 is _____'

(You may still not have gotten rid of all your rants
or turned them into wants yet, so keep going until you do.)

STOMP! STOMP! STOMP!

'My RANT No.4 is _____ because _____'

'My RANT No.5 is _____ because _____'

'My RANT No.6 is _____ because _____'

STOMP! STOMP! STOMP!

Because Y♡u Matter

Chelle Verite

'My RANT No.4 is _____ because _____
which means my WANT No.4 is _____'

'My RANT No.5 is _____ because _____
which means my WANT No.5 is _____'

'My RANT No.6 is _____ because _____
which means my WANT No.6 is _____'

STOMP! STOMP! STOMP!

Shoulders Up. Shoulders Down.

STOMP! STOMP! STOMP!

Shake your hands out in front of you like a medicine man.

STOMP! STOMP! STOMP!

What are your real WANTS?

'I WANT _____'

'I WANT _____'

'I WANT _____'

Now stop and think clearly about what you have created and what you actually want. Instead of Bitching, Moaning and Whining about all the shitness that is going on (driving that BMW of life as I call it).

What can you do more of, or less of, to create a positive difference?

While you are thinking about what actions you can, and will, take to stay present, empowered and positive in your world.
Finalise the dance with the following breathing actions.

Because Y♥u Matter
Chelle Verite

Breathe In. Relax.

Breathe Out. Relax.

Shoulders Up. Shoulders Down.

Breathe In. Relax.

Breathe Out. Relax.

Shoulders Up. Shoulders Down.

---End Dance ---

Stomp, Rant, Breathe Dance

Whoop, whoop, you did it!

There you have it. Your first **Stomp, Rant, Breathe Dance** is complete. And if you just whizzed through the instructions, write down a list of your *rants* and *becauses* and head back up to the start. After five minutes of that dance not only will your grass have accumulated many more worms in your garden (they think the stomps are rain you know), you will have channelled **Externalised Anger** into something useful too. You will have calmed your adrenaline rush and your mind, and refocused. **Anger** should feel like something you can express in a good way, so you can use the energy it is giving you. Not something that takes over your existence. It's possible (if you really stomped) that doing the **Stomp, Rant, Breathe Dance** will have given you the giggles too (when the adrenaline rush started to wear off, that is). 'Ye cannae beat a bit of humour, especially when you're peed off.' To be fair, I created this dance as an excuse to get you to do awesomely different things.

Because Y♡u Matter
Chelle Verite

Let in newness. Well, hello. This is a nice introduction to starting afresh, isn't it? And no, we are still not normal! If stomping and ranting seems a bit too high volume, you can of course always sit crossed legged, calmly instigating Buddha meditation, and reeeeeelllllaaaaaaxxxx instead. Whichever works is absolutely fine by me. (Realistically though, you are channelling **Anger**, so if you were already Buddha you wouldn't be reading this book). All I ask is that when you do the **Stomp, Rant, Breathe Dance** be sure to take a selfie and pop it over to me. I'll put it up in lights in our *'Lets Get BOMBCHELLED!'* Facebook Group, where all us crazy kids get together and celebrate our abnormalities.

- ✓ **Feeling Hungry**
- ✓ **Feeling Angry**

Well done. World of positive disruption and empowerment here we come.

Now where is that wine? We need it for the next bit. Be sure to have a glass (or nice cuppa) in hand for this one. Especially in the new COVID world. Who would have thought we would feel so **Lonely?**

L = LONELY

Lonely, I am so lonelyyy. That emptiness, void, missing someone or something can be fatal, not just a means of fuel. It's the gap between a person's desired level of social contact and their actual level of social contact. According to the American Psychological Association the negative effects and physical stress of loneliness on the body can be compared to having fifteen cigarettes a day, or even alcohol abuse. That's a bit of a headf*ck, isn't it? All the hugs we crave, connections

Because You Matter
Chelle Verite

we desire, those little 'Hellooo, how are you?' micro-lift moments. If we don't get them, the likelihood of a whole host of mental and physical health problems increase.

Connections and public displays of affection (PDAs aka those hugs!) are so important for a lot of us (and even us extroverted introverts need that refuel element too. In fact, surprisingly, I'm a bit of a hug and a kiss monster (line up, line up, that's my God complex coming out again). I really do love hugs. I think they're great. It may be because I don't remember getting many as a child so now, I'm making up for lost time. In fact, thinking about my son Oli's childhood, I used to spend a lot of my time chasing him around when he was a toddler saying, 'Mummy kiss and hug monster is coming!' To which he'd run squealing and laughing around the house, as only little ones can do (I do love the noise of children being happy, don't you?). I'd catch up with him and literally kiss, squeeze and hug him until we had to stop in fits of smiles and giggles. Even now it's one of his favourite bedtime routines, along with quiet hug and cuddle time. I have to say this with motherly pride as he tells me, 'Mum, I'll never be too old, or too big, to give you a cuddle.' Seeing as he's already a size eight in shoes and has almost taken over me in height (he's only eleven!), that has indeed made me smile many times over.

That's what having a hug and physical contact is about to me. It's like that *'Ah Bisto'* moment of contentment. Studies completed by post doctorate researcher Michael Murphy also reveal that a good hug can soothe you through the day and help you feel less affected by conflict. Bring it on. Family therapist Virginia Stair (and no, I'm not suggesting we all lie down on her couch) once said, 'We need four hugs a day for survival. We need eight hugs a day for maintenance. We need twelve hugs a day for growth.' That's a lot of hugs. However, I can see exactly where they are both coming from (Mummy hug monster at the ready. I think to avoid that infamous white coat, perhaps I need to stop waving my arms around and saying that out loud in public.

Because You Matter
Chelle Verite

Ah, but it's soooo much fun!).

Now here's the challenge. As I write this, the dynamics of our world have shifted dramatically. Those *micro-lifts*, those little *helloooo I see yous*, those touch point hugs, well, thanks to our enemy COVID-19, they have been in f*cking short supply whilst I'm writing this. Unless you're in a family or friend support bubble, of course.

It doesn't take a rocket scientist to figure out the hugs we need. If Michael and Virginia are anything to go by, if we don't get the connections we crave, it will have a potentially huge negative impact on our well-being and how we function in our day to day. I am not just talking good wolf here. This is serious stuff.

Feeling **Lonely** increases mental and physical health problems, including stress, low self-esteem, loss of memory, poor sleep quality, helplessness, more colds, aches and pains, depression, risk of heart disease, strokes, and personal and psychological functioning. Feeling **Lonely** reduces our 'bounce back' ability, our resilience, and reduces self-esteem. This cognitive decline can affect how we perceive others and how we see our place in society, causing us to withdraw (or be forced to withdraw). This leads to loneliness, which leads to physical effects, which leads to cognitive decline, and the negative downward spiral continues. Not a great picture, is it?

Which is why I say **HALT**! Before we get all doom and gloom the world is a terrible place (*I can't exist. What will we do? It's a disaster!* **Catastrophising Chris** and **Meltdown Mary Moments**. I know, I know, I'm normally so upbeat; either that or swearing like a trouper), let's wake up, shake up and positively disrupt ourselves back into action. Let's get our backside off the sofa, our brains engaged and be ready to choose our **Responses** instead.

What type of Lonely are you?

For ease I've called this **DIPPSS**. It was either I gift you a memorable acronym or bombard you with a whole load of psychobabble about studies and research. I've already suffered the latter to write this Life Lesson so I thought I'd save you the trouble. Aww, I know, I'm so lovely. (And I also have very little attention span for detail. Especially when it's time for a break!) Right, now we are all refreshed (please tell me you got a refuel snack and a drink too) and feeling **Hungry** and **Angry** are sorted let's find a way of sorting out your **Lonely DIPPSS**.

Lonely DIPPSS	
D	Developmental
I	Internal
P	People
P	Physical
S	Social
S	Situation

Because Y♥u Matter

Chelle Verite

So, let's explore a little further.

You feel **Lonely** when

   a)   you would like to have more people to talk to

and / or

   b)   your relationships aren't as meaningful as you would like

So, let's explore a little further.

♥   **Which of the Lonely DIPPSS categories do you recognise in your world?**

Have a read through the descriptions and give yourself a rating out of 10 as to how much loneliness is in your life when you are.

   a)   Having a 'good' day

   You're calm, confident and content.

   b)   Having a 'bad' day

   Things are not going to plan.

   Things are negatively impacting on your world.

   c)   Having an 'Emotional Turmoil' day

   You are in a state of great commotion, confusion, disturbance or are dealing with difficult decisions.

Rate how often you feel this way out of 10

(10/10 = I feel this 100% of the time to 0/10 = I feel this 0% of the time)

Because You Matter
Chelle Verite

	What type of Lonely do you experience?
Developmental	You feel like people are ahead of you and that you are missing out or being left behind. You feel and think their life is more on track than yours. You suffer from **'Keeping up with the Jones'** syndrome. Other people have a better job, they got the promotion first, even though you were there longer. They have the better house, were married / engaged first, had kids first, travelled further, visited better places, and went to more exclusive places. In comparison to you their social media shows happier lives that are way better than yours.

Good day	Bad day	ET day
/10	/10	/10

Internal	This is **Feeling Empty Within**. It is emotionally led and linked, as I mentioned before, to feeling **Emotionally Hungry**. A void, feeling like an empty shell (no pun intended). Missing someone or something. You feel utterly shit, empty, unworthy and not good enough. You have bucket loads of respect for everyone else and very little / none for yourself. You often experience passive aggressive **Internalised Anger** in the form of self-damning reactions and self-destructive behaviours. You are triggered by fear of rejection and fear of failure (Atchiphobia), and feelings of being overwhelmed feature a lot in your world.

Good day	Bad day	ET day
/10	/10	/10

Because You Matter
Chelle Verite

People	Also called **Objective Loneliness**. This is being around people, yet feeling utterly alone and disconnected from friends, family or the people you love. Intimacy is often missing or when it is present it causes fights, or conflict. You often feel like you aren't seen, feeling like you don't fit in, that you are invisible, or don't exist. You hold the perception that you are alone in any, and every, situation. You don't trust others. You often have demanding or toxic friendships / relationships where your views don't count, or you aren't listened to, even when you shout loudly.

Good day	Bad day	ET day
/10	/10	/10

Physical	Also known as **Subjective Loneliness**. When you are stuck in a pandemic lockdown, alone or physically away from other people. Or the alternative, when you choose to isolate yourself through choice, or when you either don't want to, or can't be bothered to, engage with the real world outside. Or as I would say, 'You've just visited Naples.' (As in you've nae pals. No friends or social connections, none, nada.) You're like a walking ghost that no one can see, that you don't even register exists, or is worth existing. (If that's the case and you score low here, call me and we can be pals.)

Good day	Bad day	ET day
/10	/10	/10

Because You Matter

Chelle Verite

Social	You choose not to engage, you are **Connection Lonely** and find being with others difficult because you feel awkward, different and / or feel like you don't fit in. You often feel shy and clunky around other people, and feel like you aren't equipped or competent, and can't be socially entertaining. You find it difficult to connect and you often feel different.

Good day	Bad day	ET day
/10	/10	/10

Situational	**Situational Loneliness** comes with major changes. It can be felt even if it is a positive change involving exciting events, for example. a new city, a new job, new surroundings, different language or cultures, or a change in situation such as becoming a stay-at-home parent. It can also be a pandemic induced situation like working from home, social distancing, lockdown, and negative events like redundancy, disability, unfamiliar faces, loss of a loved one, relationship breakup or caring for another.

Good day	Bad day	ET day
/10	/10	/10

Because Y♥u Matter

Chelle Verite

♥ What are your Lonely DIPPSS scores?			
	Good day	Bad day	ET day
D = Developmental	[ ]	[ ]	[ ]
I = Internal	[ ]	[ ]	[ ]
P = People	[ ]	[ ]	[ ]
P = Physical	[ ]	[ ]	[ ]
S = Social	[ ]	[ ]	[ ]
S = Situational	[ ]	[ ]	[ ]

Because Y♡u Matter

Chelle Verite

Understanding what triggers your feelings of **Lonely DIPPSS** will mean that you can positively impact on them to create a different **Outcome**.

♥ **What do you notice are your main areas of Lonely DIPPSS?**

♥ **What patterns have emerged?**

Because You Matter
Chelle Verite

♥ **What events or situations, up until now, have triggered your Lonely DIPPSS in the most negative ways?**

♥ **What, from now on, can you do more of (or less of) to positively impact on your experience of Lonely DIPPSS?**

BE REAL... SHOW UP... BE SEEN... Truly look at yourself. Discover your reality and **Take the Leap** to create newness. Yes, that journey is an emotional rollercoaster in itself. However, when you can be clear on things you can do differently to enhance your life, it makes a huge difference to you, your family, your work and your world. You will actually be able to enjoy the ride and exhilarating adventure without projectile vomiting with fear, anxiety or worry.

Because You Matter

Chelle Verite

Finding new ways of **BEing Human** can be daunting, but that doesn't mean it needs to be hard work. You don't have to reinvent the wheel. You can pinch with pride and snaffle what other people offer too. In terms of replenishing yourself and putting a **HALT** to feeling **Lonely**, you've now got **DIPPSS**. To make your empowerment journey easier on your stomach (and your nerves), I thought I'd be kind and offer you some suggestions below (in *Blue Peter* style, here are some I made earlier). You can thank me later. For now, relax.

In addition to your own ideas and actions to positively impact on feeling **Lonely**, please feel free to use any / some / none of the following suggestions.

Lonely D = Developmental

Instead of feeling **Lonely *'Keeping up with the Jones'*.**

♥ **Look at your life objectively.**

Keep things in perspective. Your life is your own. What will you do more or less of to ensure you stop doing a 'go compare' on your life?

♥ **Identify and focus on your goals.**

Keep your eyes on your prize. Physically writing your goals down will help to ensure that they are a reality list and not a 'pie in the sky' wish-list. Writing them out will help you action them too. Be your own accountability partner (or call me and we can do it together).

Because You Matter
Chelle Verite

💜 **Switch off social media.**

Do something way more interesting instead. Reading this book is a good start. So too is connecting with people who matter to you. TikTok and Instagram are not real.

💜 **Ditch the 'mood hoover' people in your world.**

Ditch engaging in situations where you feel pressured to 'perform' like a barking seal. If you don't feel energised being around certain people, or doing a particular task, or being in a specific situation, get rid. The gift of your tea is far too important (have a read of the next Life Lesson that last statement will make total sense).

💜 **Complete the Crown of Acceptance.**

Head back to Life Lesson 5 and focus specifically on where you are giving your power away and who you are giving it to. This will make you feel good and help alleviate **Developmental Loneliness** too. Your hands will untie, I promise.

Lonely I = Internal

Reducing your experience of feeling empty and **Lonely**.

💜 **Focus more, worry less.**

Internal Loneliness is about focusing more on what is truly going on, rather than what you think and assume is going on. Using your **FU Worry Time** and the **Worry Dissolver** (Life Lesson 6) will keep you focused on what truly matters, and a focus on what is real and what is not.

Because You Matter

Chelle Verite

💜 **Kick your SDM into touch.**

Get your rugby kicking shoes at the ready, and review Life Lesson 14 **Kick your Critical Mind** again. Be sure to kick that **SDM** far far away. Concentrate on what you can choose to do more of and less of that will add value to your life and to your world. Come on **PAM (Pioneering Angel Mindset)** we can do this!

💜 **Be your own Superhero.**

You can also choose to positively add value and empower yourself by being your own **Superhero** (Life Lesson 11) so you feel good rather than empty. If you want to, that is! If you'd rather be like my Aunty M ('I like my life the way it is so I can moan about it all and I cannae hang ma washing oot.') then I suggest you stay in bed. However, I'm sure, despite the fact that some of your head and heart will want to stay in bed, that you'd rather get a handle on empowering you now, wouldn't you? (The fact you've read this far into the book tells me you really do care about you.)

💜 **Stay present.**

Focusing on the here and now whilst avoiding the **Unchangeable Past** or the **Imagined Future** (Life Lesson 16) will help you reduce **Internal Loneliness** too. Ask yourself, 'What does that actually mean for me right now? What do I need now?' Cut yourself some slack. Beating yourself up about how awesome you should / could / ought to have been does not work. You are you, here in this moment.

Lonely P = People

Reduce **Objective Loneliness** and that feeling of being disconnected or invisible by.

♥ **Gaining appreciation of who you are and what you represent.**

This is about recognising and acknowledging your own self-worth. Revisiting **Valuing LOVE and HATE** (Life Lesson 13) will support you with this.

♥ **Say no to patterns and habits!**

Choose empowerment. Ditch the pattern of engaging in toxic or unhelpful relationships. Instead, **Be your own Superhero** (Life Lesson 11) and empower your own value. You rock!

♥ **Use logic and emotion to feel good.**

Gathering real information on how to value your accomplishments and feedback positive things about yourself (Life Lesson 15) will increase your connection to the world. Get those fabulous **BUNCHES** at the ready.

♥ **Building relationships with trust and confidence.**

Allocate 'trust buddies' in your world who understand your triggers of feeling overwhelmed or rejected, or your fears of failure and success.

♥ **Using the Worry Dissolver**

This will help you focus on what's real, and what isn't (Life Lesson 6). You will be able to stop worrying, focus on what's fundamental to your needs and create a reality list of wants, rather than disappearing down a rabbit hole of disappointment to be constantly haunted by pretend wishes and what ifs. You can also have a good old **Stomp, Rant, Breathe Dance** that we've just done in this Life Lesson too.

Lonely P = Physical

Reduce the negative impact of **Physical Subjective Loneliness** aka 'nae pals' situations by.

♥ **Creating positive *This is Your Life* moments.**

(Life Lesson 7) It's all about choices. Your choices for you. Make them limitless, the world is your oyster.

♥ **Staying clear of Devastating Dave *f*ck you and f*ck me* moments.**

Focusing instead on the here and now. Invite **Motivating Matt** positive reactions into your life, especially when interacting with others. Be a positive influence in the world rather than a negative one (Life Lesson 9).

♥ **Deciding what contact you actually need.**

Clarity on give and take, give and take, and how, and from whom, and sticking to it (You'll get this from Life Lesson 19 **Making 'It' happen**). This approach will help increase internal glow and appreciation in your world.

Because You Matter

Chelle Verite

Lonely S = Social

Instead of feeling awkward or shying away from connection focus on.

♥ **Using God ERR☺ME.**

Remember, if you do the same things, you'll get the same **Outcome**, so positively disrupt this habit. Instead of acting on your automatic **Reaction** to shy away from others, recognise and acknowledge what you are doing, then choose a different **Response** (Life Lesson 7 **Choice is limitless**). Connect with someone new. Be the change. Leave the fear of failure (Atychiphobia aka chip butties) alone. Be brave. I am rooting for your success.

♥ **Focusing on what areas of expertise you offer.**

Feedback the good stuff to you so you can communicate it with others (Life Lesson 11 **Be your own Superhero** and Life Lesson 15 **Feeding back to self** will help you here).

♥ **Finding likeminded places with likeminded people (remember, we are NOT normal).**

There are so many people out there who will understand who you are. Remind yourself why you wanted to start this empowering, positive action journey in the first place (Life Lesson 2).

♥ **Building trust and finding people who share your passions.**

People you can rely on who you can help by keeping their world safe, as well as them helping you. You need to know what you love. Valuing what you love and hate about you is a great place to start (Life Lesson 13).

Because Y♡u Matter

Chelle Verite

Lonely S = Situational

Dealing with change and feeling **Situational Loneliness** can be minimised by.

💜 **Having a supportive friend to talk to that offers no judgement is key here.**

If you can't locate **PAM** fast enough or often enough, find a friend, a coach like me, or a counsellor, we will help you channel your energy.

💜 **Making 'It' happen.**

Understanding yourself and how much you give and take in situations so you can replenish your energy. (Life Lesson 19 will explain more about how to let in the new you and set goals).

💜 **Taking the leap.**

Not being a **Woe-is-me Walker** or a **Talker Exhauster** and actually **Take the Leap** (Life Lesson 12) and help yourself to **HALT** the **Situational Lonely** feeling.

See, so many great things on offer. And the best bit, depending on where you are feeling the most pain, is that you can dip in and out of any Life Lesson that you wish. The joy of books. That and it'll keep you away from losing your life to social media. **Lonely**? As if! Unless you are choosing to be alone, which is different to feeling and being **Lonely**.

Being **Lonely** means you can be consumed by emptiness, unworthiness and belief that you lack value. Being **Lonely** often causes moments of **Emotional Turmoil**, where your emotions can easily overwhelm you and leave you feeling inadequate.

Therefore, identifying how you want to positively impact on your world so you can love the life you live, and getting a handle on **HALT**, is vital.

- ✓ **Hungry.**
- ✓ **Angry.**
- ✓ **Lonely.**

That leaves us with one final element we all know so well. being **Tired.**

T = TIRED

Hands up how many of you are like a bear with a sore head when you're **Tired**, especially without sleep? You only have to ask a parent with a newborn baby what life is like for them to say, 'Life? What f*cking life?! Jet lag is preferable to having a baby. I am practically a walking zombie!' Oh, don't get me wrong, babies are awesome. Their big eyes... their squidginess... that baby smell... You can't keep me away. However, broken sleep, not enough sleep, can't sleep because you're mentally stressed sleep (hello pandemic world), or just can't seem to recoup from feeling knackered / exhausted / depleted can leave you feeling overwhelmed and downtrodden with no oomph or va-va-vooom, or full of anxiety, or like a fire ball of impatience. Yup, we all recognise that level of **Tired**, don't we? Don't even get me started on feeling **Tired** coupled with a firepit of **Emotional Turmoil** too.

On a brighter, fluffy, marshmallow note, there were/are times (albeit few and far between) when you didn't / won't feel **Tired**. (Ermmm, I can't recall exactly when that was for me. However, I'll stay in the room of denial and blame that on greying brain cells rather than the fact feeling anything but tired hasn't happened in about a decade.) Right, think of those times that you felt full of the joys of the world,

Because Y♥u Matter
Chelle Verite

completely energised and totally refreshed. Times when you were so energised that you could stop flash, emotional, damaging reactions, harsh words and patterns of beating yourself up. Times when you could stop that critical **Sabotaging Devil Mindset** going to town on you with ease. Your mental and physical energy has a huge impact on how you deal with emotionally driven situations. Ridding yourself of feeling **Tired** and gifting yourself with mental and physical energy is often forgotten. Self-care is all about resting and recouping. Stopping the **DOing** and concentrating on **BEing** instead. The simplest way to recharge is go to bed. Like when you were little. Bath and bed.

In adulthood, satisfying the physical tiredness is all about gifting yourself something relaxing, such as low lighting, quietness, reading, being with people you love, physical touch, massage and switching off. (Get yourself a fluffy terry towling bedspread. They cuddle you in the night and even James likes ours, so men you have no excuse! Hello again Amazon!) A minimum of 10% of your day should be self-care. Without it you won't be able to re-energise. Oh, and that 10% doesn't include at least seven hours of good sleep, with no mobile phone, laptop or screen time. You are living your life through our own eyes (not the eyes of social media).

What I will say is that living in a new COVID pandemic world, full of unknowns, newness, restrictions, no get away breaks, working from home, home schooling, financial stresses, changes in our cultural and economic approach to things, no get out of jail free card, life can be f*cking hard. We are all **Tired**. We are mentally lacking energy and even getting out of bed takes it out of us. We are also, for the most part, bored. Continually feeling like we are on a life diet of rice cakes or Ryvitas. However, despite the continued adrenaline fuelled approach to our new world, we have still had to empower our emotional **Responses** and generate mental energy. Rather than feeling completely **Tired** and wiped out all the time, we need ways to reinstate our mental energy for innovation, newness, and to make sense of our world.

Because Y♥u Matter

Chelle Verite

Not to mention to look after our sanity and a change in diet choices. Head to the **Take the Leap chocolate muffin cakes** in the back of this book for some healthy inspiration.

How Tired are you?

Let's take a snapshot of your world. Just how **Tired** out are you?

On a good day, a bad day, and on a day fuelled with **Emotional Turmoil**.

♥ **How Mentally Tired are you, and why?**
Good day?
Bad day?
ET day?

♥ **How Physically Tired are you, and why?**
Good day?
Bad day?
ET day?

Because You Matter
Chelle Verite

♥ **What do you notice about what makes you Tired?**
What makes you **Mentally Tired**? What Makes you
Physically Tired? What just makes you plain **Tired**?!

♥ **What do you need to do more of (or less of) to enhance
your energy levels and HALT the negative impact feeling
Tired is having on your world?** (Be real here, only put things
down that you will, and truly want, to do.)

It's all about ensuring that you gift energy back to yourself. How can you effectively gift yourself energy and avoid feeling depleted and overwhelmingly **Tired** out with life? You are the only one who can do this. It does, however, take time for you to be honest about the patterns of behaviours you engage in that are helpful, so you can do more of them. Also, your awakening of self-awareness requires you to be able

---

to recognise the behaviours that are hindering you too. Understanding the component parts of **HALT** will absolutely help. Creating glow and having a nice cup of **'Giving and Taking Tea'** to celebrate will help too. (I'll gift you with that lovely nugget of empowerment in the next Life Lesson.) I told you, I will always tell the truth and I will never leave you in the lurch. I mean, it would be a bit shit reading a book that gave you all *look at what you could have won* theory and then didn't give you any help in getting there, wouldn't it? Besides, you'd only beat me up if I didn't help. That's **BYM Fight Club** for you.

HALT Reminder

For ease here's a reminder of them of our amazing **HALT**.

H	Hungry
A	Angry
L	Lonely
T	Tired

As you read through have a think about just how many of them you have in your world right now.

Because You Matter
Chelle Verite

Hungry	♥ **Physical** = What food are you hungry for? (good / bad wolf). ♥ **Emotional** = What is little you hungry for?
Angry	♥ **Internalised** = Frustration at self. ♥ **Externalised** = Frustration at others. ♥ **Stop and Breathe -> Think and Focus -> Listen and Express.** ♥ **Stomp, Rant, Breathe Dance** (Rant, Because, I want!).
Lonely	♥ **Developmental** = 'Keeping up with the Jones.' ♥ **Internal** = Feeling Empty Within. ♥ **People** = Objective Loneliness. Alone and disconnected around others. ♥ **Physical** = Subjective Loneliness. Naepals, pandemic lockdown. ♥ **Social** = Connection Lonely awkward, difficulty, choosing not to connect. ♥ **Situational** = Major changes and loss associated as a result.
Tired	♥ **Physical** = Sleep and rest required. Go to bed! ♥ **Mental** = Lack focus / energy.

What is this snapshot of your life and energy telling you?

Because You Matter
Chelle Verite

♥ **What level are you experiencing each element of HALT?**
(Low, medium, high or extreme?)

Hungry?

Angry?

Lonely?

Tired?

Having one of these elements out of kilter in your world is just about manageable.

Having two of these components out of sorts becomes a tad more difficult to deal with.

Having three or more is a major, major **Red Flag**. Eat, sleep and **Focus** on what you need to readdress the balance immediately.

Because You Matter

Chelle Verite

Remember, you matter. The more elements that aren't in balance, the more you won't be in the right place. When you aren't in the right place, the world becomes like pushing treacle up a hill. Sticky and unmanageable, with really messy feelings, like being buckled up on that rollercoaster of life with absolutely no means of getting off. Except, you are now equipped to press the emergency stop button. To **HALT** the negative impact of **Emotional Turmoil** on people, relationships and your world, you need to be equipped to re-channel the negative and automatic **Reactions** that cause you discomfort, pain, loss, suffering and negativity, and choose **Responses** that will promote a positive **Outcome** instead.

So, look at your **HALT** combinations. The patterns you notice. The elements of your world that you continually deny yourself or don't want to recognise. You might be feeling **Tired** due to a lack of sleep, or **Hungry** due to lack of good food. Perhaps you are ignoring feeling emotionally **Hungry** which will trigger feeling **Internalised Anger**. Which leads you to feeling **Angry** to the point you throw all your teddies out of the pram, and your world implodes with the appearance **Externalised Anger** and **Devastating Dave** appears to cause havoc. Or perhaps you're feeling just feeling downright **Lonely** and having **Catastrophising Chris** and **Meltdown Mary Moments**.

Just BREATHE!

The world is definitely a harsher place when you are **Hungry, Angry, Lonely** and **Tired.**

However, now you know what they are, you are in control of how their negative impact can be minimised.

Because You Matter

Chelle Verite

It's about recognising what's going on. Recognising and acknowledging which **HALT** element is out of sorts. It's about making a conscious choice to engage in creating a different world where when **Events** happen you can **Recognise** your **Red Flags** and choose to **Respond** positively so you get the **Outcomes** you actually want and get to enjoy your life, rather than endure it. The definition of insanity is doing the same things over and over again and expecting a different **Outcome**. You may not be normal, however, you are definitely sane! You're also human.

See, here we are learning how to look after you. Here we are asking the right questions. Here we are noticing and focusing on the right things and engaging in choices to create the right **Outcomes** for you. This is about you growing up and creating a world that makes you smile and feel good (and having fun at the same time). Just wait until the next Life Lesson and we put that glow back in you too.

Why do it?

Why put a **HALT** to **Emotional Turmoil** in your world?

Why put things in place to **Live Life** and **BE**?

Simple.

Because You Matter

> Life is like
> a cup of tea.
> It's all in how
> you make it.

IRISH PROVERB

LiveLifeBE

BE REAL... SHOW UP... BE SEEN...

LIFE LESSON

18

Who's for tea?

GIVERS, TAKERS, CREATING GLOW

Because You Matter

Chelle Verite

Want a cuppa? Ooooh, yes please. A nice cup of tea. PG Tips or Yorkshire? Mug or teapot?

A reward for finishing a life admin task = have a cuppa.

A work task completed = have a cuppa.

The British way of talking / chatting / chewing the fat = have a cuppa.

Discussing how the world has imploded, dealing with **Emotional Turmoil**, taking time out, thinking about life = have a cuppa!

'Ooooooh, let's have a nice cup of tea.' That hug in a mug moment. A good **Meltdown Mary Moment**, cry it out, or 'chin wag' as we say in Scotland = 'Aye, lets hae a cuppa, a wee blether, and put the world to rights.' (There is of course a slightly different moment which is the *f*ck I need a glass of wine* moment, however, for now, let's stick to that nice cup of tea.)

Because You Matter
Chelle Verite

We get our favourite cup, mug, teapot at the ready in our favourite place and have a nice cup of tea. My favourite mug is my *Keep Calm. You've got this!* mug. When I'm feeling particularly girly, I opt for my *Lady of the Manor* mug (which is pink, and I love pink). Mug at the ready, kettle boiled, tea made. 'Ahhh that's nice!' as we smack our lips and relax into our chair. Our shoulders drop, tension releases and we feel slightly more human again. Yes, feeling human. So important.

At this point you're probably thinking. *What on earth is Chelle going on about again? Cups of tea and hugs in mugs?* You're likely thinking. *there she goes again, off on one of her many digressions.* Yes, that might be true, but actually I thought *let's make navigating life a bit easier to digest and make it all about a nice cup of tea.* After all, I have been saying I want to make things easy for you throughout this book. You'll have got the gist of this seeing as we are on Life Lesson 18 already. Where has the time gone?! Well, this Life Lesson is all about ensuring you stay replenished. It's about how you feel good. How you are, and can be, seen by yourself and by others. It's none other than a bit of 'Shall I be mother?' making and drinking tea.

The amount of energy you create in our world is up to you. Just like how many cups of tea you decide to make, gift, accept or take (similar to the apple pie analogy). Yet many of us don't know how to replenish ourselves. Some of us don't know what to do with that nice cup of tea. That hug in a mug moment that we create. We often aren't taught how to value ourselves, or exactly how to recharge our batteries. Neither are we taught that it's a good thing to replenish ourselves by creating and experiencing that warm hug in a mug glow. Some of us are great at giving that glow to other people, to the point where we give too much of our energy away and forget that we need to stop and have recharge time for ourselves. Also, we often lose energy because even when others offer us those little gifts of warmth, we're simply not able to accept that hug in a mug glow.

We either give too much away, or don't accept its warmth.

Sometimes however, we might feel the other way inclined, in that we can be a little selfish and disregard completely what others need. Instead, we are hell bent on taking that hug in a mug glow energy that's meant for other people for ourselves. (Although, to be fair, if you really were like that all the time, I doubt very much you would have read past Life Lesson 2 in this book, or even picked it up!). Being selfish and disregarding completely what others need in the world of tea making means using the last of the milk and not giving a damn. We all know when we've done that, and when other people do it too. We also know just how much of a detrimental effect those types of relationships have on us now, don't we?

Life Lesson 18

RECHARGING, TEA

AND GIFTING GLOW

The relationship you have with yourself, and how much energy and replenishment you gift, is just as important as how much you accept and take from others. However, I ask you, how good are you at recharging and gifting energy? How good are you at generating, giving or taking that recharging glow? Let's take a moment to find out. I'd encourage you at this moment to pop the kettle on too; it'll give you that nice 'ahhhh' moment.

Excellent. Tea in hand?

Because Y♡u Matter
Chelle Verite

STEP 1. WHAT TYPE OF GIVER, ACCEPTOR AND TAKER ARE YOU?

Have a look below at the different glow types. See which ones you recognise. Rate each one out of 10 (10 being you do it all the time and 0 being you don't do it at all) and complete the continuum that follows. Be honest with yourself. It's not an exact science or a test of your goodness as a human being. What's your approach to replenishment, and feeling good?

Giver of too much	Are you a **Giver of too much** energy? To the point where you feel good but your internal glow suffers because you give too much energy away? You give out, even when you're feeling bedraggled, like life has dragged you through a hedge backwards, or feeling beyond jet lag tired. Deep down you're working on the premise that giving your energy out to experience the joy on other people's faces is way more important than receiving it.	/ 10
Giver	Are you a **Giver** of energy? To the point where you have balance in your world with others, and still have enough energy for you too? Aww, that's nice. You are zen and balanced. Cup of tea for us both.	/ 10

Because Y🩷u Matter

Chelle Verite

Willing Acceptor	Are you a **Willing Acceptor** of energy? When that energy and a gift of presence, compassion or listening comes your way you lap it up like a gift from the Gods, like it is the best thing since sliced bread. 'Ah yes, a nice cup of tea and a wee blether.' Conversation is so good for the soul.	/ 10
Reluctant Acceptor	Are you a **Reluctant Acceptor** of energy? You know that you ought to accept that lovely hug in a mug niceness from others, however, you'd much rather avoid that squirming sensation in your toes when people are being nice to you. 'Accept? I'd love to, except there are a million and one other things to do.' (You mean be distracted by.)	/ 10
Once in a while Taker	Are you a **Once in a while Taker** of energy? Those days when you just switch off the compassionate Mother Teresa approach to the world and have to take a cup of tea. You don't give to another person. Instead, you do something that takes just a little bit of energy, or glow, away from someone else. You don't mean to be mean, but you really do just need to take it. So, you do. Except the guilt of taking energy from someone else ends up consuming you. So you say sorry, replace what you took as soon as you can, and redress the balance.	/ 10

Demanding Taker	Are you a **Demanding Taker** of energy? 'Hello! There is no I in team so come on, cough up people.' You need what you need. Afterall, you work damn hard to ensure everything operates smoothly. You need that energy. The demanding taker of energy takes whatever glow there is on offer. Even if that means taking the last bit of milk, and the biscuit to go with it.	/ 10

STEP 2. WHAT DID YOU SCORE?

Giver		Acceptor		Taker	
Giver of too much	Giver	Willing	Reluctant	Once in a while	Demanding

Because Y♥u Matter
Chelle Verite

What do you notice about you?

♥ **Giver?**

Are you more of a **Giver** of energy at the expense of yourself? Or are you able to give energy to others in a way that still keeps your glow?

♥ **Acceptor?**

What about graciously being the **Acceptor** of energy? Accepting another person's presence, attention or gifts of energy to recharge your glow? Is it something you can relax into or does it make your skin crawl with the uncomfortableness, and unfamiliarity, of it all?

♥ **Taker?**

How do you fare when you are a **Taker** of energy? Is it 'My way or the highway! That's mine!' like a young child that snatches and won't share? Or perhaps you are more of the quiet, pursed lips at the ready, **Once in a while Taker** type. 'I'll just have a bit of that, thank you.'

STEP 3. WHAT DOES YOUR STORY TELL YOU?

> ♥ **How does your current Giving, Accepting and Taking of tea...**

a) **Gift your world?**

b) **Detract from your world?**

c) **What do you want more of, less of, that will empower and enhance your life?**

Because You Matter

Chelle Verite

Whatever story you came up with about how you conduct yourself, the most important thing is not which one you mostly are or aren't. (I'm not here to chastise you.) It's all about how you get more of the good stuff in your life, for you and, as a result, the people around you too.

- 💙 **Welcome to navigating who's for tea and the world of Givers, Acceptors and Takers.**
- 💙 **Welcome to understanding and discovering how to create that glow so you stay fed and whole.**

This is about generating self-awareness. It's about recognising what's currently going on and acknowledging the choices you make, so you can authentically empower all that you create. That does mean you need to spend time with yourself to understand what drives your current behaviours, and what choices to make to get what you actually want. That means paying attention to the relationships in your world. Bring it on.

So where exactly do your hugs in mugs go? Where does your energy and your ability to replenish yourself go? I've been thinking about this, and from what I can see there are four options.

1.	Give Me Tea
2.	Give You Tea
3.	Accept Tea
4.	Take Tea

All hugs in a mug. Just with varying degrees of impact on your life energy. Some positive, and some negative. You recognised all the different types of hugs in mugs, didn't you? I know I did. Let's be honest (which by now you know I am) and look at this objectively. Some of the hugs in mugs have a more positive impact than others. It really depends on how self-centred, selfish or selfless you are. Let's have a look in more detail. While we do, I need you to be honest with yourself.

How exactly do you put the kettle on and make your tea?

and

What impact on your world does it actually have?

Because You Matter

Chelle Verite

OPTION 1. GIVE ME TEA

The first option is the **Give Me Tea** hug in a mug. Where you choose to take a moment to stop and make that cup of tea just for you. This is all about putting the kettle on to stop, breathe and focus only on self-appreciation. 'Me, myself and I' time. Where it is just you that gets fed and has sustenance. Where you take a minute or two to put warmth back into yourself, look at the world and appreciate all that you bring. Where you can look at solving what's upsetting, creating, breaking and making you. **Give Me Tea** is taking a moment to feed yourself with strength, appreciation, wonder, love and time to grow. It's knowing that you are good as you are, and a valued, respected, creative, resourceful and whole human being, which results in a lovely feel good glow.

Because Yǒu Matter

Chelle Verite

Have a think... when do you actually stop and gift yourself that type of cup of tea? When do you get properly self-fed and replenished? When do you take time to feel better and become more focused and more productive? When do you consciously choose to add to your own self-worth?

When we feed ourselves, we actually feel a little more valued, a bit warmer, and we glow. When we are less **Tired** we feel less critical about the world we live in. We all need that, don't we? To run on full energy, rather than running on empty. To have a way of increasing our feel good life fuel gauge so we feel happier, more focused and more prepared for life. Visit the land of contentment and vitality rather than wallow in depletion, depression, stress, anxiety, disappointment and disillusionment.

So, that's **Give Me Tea** hug in a mug. Sit, relax and drink. So easy, isn't it?

Now, from a real person's perspective, life is not an everything-is-awesome-happy-clappy-sing-song-Lego-movie moment. Nope. If we are really honest, most of us are completely f*cking knackered. We are so tired, aren't we? How many days off have you actually had over the last month? Three months? This year? And that's without the addition of a global pandemic, working from home and home schooling.

Until I started writing this book, I didn't take time off at all. Well, perhaps at Christmas, or for my birthday. I might have had the occasional couple of days without logging into work. Give back to self? Be kind to me? Me, myself and I? Don't be ridiculous! I didn't take a moment to give anything back to me and truly stop to replenish myself. And why not? Well, it was all tied up in low self-worth and that **Worry-woe-is-me Fear Monster** pressure about what others would think, and the fact that I didn't love myself enough to gift me a hug in mug.

Because You Matter
Chelle Verite

You'll likely recognise the traits. running around after everyone else, providing for others before yourself, busying yourself with pointless and exhausting life admin tasks, not having time to do anything other than collapsing in a **Tired** mess.

Except now we are learning to look at our reflections and value self. Love one. Hate nil. We can do this. Give yourself permission to have that hug in a mug. Come on, peeps. You don't need me to tell you how awesome and deserving you are.

Get that kettle on, milk and sugar at the ready, and make a nice cup of tea in your favourite mug. Get that hug. Wrap your hands around your mug and think for a moment. Be present in the here and now with you. With all that's going on in your world. The world of you. **Give Me Tea** hug in a mug is all about being a little selfish, but in a way that doesn't do anyone else any damage. It's about looking after you. It's not selfish in the traditional sense of the world, it's about being what I call '**BEing Selfwith**'. It's about recognising what you truly need and focusing on yourself. Instead of ignoring what you need, you're choosing to give to yourself what you need and feeding you.

Give Me Tea BEing Selfwith

Take a moment to think about how **'Selfwith'** you are and what you can offer you.

Grab a nice cuppa and spend a moment sitting and reflecting and valuing all of you. Sit still with you for a moment and enjoy that hug in a mug.

Ask yourself the following questions, think about your answers, then scribble them down.

Because You Matter

Chelle Verite

♥ **What's creating me?**
(What makes me, me? Why do I like it? What is it about me that gives me joy?)

♥ **What's breaking me?**
(What's causing me pain, upset or alarm?)

♥ **What's making me?**
(What actions have I created that I am proud of?
What good things do I offer me that make me feel good?)

Because Y♡u Matter
Chelle Verite

It's likely you have never thought about these things before; however, this is about letting you have a moment to appreciate the good things that make you, you.

When you're done (which will likely mean going back and asking yourself those questions again), stop, think and sit with them for a while. When you have digested the questions and written some of your thoughts, use the following questions below and head back to **BUNCHES** approach of feeding back to self and really let your logic and emotion help you feel good.

Take a moment to think about the following.

♥ **What have I done well...**
In this moment?
Today?
Yesterday?

Because You Matter

Chelle Verite

♥ **I did well in these moments because...**

♥ **What I can do more of to re-energise me is...**

♥ **What I can do less of to re-energise me is...**

Because You Matter
Chelle Verite

Ahhhh, that is nice, isn't it? Having some **'BEing Selfwith'** Tea time. See, you're already equipping yourself with newness.

To be fair, I know you've just whizzed through that Life Lesson like the fast opening of Christmas presents. I know asking yourself to have time with you can be quite a challenge. It means that you have to take time out to recognise, acknowledge, make choices and engage in new things.

When you're ready to have a **Give Me Tea** hug in a mug moment and really take some well-earned time out, put the kettle on and relax into spending time with you properly.

You matter remember!

So, now you are more sorted to give to self, let's have look at **Give You Tea**.

OPTION 2. GIVE YOU TEA

The second option is the **Give You Tea** hug in a mug. Where you give to others by taking time out of your day and putting energy into making a nice cup of tea for another person. You think about them. You make and create that cup of tea, that hug in a mug, just for them. By doing so they benefit, and you benefit too. It's the rich tea biscuit and chocolate digestive of being nice. When you've recharged your own batteries and have enough equity in your energy bank then be sure to offer the people in your world the **Give You Tea** treatment. It does exactly what it says on the tin. This is all about being selfless and giving to others. Some of you may do this all the time. Some of you may gift far too much of your energy and time. Others of you might not be that well-rehearsed in giving tea (you'll recognise the **Take Tea** option) and take too much to the detriment of others.

Because You Matter
Chelle Verite

Give You Tea isn't about putting you first, it's about generating energy and sustenance by thinking of others instead. You make and create that cup of tea, that hug in a mug, for someone else and give it to them. When they drink it, they feel good, and when they feel good, you feel good too.

The feel-good factor does rather depend on whether your gift of giving the cup of tea, your hug in a mug, is accepted by the other person or not. (There could be a chance they will reject it due to that squirming in the toes feeling I mentioned earlier.) Whether your gift of tea is accepted or rejected also depends on how the tea is made. However, if you are in luck and you make their tea exactly how they love it, the odds are good that they will accept it and drink it. However, if you have not made it with tlc, or been careless or lackadaisical in your approach, and presented them with tea and your presence as grey as dishwater, then it's likely the desired positive effect of feeling good by gifting will be null and void. If your heart's not really in it you're wasting everyone's time, and it will be turned away.

If you haven't already guessed, this isn't just about making the tea either. The actual tea making is only part of the story. It's about whether you provide the whole service too. **Give You Tea** is about making yourself truly available, being truly present, for you and the other person you are providing the replenishment of energy for. Sitting down and listening and being there with them because you want to, not because you want something or because you have an agenda. It's about being present for them and acknowledging what's going on for them, in their present moment, with no other noise going on.

And that's Option 2 **Give You Tea**. Depending on what type of mood we are in, we can all do this option. For me, if I'm in a *yes, I can be present and think wholeheartedly about what the other person needs* mood then making a nice cup of tea with love and care is easy and

Because You Matter
Chelle Verite

a great option. I find my greatest **Give You Tea** moments are with my lovely coaching clients. I get so much energy from them when I'm truly listening and being present. However, there are times when I screw up and give them grey, dishwater tea moments. Yes, I am human.

I sometimes give my husband James grey, dishwater tea too. Don't get me wrong, I love spending time with him. However, he has the most logical and detailed brain. Sometimes when I give him tea just the way he likes it (accompanied with a sit down, truly listen and be present moment), my brain just can't compute. It completely falters with the intellectual detail of what he's talking about. And yes, on a bad day I don't do so well with my hug in a mug offering. My patience levels can be a bit on the **Take Tea** side. I tend to interrupt his stories and reroute them towards shoes, cake or "Is it pink?" conversations instead, which means that even being in my caring and compassionate state, I know I am not fully present. I am not gifting my energy to him. I'm creating and serving up grey, dishwater tea. You'll all recognise this type of tea. Yes, it's **Give You Tea** but you're not really present. You're vacant. You've left the building. No-one is home. Your brain has decided not to pay attention to creating that awesome hug in a mug for another person.

As you are reading this, you now realise it's not really just about a cup of tea, is it? That's an analogy. A metaphor for being present and offering your time to support another. Your energy, a kind ear and advice. General investment in another person. Sometimes it's an easy task and only takes a few minutes. Sometimes it's longer. However, when you give it freely it's something that should make you and the other person feel good. So here it is. Even when you feel utterly rubbish, even when the whole world is imploding around you, remember **God ERR☺ME**. Instead of automatic **Reactions** you can create choices and **Responses** that will positively impact on the **Outcome**

Because Y♥u Matter
Chelle Verite

to create that feel good factor for you, and for others. **Give You Tea** hug in a mug is a great opportunity to do so (so long as you have enough energy by gifting those tea moments to yourself too). Make it with pride. Be sure that you know what they like, how they take it and what they need. (So long as they are worth the investment of course; no point banging your head against a brick wall if your cups of tea will continually be thrown back in your face. I'll go into more detail about that in my next book. For today's life lesson we'll focus on how we are choosing to put the kettle on.)

Life is tough on us all. Being available and getting out of bed can be an almighty challenge. As I used to say, it's like a life tightrope. One minute we are there, thumbs up and balancing it all okay with a smile on our face, the next minute we have a rope sandwiching us in our bits, and we are dangling precariously in the steps of life. It's f*cking hard that tightrope of life. Look one way and we can recognise our world but turn the corner and the world as we know it is simply gone. Poof! Up in smoke in the click of fingers, or a Prime Minister's decision to lock us down. Meaning we can feel totally drained just with the effort of opening our curtains and that's just facing the day, let alone facing our reflection of reality.

Because You Matter
Chelle Verite

Give You Tea

♥ **When can you Give You Tea, and to whom?**
(What can you do to support another?)

♥ **What does that person actually need from you?**

♥ **How are you going to be truly 'present' with another?**
(Even when it's not a message or topic that you like,
want to hear or have time for? This is truly **Giving You Tea**.)

Because Yꝋu Matter

Chelle Verite

♥ **How can you help another to get through what they need, in order to BE Human?**

Give You Tea is an opportunity. Instead of being self-focused or selfish, you can choose in that moment to be authentic and present with yourself and another person. Another who needs you (and yes that person will be you too at times). Another who may not welcome or accept your energy, but when you decide to help them and make that cup of tea anyway, you are absolutely there for them, with all that you are. Not a pink shoe in sight. Trust me, **Give You Tea** is harder than you think. You will have to choose to do it, to gift your tea. You'll need to avoid creating dishwater and engage with tlc. You'll need to be aware of when you make this type of tea, and who to, and why. You never know, this selfless act might just make your day too.

OPTION 3. ACCEPT TEA

Here's the thing. If you hadn't already realised it, it's about balance. Getting the balance right to notice what and how much energy you are gifting yourself and others in the world.

There's **Give Me Tea**, **Give You Tea**, and **Accept Tea**. The third option, **Accept Tea** depends very much on your situation and personality, and is when you choose to graciously accept the cup of tea that's offered. That's the **Accept Tea** hug in a mug. When someone wants to **Give You Tea** you have to be able to accept it. This means taking and accepting investment from another person.

This, my friends, is something I'm not best practiced at doing. I'd much rather kick up a stink or distract myself, or the other person involved, so I don't have to give myself that self-acceptance time.

Because Y♡u Matter

Chelle Verite

Although I am learning. Being gifted attention, up until recently, made me feel uncomfortable. Me being able to invest in me? Me being able to accept someone else investing in me? It's like accepting a compliment. When people say to me, 'Chelle, ooooh, I love that dress / new suit / shirt / hat!' I look at it and go, 'Really? What, this old thing?' when in actual fact, I should be acknowledging what's being offered and learning to say thank you in **Response**.

Those two, teeny tiny words will make all the difference to your self-value. Thank you. And that's it. It's not difficult now, is it?! Except, how often, and how un/comfortable are you at accepting compliments or kindness? The **Accept Tea** option means we need to learn how to accept attention, presence, and energy from others. It's about saying thank you and being okay with someone doing something for you that's nice.

Yet, what you need to realise is that if you don't accept it you may deflect attention for a while. However, you may also deflect the feel-good factor from someone else, which simply isn't fair. This isn't all about you, this is about the other person too, and it's about finding ways to make life better, more rewarding and easier.

Be sure too not to give all of your tea away and keep some for you too. If I can do it learn to **Accept Tea** graciously then you can learn it too! It's like a full circle. To **BE Selfwith**, you need to know how to gift that hug in a mug to yourself first, then **Give You Tea** to others, and the bit that glues it altogether is the **Accept Tea**.

Now we are getting to grips with the concept of how our tea is served in life. Before this conversation you didn't have a clue that there were different types of tea, did you? (Except for all the different coloured packets on a supermarket shelf, or on a posh uber cool restaurant menu.)

However, before you get all, *'Yay, I understand the world now, Chelle! I've got a handle on putting the kettle on situation!'* The real deal here is that it's not all sunshine. We don't always give. At times, we will **Take** as well as **Give**. Recognising the **Take Tea**. moments is important. So too is analysing the impact of them, which at times isn't good. If we **Take** all the time, we can annihilate our world and the relationships in it.

OPTION 4. TAKE TEA

The last option is **Take Tea** and encompasses a whole range of stroppy child / controlling parent expectations of tea, demanding it, and taking it come hell or high water. This **Take Tea** for me is the flipside of **Give You Tea** and **Accept Tea**. When you use this option you decide you need a cup of tea so you'll expect it and demand it from another person who might not be in a position to make it for

Because You Matter
Chelle Verite

you, but they will anyway because they are a giver and will put what they need to one side. The difference between giving to self and being there for another is that if you just do a **Take Tea**, it's because you need it at all costs and decide to put yourself first (regardless of the costs or consequences).

Hello to the people in the world who want stuff and enjoy the stance of **Taking** rather than **Giving**. They get stuff from others because they **Take** to get what they want. They wait expectantly for a cup of tea from someone and always **Take** it from whomever they can get to make it for them. Then they complain if the cuppa wasn't quite right or didn't fit with what they wanted so they shout louder about what they want next time. Okay so it's effective self-preservation. They get what they want and a quick solution. **Take** and **Take** and **Take** some more. A short cut to taking control of life, without much effort or energy.

Don't get me wrong, everybody to some extent is a taker. It just depends on how much you take from another person, and how often. That, and the balance of **Give**. If you take all the time, you'll get so much tea your teapot overflows and you won't want to drink it, or you'll disregard it because it doesn't taste good anymore. But herein lies the subtle difference. It's not about taking for your own sake. It's about accepting what is offered. Or when you do need something, it's about making sure that you **Give** back too, creating an equal balance. When it's equal and you balance **Taking** and **Giving** life feels good, and we could all do with a bit more of that now, couldn't we?

So, if you do **Take Tea** just for taking what you want's sake, then you are being selfish. In short, if you're doing it a lot of the time to the detriment of others then you need to stop being a twat. However, I have a smile on my face as the mere fact that you are reading this book means that you are not irredeemable. You are looking to recognise what you are doing and how you are being so you can make better and more positive choices.

Because Y♡u Matter
Chelle Verite

How much 'Tea'?

Looking at your world, how much tea, and those fabulous hugs in mugs, feature in your life?

♥ **How much Give Me Tea do you experience in your world?**
(Is it enough, what can you do to enhance it?)

♥ **How much Give You Tea do you experience in your world?**
(Is it balanced, or too much, or too little?)

Because Y♥u Matter
Chelle Verite

♥ **How much Accept Tea do you experience in your world?**
(Do you graciously accept? How can you enhance the
experience for yourself and for others?)

♥ **How much Take Tea do you experience?**
(When, and why, does it happen? What do you want to do
about it that will create more positive glow in your world,
rather than detract value from the relationships you have?)

Because You Matter

Chelle Verite

♥ **What impact does each option of 'Tea' gift you in your life?**

(Positive / negative?)

♥ **What will you do now that will empower the way you create your energy glow?**

(How will you choose to put the kettle on?)

Because Y♡u Matter

Chelle Verite

There you have it.

Not rocket science, is it?

In short, we can all be **Givers**, and we can be **Takers**. The types of life energy and creating glow are all dependent on how you make, and take, your cup of tea. **Givers**, **Acceptors**, and **Takers**. Some of us are perfectly balanced in our approach to life and creating energy. Others of us are a bit out of kilter, and either **Take** too much or **Give** too much away. However, remember, life is what you choose to make it. As our fabulous **God ERR☺ME** always says. you are not defined by your automatic **Reactions**. However, you can enhance your world by consciously choosing positive **Responses**.

Here's to you giving yourself, and others, that lovely *Let's relax have a nice cup of tea and be present time.* Being present time gifts a glow of energy in your world, rather than detracting or taking energy from others or yourself. So long as you aren't running on empty, or making other people run on empty, the world will be a more empowering place.

Why do it?

Why **empower yourself** to make **conscious positive choices**?

Why consciously choose to balance **Give, Accept** and **Take Tea?**

Why **create glow** for you, and for others?

You know why!

Because Y♡u Matter

"

Courage doesn't
happen when
you have all
the answers.
It happens when
you are ready to
face the questions
you have been
avoiding.

SHANNON L. ALDER

LIFE LESSON

19

Making 'It' happen

THE MEANING OF LIFE

Because You Matter

Chelle Verite

The meaning of life, or indeed the answer to life, the universe and everything. It's 42 isn't it? (That's' just for all you *Hitchikers Guide to the Galaxy* fans out there. I don't actually remember much about that TV series. However, I do recall my parents always having a wry smile when they talked about Monty Python.)

I always thought it would be great to have a book about all the rules, about how it's all done, so I could plan, relax and **BE**, rather than reflecting back on things and having those 'oh shit' moments when I did something spontaneous then realised that nope, that definitely wasn't the right thing to do.

I've discovered a few very important things about the meaning of life on my somewhat bonkers life journey, including Scottish Tourette's storytelling. Oooooh, I need to use the sensible voice of reason.

THE MEANING OF LIFE

---

1. **You will never have enough time to do everything you want unless.**

    a) you know what you want.

    b) you stick to it, don't get distracted, and do it.

    c) you make time to do it and enjoy it, otherwise what's the f*cking point?

2. **Seriously, life does not make sense to anyone.**

    ♥ **No matter what they say or how they do it.**

    ♥ **Nobody has a clue.**

    ♥ **Not a Scooby Doo.**

3. **Unless you're laughing, life gets very serious and boring.**

    I mean, even doctors use laughter therapy to help cure cancer. Laughter doesn't make you fat and can be a great work out, especially if you laugh so much you can't stop, and your stomach muscles get a really positive going over. It's often better than sex, and it's free. The laughter, not the sex (do not be fooled). Oh, and the best thing about laughter is that it's contagious. If you laugh other people will too, or at least smirk. You should be with us when we go food shopping, we have the whole queue in stitches most visits. However, you do have to be mindful of exactly where you laugh, and with whom.

Because You Matter

Chelle Verite

Laughing at people (unless they've told a joke or are in the same mood and have the same life experience as you) will only serve you a big **Devastating Dave** 'F*ck you.' I've avoided most of these up until now. It has, at times, been a very close call.

Joking aside (ah yes, I reminded myself, be serious, Chelle, be serious!), it's not always a laugh a minute this life stuff, is it? It's difficult being real, **BEing Human**, **BEing Seen** for who we are, and for showing up. Just like I said, it can be difficult enough to get out of bed most days. You need to speak to my wonderful friend Angie Barnes about just that. She spent four years in bed for many reasons and wrote her book to explain it all. (I won't spoil the punchline however, the book is on Amazon too.) Right, back to the meaning of life. Ta-da. If the last 18 Life Lessons have told you anything, you now know that it's you that **Make 'It' Happen.**

End of Life Lesson.

Because You Matter

Chelle Verite

End of book.

Kidding!

Because Y☺u Matter

Chelle Verite

However, you really do **Make 'It' Happen**. It's all about the ever-powerful **God ERR☺ME**. How you choose to consciously **Respond**, rather than automatically **React**, to your life events determines your world. It's about how you choose to empower you. **Making 'It' Happen.**

Come on. **Take the Leap!** Ah ha, I've now fast forwarded your *'Oh, darn it'* moment. There is a sudden dawning realisation that you actually have to do something with this shit. That's right, it's not just a sit back, read and enjoy Chelle's little stories. 'F*ck!' I hear you say. 'Isn't it just enough that I have got to the end of this book and paid attention?'

Now you have read almost all the Life Lessons, your awareness has just woken up. This is where the real work begins on **Making 'It' Happen**.

I used to hate maths. All those scientific calculators, protractors, and algebraic equations $a^2 \times C^2 = xyz$. My maths teacher, Mr Findlay, was a good man, however, I sadly had to leave Currie High School in Edinburgh in my first term of sixth year. (We moved to Edinburgh from Shetland when I was eleven.) Yes, Mum and Dad, why on earth would you opt to move cities so I had to change school? Then again, we moved again just as sixth year was kicking in, and all the shitty

Because You Matter
Chelle Verite

bullying had stopped. Instead of bullying it had been replaced with a quiet *I know where I am, and where I live in this angst filled teenager world. I will survive.*

Mr Findlay had to write a report card to tell the next lovely, unsuspecting poor sod of a maths teacher in my next high school what he was in store for meeting Rachel. I remember that report to this day. My report card said. *Rachel tries really hard. Lovely girl, nice smile. However, just doesn't get maths. Forecast for her higher exam D.* And yup, I had to hand it to Mr Findlay as that's exactly what I got; a D. Well, to be fair, I did get 2% off a C (despite private tutoring and attempting to get my brain into gear), but it was still a big fat fail. My brain development on the mathematical front just hasn't quite caught up with the rest of my body. However, now I realise it's because all the energy had been taken up with the right side of my brain; the creative, emotionally intelligent, press-the-button spontaneous side, rather than the mathematical, logical bit.

It does mean that there is absolutely no foundation whatsoever to the equation for success that I am just about to introduce you to. So, to all you left brained theorists out there, there is no reference point here. No encyclopaedia. No proven theoretical reason as to why this equation will work. Other than in my infinite wisdom. Other than in my forty three years of watching, examining, investigating, and analysing people. (I started when I was three years old so I really must know my shit, otherwise what on earth have I been spending my time doing?). Other than my time studying Communications, Psychology, and working for the last twenty two years with Olympic Athletes, business owners, leaders, managers and specialists. All in the name of making people happy and getting them what they actually want. So, as far as I'm concerned, $O + D + C \times F = \textbf{'It'}$ really does mean something.

Because Y♡u Matter

Chelle Verite

Here you are, the **Making 'It' Happen** life equation for **Success**.

$$O + D + C \times F = \text{'It'}$$

I could make you guess what it means all day but

a) **You'd get bored.**

b) **You'd just get f*cking bored.**

I'd rather keep you awake, and on your toes. Let's get on with the good stuff. This is what '**It**' and success is all about. I have subtly introduced you to the concepts all throughout the book.

♥ BE REAL

A **Human BEing** who stands up tall and is recognised for all that you are. It means making decisions choosing to **Respond**, rather than automatically **Reacting**, to life **Events** that happen. It means engaging and positively influencing the **Outcome** you crave in this world.

♥ SHOW UP

Yup, actually getting out of bed and doing the day. Engaging with it. Deciding to have it for exactly what it is in every way, creating it and experiencing it as your own. Choosing to **LiveLife and BE You**.

♥ BE SEEN

Telling your story, being proud of it and wanting to persevere with it. **Success** takes guts, hard work and a bucket load of tenacity.

However...

None of this will work, make sense or make a difference if you don't actually do something with it. Remember what I said.

'If you can create it, you can f*cking make it.'

So here's to you choosing to empower you. Here's to you creating and **Making 'It' Happen**.

Life Lesson 19

MAKING 'IT' HAPPEN

Creating success and **BEing the change** you want to be can be tough. However, walk through it with me and we will get there. Refresh your mind with the areas that you want in your world. Make maths magic.

$$O + D + C \times F = 'It'$$

O = OPEN

Ah, **Open**. Being **Open** to ideas. **Open** to suggestions. **Open** to being available to new things to grow. Being **Open** to learning. Easy that, isn't it? Erm nope, it isn't. Being truly **Open**, available and accepting is beyond difficult. If it was easy, everyone would be doing it, and that's simply not the case. What I will say is, you can do **Openness**. If you want to, that is. You do, however, need to bypass the automatic **Reaction** of your previous **Non-DOing**, **Wrong-DOing** and **Their-DOing MindF*ck** states. Instead, make the decision to **Focus** on creating positive action and being available to opportunity and creation.

Because Y♥u Matter
Chelle Verite

> ❤ **How Open are you?**
> **Open** to ideas, suggestions, newness, being available
> to new things so you can grow. Be honest!
> 1 = Not **Open** 10 = Completely **Open**

	Score	Reason
Bad day	/10	
Emotionally Turbulent day	/10	
Relationships	/10	
Career	/10	
Life	/10	
Friends	/10	
Health	/10	
Aspirations	/10	

Because You Matter

Chelle Verite

♥ **What do you notice?**

♥ **Are you truly Open, and available to make and BE the change you want?**

☐ Yes

☐ No

☐ Other (please explain)

♥ **What is it that you actually want in life?**

Because You Matter
Chelle Verite

Look at what it is that you want, face your reflection, and choose you.

Are you really ready to truthfully **Take the Leap** and fling yourself wholeheartedly on that trapeze, rather than stay as a **Woe-is-me Walker** or **Talker Exhauster**?

If you're still not at the **Trapeze Take the Leap** stage, admit it.

Shelve it and focus on something else.

Alternatively, **JFDI!**

Either way, all I ask is that you do the **Stomp, Rant, Breathe Dance**. Talking incessantly about what is on your wish list and not putting it on your reality list is sooooooo yesterday.

I ask you again.

- 💙 **Are you Open to change and creating your success?**
- 💙 **Are you truly available, to create and make it?**
- 💙 **Are you ready to Take the Leap?**
- 💙 **Are you ready for people in your world to tell you like it truly is (including yourself) and accept it, Fear Monsters and all?**

If yes, then whoop! You get to move on and head to the world of **Desire**.

If no, or a not yet, then ask yourself the questions on the next page repeating the above questions (and whatever Life Lessons of this book you need, until you are ready to **Take the Leap**).

Because Y♥u Matter

Chelle Verite

♥ **Why is it a no?**

♥ **What areas of your life are you specifically referring to?**

♥ **What type of no is it?**
(For example, is it a *definite no*, a *no, not now* or a *I should, but I can't be arsed* no? Be truthful, you've got this far.)

Because You Matter

Chelle Verite

♥ **What are the reasons you aren't currently ready to be truly Open, face your reflection, and BE your change?**

♥ **How do you want to BE?**

Because You Matter

Chelle Verite

♥ **What do you need to get out of your own way, ditch your kryptonite and catapult your life into positive action? (Bring on that Superhero!)**

(After all, the only person that's stopping you is you.
Up until now, that is. I'm not talking *should've*, *could've* or *wish I had*. What do you really need to do for you? If this bit is a stumbling block I'll happily accompany you on your journey, just shout and we can arrange the first of your **'Empower BE Me'** 121 sessions.)

♥ **What are the first things you now need to do so that you are Open, and can truly BE you? 'Do it! Do it! Do it!'**

1.

2.

3.

$$O + D + C \times F = \text{'It'}$$

✓ **O = Open. Yes, get in!**

+

D = DESIRE

Desire means you have to actually want to do it in the first place. The **Desire** to do something you actually want to do. I mean, people say they want to do something all the time. 'I want to lose weight.' or 'I want to get fit.' or 'I want to be successful.'

Except, here's the thing…

If the juice ain't worth the squeeze, or the cake is worth more than the size ten dress or sitting on the sofa is simply more pleasurable than going to the gym or taking that walk, then you know exactly what will result. In other words, if the cons outweigh the pros, then **Desire** is low and it's a no go. It simply won't happen. We are not going to kid ourselves with a pretend 'wish list'. You are **BEing REAL**.

Because You Matter
Chelle Verite

Desire is a killer. If you truly want something, you know you will go get it, come hell or high water. Just ask anyone who clambers over crowds and bats people with a handbag in a sale, just to get to those pink shoes they 'have to have'. This is life. It's about being brutally honest with yourself.

♥ **What is it you actually want?**

and

♥ **Do you truthfully Desire the end state?**

Figure out your Desire in 10

Let's give it a go. Think about what you actually want, really want. Write it in the *What I want for me* column. Then think about what the end state of that will give you. How much do you really **Desire** the end state over the immediate **Desire**? Let's see what happens.

Because You Matter

Chelle Verite

1	**What I want for me is...**

2	**The end state of what I want is...**

3	**How much do I really Desire it? (out of 100%)**

4	**What do I do that sabotages or gets in the way of my success? (What habits / behaviour patterns?)**

5	**What happens to my Desire score if things get in the way?**

Because Y♡u Matter
Chelle Verite

6	**Looking honestly at what I want (Question 1 & 2) What is my Desire level now?**

7	**What have I realised by doing this exercise?**

8	**What do I need to do more of, or less of, to get what I want?**

9	**What does this really mean for me now if I am to LiveLife and BE an empowered me?**

10	**Now I know what I know, what does this really mean for my life?**

Well done. See, without **Desire** it's not real.

Chelle's Desires
(Just so you know I'm human too)"

1	**What I want for me is...**
	To be fit and healthy.
2	**The end state of what I want is...**
	To have a slim stomach so that I can wear a bikini with a smile and be a size ten.
3	**How much do I really Desire it? (out of 100%)**
	85%
4	**What do I do that sabotages or gets in the way of my success? (What habits / behaviour patterns?)**
	I drink wine, eat chocolate and crisps and don't do exercise consistently.
5	**What happens to my Desire score if things get in the way?**
	It goes down. I like wine and chocolate a lot more than being slim... Ooops.
6	**Looking honestly at what I want (Question 1 & 2) What is my Desire level now?**
	60%

7	**What have I realised by doing this exercise?**

I've associated being fit and healthy with being a size 10. That's not true. Being fit and healthy is about balance. Accepting that I like wine and chocolate and enjoying them and keeping active so I stay within a healthy weight range. Having a six pack stomach would mean giving up wine and chocolate. I like wine too much to do that (you may have noticed on this journey).

8	**What do I need to do more of, or less of, to get what I want?**

I'll stop driving my life BMW (Bitching, Moaning, Whining). I'll start enjoying exercise when I do it. I'll enjoy the glasses of wine when I drink those too. I'll bake and eat the **Take the Leap chocolate muffin cakes** for breakfast so I can feed my good wolf. (I love doing that. Eating cake for breakfast, it's so wrong, yet so right!), and I'll start shopping in Next as their size ten is really a size twelve = ☺

9	**What does this really mean for me now if I am to LiveLife and BE an empowered me?**

I'll relax and enjoy what life offers me instead of putting restrictions on myself. I'll look forward to having a glass of wine or a cocktail on holiday rather than stressing about being a size ten. Life is for living after all?!

10	**Now I know what I know, what does this really mean for my life?**

I can start looking realistically at what my health and fitness goals actually are without pressurising myself into unrealistic expectations.

Now it's your turn. Revisit the 1-10 you completed earlier and do it properly. You know you want to.

So, do you really truthfully Desire the end state?

☐ **Yes**   ☐ **No**

If yes, terrific.

If it's a no, you are wasting everyone's time and I for one would much rather go shopping for shoes, than listen to you saying you do, really do **Desire** it, when I know deep down you don't.

However, if the pros outweigh the cons, then I will happily forgo the shoe shopping and sit down and play the game with you. Then you can pass go and collect two hundred pounds. Yay! Get the item / action / goal that you want. You get to play the new game of *Let's go get success!* Only if I get to be the top hat or car (I do not want to be the old boot). Remember, this is about creating a Reality list, not just a pretend **Talker Exhauster** wish list.

$$O + D + C \times F = \text{'It'}$$

✓ **O = Open. Yes, get in!**

+

✓ **D = Desire. Done.**

+

C = COURAGE

Because You Matter
Chelle Verite

Courage. Or being brave (as I like to call it). Aka getting your lazy *I don't want to face the world* arse out of bed. Sticking your head above the parapet and doing it. Having **Courage** and being brave means you making and taking the decision to do, and **BE** something different. It means stopping doing what you know you don't want, and instead starting something that you do want and are **Open** to. Something that will have a positive impact on your world, catapult you into action and create a hugely positive **Outcome**. God ERR☺ME isn't here just for kicks. He's here to encourage and empower you to make the right decisions. To choose the right **Outcomes** that make a positive difference to your world. Something that's new. Something that inevitably scares the shit out of you. Something that makes you want to go, 'No, it's too much effort.' The bit that makes you go, 'Urghhhh, really? Do I have to?' The bit that's out of your comfort zone. Like when your mum made you eat your sprouts as a child. You didn't really want to; you'd much rather eat chocolate biscuits. However, you ate those sprouts and were Mummy's brave little soldier. Step out of your comfort zone. Feel the fear and **Take the Leap** anyway.

Be brave, have Courage

What is it that you really want for...

♥ Life?

Because You Matter

Chelle Verite

♥ Home?

♥ Work?

♥ People?

Because Yöu Matter

Chelle Verite

♥ Finances?

♥ Health?

What is Courage to you?

How are you going to say it out loud to the world?

How are you going to show up with **Courage**?

What do you need to do more of, or less of?

Because You Matter

Chelle Verite

> Be brave, people. Be brave!

$$O + D + C \times F = \text{'It'}$$

✓ **O = Open.**

+

✓ **D = Desire.**

+

✓ **C = Courage.**

All great competent parts to creating success.

'YES!' I hear you say. 'See, Chelle, I am actually doing it. I'm **Open** and available. I **Desire** and want the success, and I'm being brave and **Courageous**.' I say well done. Pat on the back. Lots of brownie points on your good behaviour chart. However, you still need to put your big girl, Yorkie chocolate pants on and recognise it's all utterly useless if you don't have the next bit which is the big F. Surprisingly, this time F isn't a swear word. F is for **Focus**. F*ck me, really? (That no swearing situ didn't last long did it!)

$$O + D + C \times F = \text{'It'}$$

- ✓ **O= Open.**

$+$

- ✓ **D = Desire.**

$+$

- ✓ **C = Courage.**

$\times$

F = FOCUS

Because You Matter

Chelle Verite

The F word of the season. **Focus**. The word that actually **Makes 'It' Happen**. This has the biggest influence on it, hence the multiplication and the real work here. **Focus**. You've got to know what it is that you want and stick to it. And I mean really, really stick to it. I liken it to having a plate. You know that old saying 'eat what's on your plate'? Well, that's just it. **Success** comes to those who completely focus and stick to what is on their plate, and only their plate. They don't add to the plate. They don't stockpile food. They don't change their mind and get a different plate. They don't stand chatting to their mates, driving the BMW of life (Bitching, Moaning or Whining) about how crap the service or choice is. They make the decision to **Focus**, and they go for it.

Failure happens when we take on too much. When we get distracted. Then we use distraction, or our inability to deliver **Success**, as a 'Woe is me I almost did it.' **Success** comes from keeping **Focused** on exactly what's on your plate. Then staying **Focused** on eating that, and only that.

It's like going out for dinner. There's a place where our family loves to go. It's called *Pontis* about a five-minute drive from our house. A lovely Italian restaurant where the customer service is simply awesome and we are greeted like long lost family. Nothing is too much trouble for Evo and the team. If you haven't already noticed there are two loves in my life (other than the family love, that is) 1. prosecco, and 2. cake. Actually, three loves. prosecco, cake, and wine. Nope, make that four loves. 1. prosecco, 2. wine, 3. cake and 4. chocolate. Phew, I am back in the room. Do not think about chocolate. (FFS, how does Henry do that?!) I simply have to have at least two of those on my list to love a place. So, when we are out to dinner, in our favourite family restaurant, the whole reason I'm there, is for dessert. OMG, I love dessert. I love the choice. In fact, if I could just have dessert (for starter, main and dessert) I really, really, would.

Because You Matter
Chelle Verite

On one occasion, there we were, sitting in our usual spot (which is tucked away in a corner so James and I can actually relax) and we had ordered drinks. Drinks sorted, we moved on to ordering food. Now remember, we specifically come to this restaurant because I want pudding / dessert / cake. That is my **Focus**. The family are debating what to eat, and they are beginning to opt for starters. Hold tight. Here's the thing: I want cake. Deep down, I know that if I eat a starter I won't have room for my dessert. Yet the weight of expectation, to order a starter and join in, or the annoyance of not having a starter when everyone else is eating one, will scratch at my head. Little voices from the children: "Mum, have a starter." Or from James: "Aren't you having a starter, honey?" Or even from me: *I'm hungry, and don't want to miss out.*

Here's the thing, people...

- ❤ If I order a starter (unless it's a dessert!!) = I've lost **Focus**.
- ❤ If I forget or compromise myself over the beginnings of my meal = I've lost **Focus**.
- ❤ If I let the needs of others get in the way because they want to eat with me, and don't want me missing out = I've lost **Focus**.
- ❤ If I eat a starter (or pinch anyone else's for that matter) and take my eyes off the prize (which is dessert for just a moment), then stuff my face full of a big main course too, when it gets to dessert time, to pudding time, to cake time, I either

    a) **Won't have enough room = I've lost Focus.**

    b) **Order a dessert and not be able to eat it = I've lost Focus.**

c) **Stuff myself so much that I carry around what Belle would say is a six-month food baby and get bad stomach cramps = I've lost Focus.**

♥ In other words, I've lost **Focus** because I was not clear about what I actually wanted and **Desired.** I did not stick to what was on my plate in the first place.

What I am saying is, for you to be successful, for you to be your change, for you to truly create **Success**, it completely depends on how you stack your plate in the first place, and what you do with it. Translated, this means that what you decide to have on your plate of life stays on your plate. It stays on your plate until you have eaten it, completed it or achieved it. It's not about adding starters or other items. It's not about adding workload to your plate. If you pile your plate, not only will your plate not be able to handle being overloaded, but your stomach for life won't be able to cope. The choices to add more to your plate and to eat more will be too much and you simply won't have the capacity to finish it.

The biggest mistake you can make is to take it all on, and then think you can cope with it. Like a gluttony competition. Keep piling food on your plate so that it becomes so overloaded you drop it. Or you have so much to eat that you burst. Worse still, it becomes so unappetising that you don't even want to eat it now that you have it. You will only achieve **Success** if you remain focused on the prize. Not the starter, or the new task you take on, even if it is delicious. Not the extra portion for your main meal, even if it is exquisite.

In my case, it was doing everything I could to ensure that I got a pudding full of cake. On that particular *Pontis* day, I was successful.

Because Y♡u Matter

Chelle Verite

- ♥ I didn't opt for a starter = YES! I chose to have **Focus.**
- ♥ That particular day I ate my main meal = YES!
  I chose to have **Focus.**
- ♥ Then yes, yes, yes, I got my dessert. My pudding. In this case
  it was Tiramisu, and I loved every mouthful of it.
  Thank you **Focus**.

Creating **Success** is **NOT** an eat-as-much-as-you-want buffet or pile-as-much-food-as-you-can-on-your-plate-and-attempt-to-keep-it-down-without-throwing-up-all-over-your-new-outfit experience.

- ♥ Success is a *'Focus-on-what-you-truly-want'*
  experience.
- ♥ Success is also an *enjoy-what-you-put-on-your-plate-and-eat-it-until-it's-gone* **experience.**

And the best bit?

You get to choose where to go for dinner and what's on your plate. In fact, why not have cake for starters, main and dessert?! Who makes up the rules anyway? That's for normal people, and remember you are NOT normal!

Ooooh, now where have you decided you're going for dinner?

FOCUS, FOCUS, FOCUS!

STEP 1. WHAT'S GOING ON NOW?

♥ **What do you truly want that you have placed on your adventure plate of life?**

♥ **What additional things / prerequisites have you piled on your adventure plate that have meant you've lost Focus of what you want?**

Because You Matter

Chelle Verite

♥ **(Other than cake which is in my world a pre-requisite to everything...) What can you do more of, or less of, to regain Focus and get what you actually want in life?**

♥ **What positive impact will this have on your life and what meaning will it give you?**

There you go. See, you did the first initial thought about what's on your mind. Let's dig a bit deeper into all aspects of your world. This may be a great time to stop for a wee cup of tea or reach for a little glass of vino, or prosecco. (If you opt for alcohol do drink responsibly; I can't be a reason your adventure plate falls!)

Because Y♥u Matter
Chelle Verite

STEP 2. DESIGN YOUR ADVENTURE PLATE

What do you want on your Focus adventure plate for...

♥ **Life?**

♥ **Home?**

♥ **Work?**

Because You Matter

Chelle Verite

❤ **People?**

❤ **Finances?**

❤ **Health?**

Because You Matter

Chelle Verite

♥ **Up until now what's stopped / blocked you / got in the way of you achieving these?**

♥ **What do you notice about these themes / patterns?**

♥ **What do you actually want to do about them?**

Because You Matter

Chelle Verite

Whoop, whoop! I'm loving your new adventure.

$$O + D + C \times F = \text{'It'}$$

- ✓ **O= Open.**

+

- ✓ **D = Desire.**

+

- ✓ **C = Courage.**

X

- ✓ **F = Focus.**

= 'It'

MEANING OF LIFE
O + D + C X F = 'IT' SUCCESS

Eh, voila! Maths magic. See, I promised (and there's not a Bob or a Brian in sight... although there is an Einstein).

Use the following meaning of life
Making 'It' Happen Success Check In to ensure you are catapulting yourself into positive action and empowering yourself so you can live the life you love AND love the life you live.

Making 'It' Happen
Success Check in
O + D + C x F = 'It'
(Open + Desire + Courage x Focus = 'It')

What do you actually want?
(not what you don't want?)

How will you ensure that you are Open
to truly achieving this?

How do you know that you actually Desire
this Outcome and Success achievement?

How will you ensure you have the Courage
to achieve it?

How will you ensure that you retain Focus
on that one adventure plate?

How will you know you have achieved
'It' Success?

Because You Matter
Chelle Verite

The meaning of life is indeed 42. No, Chelle, it isn't, but it is maths magic. Thank you, Mr Findlay, I knew I'd pass someday.

Thank you too for your perseverance on that front. We've had some fun deciphering exactly how **Open** and available you are to the change you want to make. You'll now know how much you **Desire** actualising that change. You'll also know if that **Desire** is strong enough to make it from a wish list to a **Take the Leap** reality list.

You'll have the **Courage** to name what it is that you want, coupled with the **Focus** to keep that (and only that) on your plate. Lo and behold, you will get **'It'**. **Success** will happen, my friend.

You will **LiveLife and BE.**

Achievemephobia? Pah! Read it and weep fear of achievement. You've so got this!

And why do it?

Why create and **BE your change**?

Why focus on your **Success** and **Making 'It' Happen**?

Simple.

Because You Matter

“

Happiness is
letting go of what
you think life is
supposed to look
like, and celebrating
it for everything
that it is.

MANDY HALE

LIFE LESSON

20

Say 'Goodbye Hello'

LET IN THE NEW YOU

Because Y♡u Matter

Chelle Verite

Right, you're **Open**. You've got bucket loads of desire to change. You are choosing to **Respond** differently. **Motivating Matt** is out, all guns blazing, and your **Sabotaging Devil Mindset** has been permanently kicked into touch. **Courage**? You have it in bucket loads. Your **Superhero** focus is laser beam sharp, and there is no kryptonite in sight. You are well on the way to **Taking the Leap** to **BEing YOU**. Waking up, shaking up and positively disrupting your world. Loving the life you live and living the life you love. All because the lady loves Milk Tray... I mean, *Because YOU Matter*. What a wonderful world. One of my favourite songs is *What a Wonderful World*. If you don't know it, look it up. You have choice of the original by Louis Armstrong, or my favourite version by that big burly chap called Israel Kamakawiwo'ole who sings whilst playing the tiniest of ukuleles. There it is. Your wonderful world. Just waiting for when you are ready.

Are you ready? It's time. Time to say. 'Goodbye Hello'. Yes, you can. It's time to ditch that **Sabotaging Devil Mindset**. Ditch those **Worry-woe-is-me** gold medals. Ditch that '**HATE ME**' mentality. Instead, truly face your new, wonderful, empowering reflection, and get on with it.

'Time to say goodbye...'

'La, la, la, la, la, la, la, la...'

As the song blasts in my ears on my noise cancelling, best buy, Bose earphones (blatant advertising product placement moment), it's time to say goodbye. That Italian Andrea Bocelli song that everyone loves but no one knows the words to. F*ck, when will this ever end? No, not this book. I'm referring to exactly what I was thinking as I was cycling up a never-ending hill. To be fair, it wasn't just any old hill. It was a hill that could be described as the biggest nemesis of my existence. It was monstrous.

Because You Matter

Chelle Verite

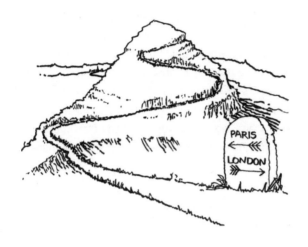

The idea was to coach and support my friend Neal (who was doing way, way better than me), on our three day, London to Paris, three hundred mile bike ride. Neal was flying high in the fast group (unbeknownst to me he was a demon on a bicycle. 'Bicycle! Bicycle. I want to ride my bicycle. I want to ride my bike...' Queen interlude. 'No Queen, I do not want to ride my bicycle,' I replied) but a dynamic duo we were not. Despite being 'Team Chocolate Orange' (Neal was sporting his ginger mop top hence the other part of the team name). I was miles behind. Miles behind and f*cking dying. I mean dying. Little old me. Team? Yes. Dynamic? Certainly not on my part!

There we were, on day two of three days of hell (as far as I was concerned). At least we were cycling in France, having already completed the London to Dover and Dover to Calais legs (the latter was the easy bit aka the ferry ride). We were supposedly rested and ready for the second day of cycling. For all you brave people out there taking on the world, and for those who want to take on a cycling or fitness challenge, be afraid. Be very afraid. My arse was literally on fire. My legs felt as if they were about to explode. My chest felt like I

Because Y♡u Matter
Chelle Verite

was beyond asthmatic. We were ninety eight miles into the hundred and twelve mile ride, having already clocked up eighty three miles from the day before. We were doing the ride of our own free will, and for charity. Except, the only charity right then was me. I mean, I only did it because firstly, I needed to support Neal because that is what a friend and an Empowerment Coach does, right? Secondly, I did it because my bike was pink. Nope, f*ckedy f*ck sticks, that awful, nasty, pretending to be beautiful sadistic hill was still there.

Then it happened.

Right in the middle of that nemesis of a hill. Right in the middle, when I thought my life had literally stopped and I had died and gone to hell. Right in the middle of that hill, that was at least seven miles long, when I was almost at the end of the slowest group. Right in the middle of the beautiful forest countryside (which, to be fair, had I been in a car I'm absolutely sure I would have said, 'Wow, look at that French chateau!' and waved my hand like a princess and picture of royalty daaaaaaahling). However, as it was, I was an overheating wreck of a person going at an utter snail's pace up a hill that was the steepest thing I had ever experienced in my life. Battling with gravity to keep my cycling shoes in their cleats. Battling crippling lactic acid in my legs, willing them to keep going round. Frantically attempting to stop my body from keeling over in exhaustion. (There is nothing worse than going so slowly on a bike that the inevitable falling-over-sideways happens. Most embarrassing. Worse than that, it f*cking hurts when you keel over whilst frantically trying to free your feet. Hurts big time. Both pride and body.)

In amongst all of that pain, the song came on. The song. The song that to this day still catapults me to a place where I think I experienced an outer body moment. It was *Time to Say Goodbye* and I cried.

Because You Matter

Chelle Verite

I cried, and I cried.

I cried because despite all the pain, despite all the chest breaking, bum shattering, lactic acid leg tearing exhaustion that I was experiencing, right in that moment I knew I could do it. Something crazy happened. I looped that song on my headphones, and I kept going.

Going and going and going.

My head went down. My legs decided that they could keep going round and my body just believed that I could do it. I was so in that moment that I didn't notice the hill anymore. I couldn't see the top or the fact that people weren't there. I couldn't see the beautiful French chateau disappearing and getting smaller and smaller on the horizon. None of it mattered, except listening to that song and knowing that anything was possible. The only other time I have ever experienced anything like it is during labour and giving birth. It's like your body just goes into *f*ck it, you can do this* mode and your brain goes. *Okay, I'm on it. I'm doing it and it is quite literally time to say goodbye to any pain, any doubts. Goodbye to anything that will stop you.*

Now I could quite easily say, 'Yay! This experience made my world. It changed my life. I did something amazing that day that made a difference.' I could big it up and tell people I was amazing and they can be too. But that isn't why I'm telling you this story. I'm telling you this story because of the reason why I ended up on that hill in the first place.

I ended up on that hill in the first place battling my own demons because a friend of mine was in a very bad way. He was hating life. He was getting ill. He was unfocused at work and didn't know how or what to do with himself. He was in his early thirties, five foot six inches tall and a whopping nineteen stone. He was in the prime of life (or at least he should have been). Except, put simply, he was miserable.

Because You Matter

Chelle Verite

Miserable and getting itchy and scratchy physically and mentally. So, here's the thing, as a coach you take on board everything when you work with a client, or at least I do. At that time, however, life for me wasn't exactly a bed of roses. I was a single mum. I was divorced following a relationship where I felt belittled and worthless. I was attempting to demonstrate my worth in a young, crazy, fast paced company. I was carving a role in learning and development and doing amazing things like single handily creating a new and dynamic, never-had-before, Management Development Programme, and literally empowering hundreds of people into positive action. All the while paying out two thousand pounds a month in childcare. I was five hundred pounds down every month just for the joy of going to work and enduring the internal battle that every working career mother has. *I think I should be at home to support my child* and *If I do stay home, how will I carve my way as a successful career woman?* and *How will I juggle everything without feeling like I'm failing?* So many negative plates!

Taking on a friend and an almost daily coaching client full time was exactly the type of distraction I needed. Focusing on someone else instead of myself and my life meant I didn't have to face my own demons. So, that's what I did. For over a year I coached, supported, helped, and retrained Neal physically, mentally and emotionally. He got the full on *'Lets Get BOMBCHELLED!'* experience. Which must have been a bit of a shock to the system for him. If any of my other clients are to go by, having an hour of my time, let alone every day for three hundred and sixty five days or more, is a bit of a head f*ck.

By the time we hit the London to Paris charity bike ride day Neal was five and a half stone down. He was fit and pumped up physically and mentally. He was making different decisions about his life. His outlook was different, and this was, as it turned out, his moment to shine. That nemesis hill I mentioned earlier was a *let's fly* moment for Neal.

Because Y♡u Matter

Chelle Verite

Boy, had he smashed that target. He had whizzed up that hill like a gazelle on speed and completed it in record time, moving into the fastest cycling group of the whole event. He was ready. More so than my little brain, or body, had banked on. I wasn't sure if I was elated that he'd got there and made it, or totally gutted that he didn't need me anymore. He was far more ready than I was. The tables had turned.

He had done it.

I had not.

Which is why I bring you back to the *Time to Say Goodbye* moment, when I found myself on that hill. I thought Neal was the reason I had gotten there in the first place, but he wasn't. The moment that song hit my head and my body, that moment was for me. For all of the fight I'd had kicked out of me as a child growing up in a place I didn't fit in. For all the time I'd spent in relationships that weren't deserving of me. For all the times I'd piled doubt on my head. For all the pressures of perceived failures that I hadn't made **'It'**. For all the times my **Crown of Acceptance** had slipped and choked me round my neck. For all the times my **Woe-is-me Worries** had gotten the better of me, and my **Sabotaging Devil Mindset** had kicked me down and down and down. It was that moment that my body, my heart and my brain went *clunk*.

It was at that moment that acceptance kicked in. I was able to consciously let go of all the nonsense that was until then holding me back. From then on, I let in something different. Something new.

What was that difference?

The difference was belief.

The simple belief in me.

Belief that I mattered.

Because You Matter
Chelle Verite

I put all of my heart, my soul, my guts and my superpower into believing.

Believing in me.

It wasn't finishing the three hundred mile cycle and standing by the Eiffel Tower in France with my bike raised up above my head that did it. It wasn't the glass of prosecco (or the many others of them) that greeted my parched throat with glee when I had finished. It wasn't the completion medal around my neck, which now sits pride of place in my bedroom. It was that day. It was that sodding hill. It was that moment that I decided it was time to say goodbye.

So, I ask you, with all the fight you have in you, with all the demons you will face and all the courage you will create, when exactly will your time to say goodbye and welcome your hello moment be? When will you rise up, put you first and start to believe you can? When will you go and get the life you deserve and love? When will you **Live Life** and **BE**?

Life Lesson 20

TIME TO SAY 'GOODBYE HELLO'

♥ When has life really kicked you down?

Because You Matter
Chelle Verite

♥ **What makes you want to rise up and stop this happening again?**

♥ **What will you say goodbye to?**

♥ **What will you say hello to?**

Because Y♡u Matter

Chelle Verite

> ♥ **What will you do more of / less of so you can truly believe in you?**

This is what it is all about.

I believe I can. I believe I will. I believe in me.

That moment of pride. That moment of connection with your own self. The moment you realise that it isn't about doing it for other people. It's not about the expectation of doing what's normal. Or what you should have done, could have done, or wish you had done. It's about celebrating exactly who you are, for you. It's about realising and recognising that your life is about choosing the way you want to live it. Having clarity for you. Making and creating change. Yes, you've got it. For **YOU**. It's about having the choice to positively **Respond** rather than to negatively **React**. It's about having the choice to face the fear of your own reflection and recognising and acknowledging **'It'**. Choosing to free your own clarity. Choosing to change and be your new reality. Making the choice to fight. Making the choice to empower, be happy and **BE YOU**.

Because Y♡u Matter

Chelle Verite

> ### To BE REAL...
>
> in all the ways you want to be.
>
> ### To SHOW UP...
>
> and feel that you are taking account of the world in the ways you want it to be and that you choose it to be.
>
> ### To BE SEEN...
>
> for exactly who you are.
>
> ### To choose to be Authentically Present,
>
> to LiveLife and **BE YOU**.

Choosing to get out of bed and ride the emotional rollercoaster of life with pride, without throwing up all over your dreams, hopes and aspirations. Choosing to **BE True** and **Focus** on what makes you, you. **Choosing to BE Brave** and choosing to **Take the Leap** and positively transform your wishes and wants into realities. **Empower YOU and Choose to BE**. Goodbye Hello. Here's to you, **Authentically Present Human BEing**. If I can do **'It'**, this thing they call life, with all my insecurities, with the shit that I've had thrown my way, with all the mistakes, Life Lessons and experiences that have made me who I am, if I can stand up here and say, 'Hello world, here I am!' then yes, Yes, YES, you f*cking can too!

- ♥ **Choose change.**
- ♥ **Choose to catapult your life into positive action.**
- ♥ **Choose to LiveLifeBE.**
- ♥ **Choose to BE YOU.**

Aww, we are nearing the end and the beginning. Yup, that means you'll have get off that lovely arse of yours and decide exactly, what do you want to do differently that will positively help you to triumphantly

Because Y🫶u Matter

Chelle Verite

LiveLifeBE. It means having the mindset that you *can*. It means choosing and **BEing the change** so you can **BE REAL... SHOW UP... BE SEEN...** So you can be that awesome **Human BEing** who chooses to stop just **Reacting** and automatically implementing that mindless **Human DOing**, which leads to the **MindF*ck** of negative **Outcomes**. Instead, it means using all of these motivational Life Lessons to help you **Focus** on how to react to things with conscious choice. Conscious choice will lead you beautifully to an array of positive **God ERR☺ME Outcomes**.

However, for those of you who have, up until now, spent the majority of your **Reaction** time visiting the **Dark Side** with **Catastrophising Chris**, **Meltdown Mary**, **Devastating Dave** and **Sabotaging Devil Mindset Reactions.** Not to mention those previously pesky **Worry Woe-is-me Fear Monsters**, coupled with a choking **Crown of Acceptance** (like I did most of my life). You are not alone. Yes, there is hope. Yes, there is a positive (cycling challenge free) way to transform. All of these Life Lessons will ensure that from now on you will enjoy your lovely, relaxing, **Selfwith Giving cups of 'Tea'**, put a **HALT** to the inner **Emotional Turmoil** of life's rollercoaster, and encourage the wonderful **Pioneering Angel Mindset** and **Motivating Matt** to the forefront of your life's adventure. Your Toblerone / FedEx reveal, rugby ball kicking insight will serve to increase your awareness of what you actually want and how to get it way more regularly (thanks to our awesome **God ERR☺ME** and your **Superhero** you). You can forever be in the driving seat of creating and appreciating a new world that, from now on, will be so empowering. You *can* live the life you love AND love the life you live.

Because Y♥u Matter
Chelle Verite

That is definitely something worth fighting for. However, it does mean being honest with yourself and deciding to commit to **BEing your positive change**. So, let's have a go. Have a look back at the wonderful event creations you have written throughout this book. Decide exactly what you are going to do to change the **Outcome** for the better. How you are going to generate those Yes, Get In! **Motivating Matt Responses** and use those positive **God E+R+R=☺ME Responses** instead. **BE your change**. Learn to let go of expectations. Learn to let go of the patterns and behaviours that, up until now, you automatically did without thinking. From now on, you will cultivate love in your world. You will **stop mindlessly DOing** and **start consciously BEing**.

Go forth and conquer, people.

This is your life.

This is you.

Let your life begin.

Remember, regardless of how it feels, you've got this!

Because Y♡u Matter

Chelle Verite

> We are NOT normal.
>
> Thank f*ck.
>
> We are NOT normal.
>
> Yes, please.
>
> We are NOT normal.
>
> Absof*ckinglootly!

This is your world.

This is your time.

- ♥ **Fight.**
- ♥ **Choose.**
- ♥ **Shine.**

It's your time to say **'Goodbye Hello'**.

You can make it when you f*cking create it.

Go BE YOU! You've got the tools. Your new world awaits.

Why do it?

Simple.

Because Y♡u Matter

66

One day you'll
wake up and
realise your truth.
To let in the
light and choose
to shine.

CHELLE VERITE

LIFE LESSON

21

Go BE

ABSOF*CKINGLOOTLY

Because You Matter

Chelle Verite

Yes, Get In! Congratulations. You read. You fought. You conquered. This is of course not the end but merely the beginning of your journey. Thank you for making it this far. I am soooooo excited to hear all about how your adventure unfolds. It's time, isn't it? Time for you to realise your truth. Time for you to shine. To make choices for you. To be that amazing human being that you are. To simply **Go BE**.

Thank you for giving me the reason to write.

Thank you for wanting to empower you. (If you didn't, you wouldn't have got this far in the book.) I am so very proud that you have.

Thank you for giving me my reason to be brave and put pen to paper. It's only taken me since 2007 when I looked in my own magic mirror and started my search for the meaning of life and self-value.

In short, it makes not one jot of difference how long **'It' Success** takes you. The fact that you have used / are using your new motivational Life Lesson toolkits in this book to help you to be you is what matters. There's so much time to enjoy how your new transformational journey will unfold.

BE REAL... SHOW UP... BE SEEN... and BE YOU.

So cut yourself some slack! Be kind about how you grow. How you develop. Wake up! Shake up! Choose to positively disrupt your world so you can live the life you love AND love the life you live. Most importantly, enjoy your **Success**. Yes, we will all have a little dance around the living room.

To help you notice, **Focus** and catapult you into positive action I thought I'd gift you a nice wee cup of tea, the last Life Lessons. We could all do with a nice cup of **Give Tea** moment now, couldn't we? Go on, accept it. I know you want to.

Life Lesson 21

CATAPULT YOUR LIFE INTO

POSITIVE ACTION

Ta-da! Not that you need it. I'm sure you're already ditching your critical **Sabotaging Devil Mindset**, slamming that self-hate and placing that **Crown of Acceptance** firmly on your head. Not to mention **Dissolving** those **Woe-is-me Worries** to within an inch of their life, **Superhero**-ing and **God ERR☺ME**-ing the hell out of your new way of **BEing Human.** However, just in case you'd like me to walk (or run) with you on the journey, I've put your **Go BE** actions all down in black and white.

YOUR COUNTDOWN BEGINS...

Because Y♡u Matter
Chelle Verite

10... Let go to let in

This is where you are now and this **Go BE** Life Lesson involves drawing an outline of your hands. The left represents all the things that you want to leave behind that have stopped serving you. The right represents all the things that make your world right. The things that make you feel good and proud. The things that will make you shine and be the best version of you.

Once you've completed this exercise, every time you look at your hands you will know what to do and, more importantly, how to love and honour **BEing YOU**.

9... Draw

Draw an outline of your hands, left hand and then right hand.

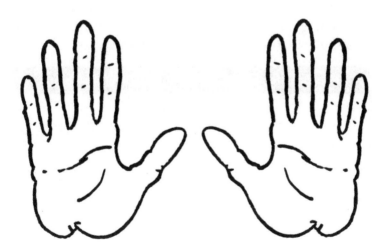

8... Reflect on what you left

Write in the left hand all the things you want to leave behind that have stopped serving you. Do this by taking a moment to really think about how you have shown up and experienced your world. What have you done to you (not what other people or situations have caused) that has caused you pain, angst, worry, rejection, **Emotional Turmoil** or negativity? This is about being real here, not projecting the blame on to others.

7... Name it

Now I want you to look at everything you have written in your left hand and decide what slogan to use for those challenging and potentially negative experiences. Like it was an advertisement. What did that year, that time, those moments mean to you? What will you name it? (Remember slogans are catchy so only choose a few words, not a novel. Yes, by all means, use Scottish Tourettes.) Write your slogan for those challenging experiences by your left-hand drawing.

My slogan for what I've left (and will leave) behind is...

6... Recognise

Now look at the drawing of your completed left hand. Take a moment to read through, recognise and acknowledge all the things that have **'Up until now'** hindered your life. Look at each of the items. Really look at them. Look at your slogan too. This **was** your world.

5... Let go

Good, you're being brave. Now you are going to learn to let go of the past and leave it behind. Look at your left hand drawing again, and all that you have written. Take a moment to acknowledge and recognise that despite all the pain and negativity these challenging experiences and moments may have caused you, there were valuable Life Lessons to be had from every single one of them.

♥ What did those negative experiences offer you that hindered your life?

Because Y♥u Matter

Chelle Verite

> ♥ **What insight and positivity can they gift you that 'From now on' will help you in life?**

> ♥ **What have you learnt about you?**

Phew. It's powerful stuff this looking at what you do for you, and not blaming anyone else.

4... Write your insight

With your new hinder and help insight, write your findings. Put the things that hindered you to the left of your left-hand drawing. Put the things that helped you to the right of your right-hand drawing (or as near as you can get it depending on your paper size).

3... Choose to engage

This is where the magic begins to happen. You're likely thinking. *Chelle, great, I've done all the work for my left hand. I get that there's stuff to be left behind. I know the things that have hindered, and things that I need to learn. But what is supposed to happen with the right hand that I've drawn? It's still blank.*

Quite right. **Success** in life isn't just about recognising and leaving things behind that have prevented you from getting what you want and need. It's about **Focusing** on creating a positive and **Focused** life plate with all the magical things that will be 'right' for you. **Focus** areas that you will choose to enlist the support of, to empower you so you can **BE** your wonderful you. The left hand signifies what you have left behind. The right hand signifies what's right for your new life. Get in!

2... What's right?

Let's look to you, as you are now. You as a creation. The newest version of how you want to be. On your right hand drawing write all the things that make your world right. Scribble to your heart's content. Think about all the things that you notice about you, that you value about you, that you appreciate about you. Write down the things that you think others would say about you on a great day, on a day when you are in full flow, and when life is making you smile and sparkle. Be kind here. Think about all the amazing things that you have done to overcome adversity and achieve your goals. Think about when you have completed the tough things in life, the things that you choose you want to (and do) get out of bed for. The things that make you feel good, that make you proud of you, that will make you shine and love you and be the best version of you. Sit with that creation. That **Selfwith Give Me Tea**.

Because You Matter

Chelle Verite

Focusing on all the good that you bring may be new to you, however, you can do it. Take a few deep and meaningful moments to mute the noise, ditch your **Sabotaging Devil Mindset** and **Recognise** and acknowledge that feel good glow. **Recognise** and acknowledge that by being on this planet you provide to you, and to others.

♥ **What do these positive experiences offer you?**

♥ **What insight can they gift you for your new you?**

Because You Matter

Chelle Verite

♥ **What are you learning about you?**

1... Recite and relive

Now decide what all these positive experiences and moments mean to you. One by one, look at everything you've written in your right-hand drawing. Re-live the experiences of them, the fight that you made for them, the experiences you created because of them, the pride that you felt because of them. Sit with those thoughts for a moment. What will your slogan be for what's right for your life? What words will you use that will catapult you into *I feel good, I believe in me, I will choose to take positive action* mode?

My slogan for what's right in my life is...

Because Y♡u Matter
Chelle Verite

Remember these words. Remember all the positivity from the words you've written on your right-hand drawing, and the feelings and thoughts they create. Carry these with you. Recite, relive and ignite them. Every time you look at your hands be clear on what you will do less of that disempowers you, and what you will do more of that empowers you.

Left hand. leave behind. Right hand. what's right for you and your life.

Whoop, whoop. You didn't realise just how gifted those hands of yours could be, did you?!

Go on. **Go BE YOU**.

I know you can do it, and I know that as a result of reading all of this book that you will.

(Even if you need a little time).

Bake some **Take the Leap chocolate muffin cakes** and that'll give you all the good energy you need. Failing that, a little more wine or prosecco is always an option. Just remember, if you opt for the latter, drink sensibly!

Because Y♡u Matter
Chelle Verite

Blast Off!

GO BE ABSOF*CKINGLOOTLY

Go BE me and catapult me and my life into positive action.

I (name in here) _____ have decided to commit to the following **E+R+R=☺ME** positive actions that will support me to positively **GO BE** and live the life I love. *Because I matter.*

Because Y♥u Matter

Chelle Verite

---

1. What I actually want in terms of my ERR☺ME
   positive actions for my life, family, work, relationships
   and world is...

---

2. To make my wish a reality and get what I want,
   I need to decide the following

   ♥ I want...

Because You Matter

Chelle Verite

♥ **I will do more of...**

♥ **I will do less of...**

♥ **I will know it's done because...**

Because Y♡u Matter

Chelle Verite

3. The reasons why I want to change and catapult
   my life into positive action so I can LiveLifeBE is...

Signed _____

Dated _____

Whoop! Whoop you did it! You read, you conquered, you committed.

The only questions left to ask are...

What will you do every day, every hour, and every minute to ensure you can Absof*ckinglootly Go BE YOU?

I trust you to

- ♥ To love and to honour you.
- ♥ Your **BYM Fight Club** pledge
- ♥ Your fight, for all of you.

Bring it on!

Because Y♥u Matter

Chelle Verite

Remember you are most definitely NOT normal.

This is your world.

These are your choices.

BE your change and choose to catapult yourself and your life into positive action.

Why do it?

Why Live the life you love AND love the life you live?

You know why.

Because Y♥u Matter

You truly, truly do.

Chelle ☺ X

LiveLifeBE

Take the leap cakes

CHOCOLATE MUFFIN RECIPE

Because Y♥u Matter

Chelle Verite

We always need decent sustenance for our new world, now don't we!

Welcome to the eat as much as you want and not get fat, 'F*ck me, is that actually a chocolate muffin? Mmmmh, it's so good let's have it for breakfast!' **Take the Leap chocolate muffin cake recipe.** All you wannabe procrastinators or sit on your ass doing nothing-ators, you have no excuse not to go and make it. You won't get (that) fat. It's made with good fat and each cake is less than one hundred calories, so you can actually have cake for breakfast. More to the point, those little pleasure domes even taste good.

Because You Matter
Chelle Verite

Here's a Chelle guarantee. if you make these cakes and they don't work, or taste yuk, then you have my permission to book yourself in for a virtual 'pop round to my house for nice cup of **'Tea'** and we'll bake some **Take the Leap** cakes together' session where you'll get my special positive disruption treatment.

This recipe makes sixteen to eighteen muffins. Officially it's called 'loads of cake'. You, however, may not want to make that many in one sitting. So, halve the ingredients if you're a family of one or if you're baking this for the first time (just in case you drop eggshell in the mixture or it goes painfully wrong). Ingredients cost money, people.

EQUIPMENT

- ♥ **Sanity** (just kidding).
- ♥ **Kitchen aid electric mixer** ideally, or some means of mixing ingredients at lightning speed (otherwise your wrists will break and you need those for a whole variety of other way more exciting and thrilling life things).
- ♥ **Bowl** for the dry ingredients.
- ♥ Pink **spatula** man tool to scrape chocolate mix ingredients from the mixing bowl (and yes if you're very lucky you can lick the bowl, just don't make yourself sick).
- ♥ Couple of **teaspoons.**
- ♥ Couple of **dessertspoons.**
- ♥ Cupcake **baking tray.**
- ♥ Cupcake **paper holders** (get some nice colours please; all plain is a tad boring).

Because You Matter
Chelle Verite

- 💜 **Oven** yes, you need one. 180 degrees C. Preheated.

- 💜 **Timer** ideally on the oven, however, your phone timer will do. You have to be very close to the oven when the timer goes off to whisk the cakes out. (Overcook the cakes and they'll be crap. You have been told.)

- 💜 **Microwave** if you've not got one ask DJ Jo, I hear his sister has loads.

- 💜 **Resting rack** for your cakes. If you haven't got one of those, Amazon is a great port of call. Alternatively, be imaginative. I used a wire rack that's part of the Jamie Oliver casserole dish set. Wedding gift sets are great, aren't they? (Except I've still yet to meet someone who uses a gift for what they were actually designed for. Napkin holders are the worst.)

- 💜 **Plastic storage box** or resealable bag. Yes, the latter does count if you tie a knot in it. So long as you can get back into it, it is indeed 'resealable'. (We always get those big bags of sweets like Revels or Maltesers. Resealable my arse, that is dependant on the fact that they aren't eaten in one sitting.)

INGREDIENTS

(For ease, measure using the scoop from Protein Powder pack, dessertspoons and teaspoons.)

- 💜 **Bananas** 5 medium size, or 4 big
  (ripe / overly ripe / definitely not green).

- 💜 **Coconut oil** 3 heaped dessertspoons.

- 💜 **Runny honey** 5 scoops (or more if you prefer!)

Because You Matter

Chelle Verite

- **Eggs** 2 large.
- **Chocolate protein powder** 2 scoops.
- **Coconut flour** 2 scoops.
- **Cocoa powder** 1 scoop.
- **Baking powder** 2 teaspoons.
- **Bicarbonate of soda** 2 teaspoons.
- **Raising flour** 2 teaspoons.
- **Chocolate (70% cocoa)** 150 grams.

HOW TO MAKE

- Put your oven on to heat. Get out materials.
- Peel bananas, snap into bits, put in a bowl, microwave on full power 1 minute.
- Take bananas out of microwave, put in Kitchen Aid and mix until baby mush.
- Meanwhile, put coconut oil in bowl, microwave for 1 minute on full power until clear liquid.
- Take bowl out of microwave (watch, it's hot) and put honey in bowl (should be up to half the oil level so it's half oil and half honey).
- Pour oil and honey into banana mush and mix again.
- Break and put in two eggs, yolks and whites (watch when you break the eggs. The last time I made cakes, I accidently dropped an egg in with shell and had to spend an eternity picking out the bits, so do the egg cracking carefully.)
- Mix together until liquid consistency.

Because You Matter
Chelle Verite

- ♥ Measure out and pour the protein powder, coconut flour, cocoa powder, baking powder and bicarbonate of soda into the mixture.

- ♥ Mix until gloopy consistency.

- ♥ Smash chocolate into small bits (don't eat too much as you'll need it for the recipe) and put the little bits into the mixture.

- ♥ Mix together.

- ♥ Eh voila, you have your cake mixture at the ready.

- ♥ Put your cupcake paper holders out, take dessertspoons and scoop in about 1.5 spoonfuls of mixture per cupcake holder. Use the spatula for any remaining mixture. Lick bowl. (It's an empty cake mixture bowl so we all know you're going to have a taste.)

- ♥ Set timer to 16 minutes and get ready to go.

- ♥ Open oven door, put cakes in, start timer and leave them alone. Once shut, do not open the oven door.

- ♥ Once 16 minutes is up, take the cakes out of the oven immediately.

- ♥ Place tray on rack and leave for 10 minutes. (Eating one at this stage is acceptable, just prepare your stomach for the molten lava chocolate bits as they are very, very hot.)

- ♥ After 10 minutes, pack the cakes in the plastic box (or bag) and close the lid (or tie the bag). This will keep the moisture in and keep the cakes nice and soft.

Because Y♡u Matter

Chelle Verite

Yes! Your **Take the Leap chocolate muffin cakes** are now complete. Eat at your leisure. I have cakes for breakfast, and as many times as I can in a day. (I even travel take them with me when I travel for work). Seriously, you can never have enough cake!!

Now all you have to do is just **Take the Leap**, eat and enjoy!

And why do it?

Simple.

Because Y♡u Matter

BE REAL ... SHOW UP ... BE SEEN

Because Y♥U Matter

21 say it like it is, no bullshit, we're definitely NOT normal!
life lessons to catapult you into positive action.

Join Chelle Verite (Empowerment Coach, TEDx Speaker, Adoptee & Divorcee)
in the creation of your very own transformational journey of honest
self discovery and motivational life toolkit so you can...

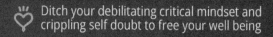 Ditch your debilitating critical mindset and
crippling self doubt to free your well being

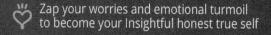 Zap your worries and emotional turmoil
to become your Insightful honest true self

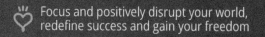 Focus and positively disrupt your world,
redefine success and gain your freedom

Chelle's heartwarming, and heartbreaking life stories about
overcoming adversity will make you laugh, make you cry, and
make you truly re-evaluate what you actually want and need.
So you too can live life and BE.

Why do it?

Because Y♥U Matter

FCM PUBLISHING